288

Whereas the Persons hereafter named are Certified by Hugh may Esq'r to be Painters and other Artists, with their families, and that they are ... dorning his maj'ty Castle at Windsor, and haue often occa... remain in London for the carrying on of their Worke, and ... all Forreigners. Wee do in pursueance of his maj'ty order ... and permit the said Persons, namely Renne Coussin Guilder with Estienne his wife, Peter and mary his Children, John Carce his apprentice and le mair his Servant, Anthony Montingo Painter of Flowers, with alice his wife; Nicholas Lauzellier Painter; John Vanderstaine Stone Carver, John Oast his Servant, and Goizen his Howse keeper; Lawrence Vandermulen, Anthony Verhuke, and arnold Quellan serv'ts to Grinling Gibbons the Carver. To remain in and about the Citties of London & Westminster Untill further order, his maj'ty late Proclamation to the Contrary notwith-standing. And hereof all Mayors, Justices of the Peace, Constables, Church Wardens, and other Parish officers, and all others whom it may Concerne are to take notice and gouerne themselues accordingly. dat 21 may 1679

Lord Chancelor   Lord Priuy Seale   Lord Chamberlain
Lord President   Marq. of Winchester   Sr Henry Capell

Whereas at the humble request of mons'r Ierome Gohory, Setting forth, that he hath ...ued in England for the Space of twenty Six yeares, and imployed his time in teaching to Daunce, And praying his maj'tie that he would be graciously pleased to permit him ... Stay in Towne for Some time, the better to recouer Certain Sumes of money, w'ch ... due to him from Seuerall Persons here. Wee do in pursueance of his maj'ty order ... Councill hereby Licence and permit the said m'r Ierome Gohory to remaine in and ...bout the Citties of London and Westminster in order to the gathering in of his debts ...y aforesaid Untill the End of next Trinity Term, notwithstanding his maj'ty late proclamation. And hereof all Justices of the Peace, Constables &c dated 21'th may 1679

Signed, as aboue.

Upon the Petition of Thomas Gardner Setting forth that by order of this Board of the ...th of December 1677, the Lords Comm'rs of the admiralty were to Consider what ...reward was reasonable to be allowed the Pet'r for his good Seruices in Virginia, and humbly praying, in regard therein to'y made no Report in the matter, that his maj'tie wilbe pleased to direct the present Comm'rs of the admiralty to examine and ...port in the Same. It is this day Ordered by his maj'tie in Councill that the

Grinling Gibbons & The English Woodcarving Tradition

Happ Birthday Dad
From Your Chips
off the Old Block
x x

GRINLING GIBBONS
&
The English Woodcarving Tradition

FREDERICK OUGHTON

Fellow of the Royal Society of Arts

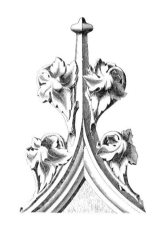

STOBART : LONDON

Published 1979

ISBN 0 85442 011 8
Stobart & Son Ltd, 67-73 Worship Street, London, EC2A 2EL

Designed by Edward Addison and photoset in Monotype Baskerville by Photocomp Ltd of Birmingham. Printed in Great Britain by Clarke, Doble and Brendon Ltd of Plymouth and bound by Webb Son & Co Ltd at Ferndale.

For Eve

—Photographic Credits—

British Travel Association, Victoria and Albert Museum, The Museum of London, Royal Commission on Historic Monuments, England, Royal Commission on Ancient and Historical Monuments in Wales, Courtauld Institute, Hermitage Museum, Leningrad, the Florence and Modena Galleries, Italy, Tower of London, Ashmolean Museum, Cambridge, The National Trust, Trust Houses Forte Ltd, Council for Small Industries in Rural Areas, Mr J. C. D. Smith, Mr Ronald A. Lee and Miss Nancy Catford.

Contents

CONCERNING THE ILLUSTRATIONS . . .

Apart from the documents reproduced on pages 101, 104, 105, 106, 108, 109, 110 and 141, and the portrait of Grinling Gibbons by Sir Godfrey Kneller, which appears on page 97, the photographs of woodcarving appear at the conclusion of each chapter, thus:

The book is adorned with ornaments in the form of line drawings which are intended to illustrate the development of carved decoration. They are not strictly aligned to the periods discussed in the text but form an independent glossary of embellishment – the vocabulary of the carver.

A descriptive list of photographs and ornaments appears at the end of the book. Details of the documents in the text appear on page *x* and the endpapers, below.

ENDPAPERS

[1] The detailed account for the carving by Gibbons of one of the most elaborate catafalques ever designed and constructed in England, for the funeral of Queen Mary on 5 March 1695. See also text, page 121.

[2] The document (top) of 21 May 1697 signed by the Lord Privy Seal and other officials which authorised the employment of Gibbons at 'his Majesty's Castle at Windsor' on the certification of Hugh May. The group included René Cousin, gilder, and Ettienne, his wife, with his children, Peter and Mary; John Caree, apprentice, and Le Mair, servant. Also specified are Anthony Montingo, 'Painter of Flowers' with his wife, Alice; Nicholas Lauzellier, artist; John 'Vanderstaine', stone carver, John Oaste, servant, and Gaizen, housekeeper; Laurence 'Vandermulen'; Anthony Verhuke, and Arn- old Quellan, 'serv to Grinling Gibbons the Carver.' The preamble states that all persons named were 'Forreiners', suggesting that Gibbons was still at this time regarded as an alien, despite his lengthy residence in England.

[3] Evidence of the association of Grinling Gibbons and John Nost in work carried out at Windsor, including the carving by Gibbons of 59 ft 10 inches of coved cornice and enriched 'members' or brackets. Nost's price for the carving of the marble chimneypiece was £20, including the coving and hearth.

[4] Entry in the works account ledger relating to work carried out by various craftsmen at Windsor. Gibbons was not treated with any partiality and his name appears in the body of the document.

Author's Foreword

CARVING is not an art, it is a trade, and for that reason its practitioners are properly classified as tradesmen. Even Grinling Gibbons remains a tradesman, despite the efforts of some writers and commentators to make an artist out of him. In contrast, primitive societies past and present regard the woodcarver as a man apart, imbued with mystical gifts.

This study is perhaps the only extended attempt to put English woodcarving into historical perspective. We are concerned with several different factors. They include the growth of carving from the earliest times in a number of places, the tradesmen themselves and the money which they earned for their skills. Part of the study will be concerned with the effects of Crown patronage, its increase and effect on the craft, and then its decline.

The products of a trade have, by tradition, always been done for reward and profit. In the historical context it is now practically impossible to relate decimal currency to medieval and early modern periods. The shrinkage of the modern penny due to inflation cannot any longer bear any relationship to the 12th century penny, and a medieval penny cannot be rendered as 0.4 new pence. In medieval times prices and wages were measured in halfpence and farthings. Prior to the Black Death sums of ½d, 1d and 1½d were common enough. At Cuxham in Oxfordshire in 1330 the daily rate for ploughing was 1½d, while mowing and reaping attracted a wage of 2d, and wheat reaping brought in 3d. If we attempt to translate such sums into decimal currency, we end up with approximately one new penny. In this study I have resisted the temptation. Actual wages and prices are quoted throughout. I trust that the reader who is neither historian nor antiquarian will keep these sums in perspective.

Frederick Oughton
London 1979

References in square brackets denote page number

[101] Accounts drafted for the Little Bed-Chamber at Windsor Castle, subsequently deleted from the account book and not resubmitted but still relating to work carried out by Gibbons. It was common custom to dispute accounts. Later validated accounts presumably contain such sums suitably disguised under other headings. Some idea of the tedium of certain types of repetitious carving may be gained from this item, which includes '48 ft running of Architrave.'

[104] Draft of details relating to the 1699 embellishment of the King's Great Bed Chamber at Windsor Castle, including approximately 25 feet of 'picture frame over the chimney.' It was customary to cost frames by total length.

[105] Actual costs of door moulding and picture frames are shown in this extract from the Windsor Castle accounts.

[106] Example of fine calligraphy which appeared in important documents. This details the work required of Gibbons at Windsor Castle and it instructs him to find 'timber and workmanship.'

[108] A reference to Gibbons' period at Windsor Castle when he was instructed to carry out sundry repair work.

[109] This document illustrates the common habit of mis-spelling Gibbons' name. It is an order for carving intended to decorate one of the Queen's rooms at Windsor Castle.

[110] Official order for Windsor Castle carving. Such documents contained a wealth of detail as to the intended location of the work, the quality being implicit and not worthy of mention.

[141] Order to Gibbons for 'a statue of wood' emanating from 'King Charles the first'. This is a good example of the fine and florid calligraphy accorded to many sovereign documents of the period. No mention of price was made because the size was not yet decided, and it would fall to Gibbons to survey the proposed site and then suggest a suitable fee.

Introduction

As indicated in the Foreword, the medieval carver was a tradesman rather than an artist. Insight into his attitudes was provided in the presentation of *Herod* by Paul Mills, first performed at the National Theatre, London, on 13 December 1978. Three craftsmen stand in the chancel of the cathedral on which they have been working. The first craftsman asks:

> 'In how many years? Another thousand —
> My little elephant of glossy wood
> Will still be carrying the world on its back.'

This is an allusion to the elephant which appeared as part of the arm-rest of a pew or stall (see plate 25). A few moments later he says:

> ' . . . Who'll notice my elephant.
> And who'll take unction from my fox
> In its oak pulpit. What is it?
> They asked me. I said, a fox.
> They said, the priest. Afterwards
> They took me off the choir. So it's there
> And stays, six weeks' work under a seat.
> Propping up somebody's bum . . . ' *

This is a reference to a misericord representation of Reynard the Fox preaching to the geese. Clearly, it was considered derogatory as far as orthodoxy was concerned. But the passage underlines the often sly humour of the carver at a time when the personality of the craftsman was crushed by the demands of his paymasters.

11

* With acknowledgements to the author, Paul Mills, and the publisher, Rex Collings, London.

Although there are no known surviving examples of their work, the earliest carvers in England were probably the pagan Saxons. But the centuries which followed left plentiful evidence. In the Norman church at South Cerney, Gloucestershire, are two 12th century fragments which may be the earliest evidence of English woodcarving. One fragment is a head of Christ, six inches long, with closed eyes, hair in tresses, and the features oriental in style. The other fragment is a carved foot. Both pieces have traces of colour as evidence of the tradition of painting carved wood. The 13th century church at Balsham, Cambridgeshire, is another link in the chain of time, with 24 carved stalls and bestiary-type creatures on the poppyheads. Elsewhere in a galaxy of carving are a muzzled bear and a stilt walker leading a dog. The medieval imagination is in evidence within a church at Dennington, Suffolk, where the carver used a bench-end to depict a sciapod — a human being with a huge foot which could be used as a parasol while sleeping in the sun. In this particular example the carver mistakenly endowed the creature with two feet instead of a single traditional mythological limb. In the 15th century a carver at East Budleigh, Devon, created dragons, a monster devouring a man and a ship on stormy seas, all on bench-ends for the parish church. The time-tapestry is clearly defined in churches throughout the British Isles. The early 16th century produced at Trull, Somerset, five bench-ends on which are carved in the form of serial imagery a complete religious procession. Later came dynasties of carvers which over the centuries became commercial firms. For instance, there was Thomas Wolstenholme, a joiner and carver, born 1759, who acquired property at the corner of Bootham and Gillygate, York, and died in 1812, leaving his stock in trade and business to his brother, Francis. When Francis died in 1833 he was succeeded by his son, John (1794-1865), who worked as a carver in York Minster. His signature appears on some of the bosses in the nave of this finest of English minsters.

Such factors characterise the English woodcarving tradition. It has traces of a main trunk, it has branches, and yet it has no specific sophistication in the sense that German and French carving suggest sophistication. Apart from the great and voluptuous fountain of work by Grinling Gibbons and some of his contemporaries, English carving has many patterns but no single overall pattern. It explains why this book is likely to develop into a piece of detective work rather than a historical survey. Apart from being a comprehensive study of English woodcarving in general, it is the first entirely new and fresh approach to Gibbons' work since David Green's account, *Grinling Gibbons, His Work as Carver and Statuary, 1648-1721* (Country Life 1964). Unlike Green's book, it is also a critique of Gibbons which, it is hoped, will enable the reader to put England's greatest carver into perspective.

This is as good a time as any to publish an historical account of English woodcarving because we are now at the lower part of the cycle in which the number of master carvers in London is less than one score and ten. A century and a half ago, it was one of the elite trades. If we disregard truly ancient history, the carving trade through its evolution and the laws of supply and demand was broken down into several branches, such as:

(1) Ship carvers responsible for creating figureheads and decorating the sterns and quarters of vessels. Judging from the quality of their work, they were muscular men lacking in appreciation of what they were about. Their work is in the naïve tradition.

(2) Coach carvers who specialised in the decoration of sedan chairs and horse-drawn vehicles. Some comments about their work and way of life can be found elsewhere in this Introduction.

(3) House carvers (including ecclesiastical carvers). They carved pieces of architectural ornamentation, including wainscots, overdoors and doors, the capitals of columns and entablatures.

(4) Furniture carvers, who were divided into two groups, chair carvers and those who carved looking-glass and picture frames. The chair carvers worked as a rule for cabinet makers and decorated such items as stools, couches, bedsteads and tables.

R. Campbell described the trade in 1747 in his *The London Tradesman*: 'The Cabinet-Maker and Upholder employ a species of carvers peculiar to themselves; who are employed in carving Chairs, Posts and Testers of Beds, or any other Furniture whereon Carving is used. Their work is slight and requires no great Ingenuity to perform it; I mean, he (the apprentice) needs no elegant Taste in the general Art of Carving who performs that used at present upon Furniture. They are generally paid by the Piece, according to the Pattern of the Work, and may earn Thirty or Forty Shillings a Week. As this Taste in Furniture has prevailed for some Time past, Tradesmen in this Way are much wanted and are never out of Business. Drawing is absolutely necessary for this as well as all other Classes of Carvers, and the rest of their Education may be as mean as they please.'

The picture-frame and looking-glass carvers worked in partnership with the gilders, and they were sometimes one and the same person. Practically all their work was gilded, not polished. They made a vast variety of pieces, including sconces, gilt stands, pier glasses and marble-topped tables and, of course, frames, using for the most part soft woods for medium class work and lime for the high class pieces. In the 17th century carvers and gilders were amongst the elite of the trade, and they grew wealthy from the commissions which they received from the gentry. Philip Broomefeild, who was carver and gilder to the Crown in the reign of Charles II, supplied 'Sheilds all gilt with burnish gold . . . Stooles Crimson and gould gilt with burnish gould . . . very Large Stands richly carved & gilt with burnisht gould . . and X gilt Branches'. In the reign of William II John Pelletier, a carver and gilder, made for Hampton Court Palace a number of gilt and 'all white' frames for marble-topped tables. A comment on the methods of working and the division of skills appeared in 1761, when Joseph Collyer published his book, *The Parent's and Guardian's Directory*. 'This business, which has been lately carried to great perfection requires much ingenuity, a lively and elegant fancy, skill in drawing, with great neatness, foliages, fruit, flowers, birds, heads &c., a good eye, and a steady hand. The Frame being prepared . . is sent to the Carver, who finishes it in two different manners, as the work requires; either carving in the wood entirely, and afterwards causing the work to be gilt, or cutting out the figures first roughly in the wood; after which the whole is covered with several coats of whiting to a considerable thickness which, when dry, the Carver wets with a brush, and finishes the figures, by making such strokes and imbellishments on the whiting as is agreeable to his pattern. After this he either sends the Frame home, white as it is, or causes some parts of it or the whole to be gilt. But neither the Frames finished in the wood, nor those in the whiting, are entirely cut out of the solid; for all the figures that rise above the plain of the Frame are glued on before the Carver begins to work'.

Between the end of the Victorian era and the start of the present century practically the entire craft of carving became moribund. Apart from a few small carving shops around the country which doubled as coffin makers and joiners, carpenters or masons, it was not practised to a great degree by more than a few hundred professionals, many working only spasmodically and forced to turn their hands between times to other trades in order to make a living. It now seems wholly deplorable that steps were not taken to stimulate the tradition by taking on more apprentices, despite the fact that we are considering a period in which there was a placid acceptance of the British Empire and tradesmen were not considered to be important except in their role as producers of goods. Wood carving practically vanished for lack of patronage, yet in its golden years it flourished on the fat of ecclesiastical patronage and the good offices of the Crown. When the Crown was all but bankrupt and there was a growing disinterest in religion, many of the crafts and the arts fell into decline and atrophy. Most of this patronage came from the Roman Catholic Church, which seemingly had an insatiable appetite for figures sculpted in wood and then thickly polychromed to hide the bare beauty of the oak

or lime. Apart from its cathedrals and parish churches, the Church of England was never very strong in the purse when the talk turned to the commissioning of carvers and the best it was able to offer was the often repetitious geometric carving which many carvers insisted on turning into veritable masterpieces of balance and precision.

At this early stage we should differentiate between good carving and wood sculpture. Carved figures can be considered sculptural in the artistic sense. They were generally executed by stone masons who specialised in the production of saintly figures and external decoration which included gargoyles. They were the craftsmen who possessed a special gift when it came to depicting the human and divine form. One major example is that of the young knight, George de Cantelupe (d 1273), to be seen in the south choir aisle of Abergavenny Church, Gwent. Carved ornamentation, on the other hand, was also provided by stone masons, but they were craftsmen of a different order and it is doubtful whether they would have considered themselves sculptors. Parish churches, cathedrals, minsters and many of the great houses throughout the British Isles are rich in this form of carving. It can be seen in Tudor, Georgian and 19th century houses, inns and public buildings. Even to the untutored eye, a random viewing discloses a wide variety of accomplishment and a good and sound knowledge of style. It is as though the craftsmen already sensed the truth of what Ralph Nicholson was to say in his *Analysis of Ornament* (Chapman and Hall 1855): 'Ornament is essentially the accessory to, and not the substitute of, the useful; it is a decoration or adornment; it can have no independent existence practically'. While the woodcarver may well have improvised, what he improvised was more often than not absolutely right in relation to the job he was doing because he created out of the instinct of the craftsman. Linenfold carving is one example. This stylised representation of linen in vertical folds was invented in the late 15th century, and it probably originated in the Low Countries. It bore no resemblance to any form of geometric carving and was entirely new. By the end of the 15th century it was in use with regional variations in Germany, France and England for the decoration of presses, chests, chimney pieces and panels. The word 'linenfold' was not introduced until the 19th century. Despite its area of origin, it is now regarded as the trademark of the English carver. During the 15th century there was a veritable mishmash of decoration and it was, all too often, crammed into a limited space regardless of the aesthetic appeal. Balustrades, pillars, testers, the ends of joists and joints and literally every inch of space were heavily endowed with carving of varying quality. There is no doubt that some sectors of English woodcarving can offer a rich treasure trove for the collector of visual whimsy. It is quite unwise to approach it

with piety simply because it is ancient or was done under church patronage. Indeed, there is a great deal of Rabelaisian humour to be found, as witness the misericords which depict bare-arsed husbands being beaten by laughing wives. Despite the treatment of the subject, such examples should not be regarded as lewd but naïve.

The men behind much of the great carving and practically all the lesser work are still anonymous in most cases, although the craft was at its zenith in the 14th and 15th centuries, and the carvers were in part responsible for the enrichment of the Gothic Age. The continuous dynasty of the Wolstenholme carvers, mentioned earlier, remains quite unusual. Apart from a few names, such as Grinling Gibbons, Arnold Quellin Jonathan Mayn and Samuel Watson, they are unknown, although a search of public records occasionally yields a name attached to a bill rendered for the job. John Ripley, for instance, was employed in 1529 to carve a set of the King's Beasts at 18s each for the Privy Orchard at Hampton Court. It is sheer accident that we know Ripley's name and those of several more, because they worked for the Crown and so every transaction was recorded in detail.

In the less well recorded world outside Crown patronage there were the anonymous carvers, probably many hundreds of them in England between the 14th and 17th centuries. They were the men who carried out the carving for a set price against a contractual agreement with the architect. There were, too, the gentry, who employed them through their estate stewards to carve the panelling for rooms in much the same way that modern man employs a decorator to hang wallpaper and paint ceilings. Then there were the often rumbustious trade carvers who were employed by other tradesmen. In the 17th century, for instance, the yards in front of the coachbuilder's premises swarmed with the journeymen carvers who bid fiercely against one another in order to get the job of adding the dolphins, the phantasmagoric or allegorical beasts, the curlicues and the swags of fruit, flowers and birds to the vehicles. In common with the artists and the gilders, the carvers were very highly paid, although their work was deliberately undervalued by the coachbuilders, who charged their clients three or four times more than the sum paid to the carvers. In retrospect we can see the carvers in this sector as the aristocracy of tradesmen, though many were chronic drunkards, not above carrying on with the job while reeling from the cheap gin which was freely available and brought to them by the flask by their apprentices. The 17th century was a good but alcoholic time for carvers because the vanity-ridden gentry vied with one another to commission the building of fine coaches and sedan chairs for town and country use. The Establishment of the day was both proud and avaricious, not satisfied with anything but the best. Plainness was at a discount. It was a period in which the carver was able to indulge his personal fancies, drawing many ideas for the embellishment of the carriages not only from the classical forms to be seen in the paintings of the masters but also the madness of their drunken dreams. This explains why it is often difficult to trace the precise origins of certain designs. The fact that these *objets de vanité* would quickly become chipped, broken and mud-splashed mattered not at all. It was sufficient to have the opportunity of helping to create them that mattered. The figures of these roistering coach carvers appear only momentarily in the history of the craft and then fade away, many returning in all probability to the furniture workshops around St Martin's Lane in London, where they earned a fair if humdrum living decorating chairs, 'sophas', bookcases and wall brackets. There were the other carvers who drifted in from the provinces, where they may have been employed on church work. This was such an intensive business that none of the church or coach carvers thought to sign their work. The money was enough.

The noticeable absence of more than a few signed pieces is itself indicative of the mentality of wood carvers as a race of tradesmen. For many centuries carvers have been satisfied to be paid without any desire for personal recognition. Even Grinling Gibbons with the prolific output of his workshops at Ludgate Hill, London, personally signed only two or three pieces to the best of our knowledge, but it should be added that some of his work may well bear cyphers or carved signatures which remain unseen within the rich foliation, scrolls, musical and nautical instruments and the clusters of fruit which typify his style. The lack of names and personalities is perhaps the weakest point of any study of English wood carving. We know practically nothing about the carvers themselves, we know only their work. There is, of course, a good reason for this baffling anonymity. Carvers were regarded as members of teams, and while they may have taken great pride in their work, it would not dawn on them to sign their finished products. While this is naturally frustrating for those who seek to write about them or study their works, it becomes easier to grasp when one looks at the parallel of modern industry. We do not expect to discover the identity of the man who designs and makes the individual parts of a motor car any more than we know the name of the worker who helps to assemble even the finest piece of furniture designed to meet the needs of a wealthy client. So it was with the carvers. They were called in to do the job, they were often provided with detailed drawings, and they duly carried out the task, and then they moved on.

Recognition did come for a time, and it occurred long before the era of Grinling Gibbons. From the ranks of the stone masons came the master carvers, men of wide talents and ingenuity who were able to work in both stone and wood, capable of building and dressing walls, creating tombs in alabaster and marble, carving organ cases or screens for churches. These versatile individuals emerged towards the middle of the 13th century, and they were called 'Imaginator' or 'Imageur'. One of the first was John of St Albans, who was King's Imageur in 1268. He and the other members of the elite were followed for several centuries by the contractors who ran their own workshops in York, Canterbury and other great centres for the special execution of carved pieces in stone and wood. Some of them were prominent in civic life, holding office as mayor of the town or city where they had their businesses.

Grinling Gibbons, who was something of an impressario, still stands at the centre of the English woodcarving tradition. It is typical of English history that he was not English by birth, for he had his origins in the Netherlands and throughout his life appears to have spoken only bad English. His association with the quixotic and self-taught architect, Sir Christopher Wren, was probably not so much a matter of detailed discussion between two masters as an exchange of working drawings. While Gibbons' life and work will be examined later, it should at once be made clear that he was not a slavish copyist as were many other carvers who mercilessly stole from one another. On the contrary, his contemporaries stole from him, because he was the originator of a rich and even ridiculous but always dazzling style. Like many other carvers, he was also a mason, but it cannot be said that his stonework was first quality. He did not, moreover, create an enduring tradition for the reason that his rich and extravagant flamboyance could not be copied or developed with success, nor did it represent a starting point for future excellence. The many reasons why this should be so will become more evident in the section dealing with Gibbons. It is enough to say at this point that many of his finest pieces were more art than craft. At the height of his commercial success, Gibbons was like a great tree without roots or future. This is, admittedly, a radical view, but it is not intended to detract in any way from his unique place in the history of wood carving. He was one of the few carvers capable of recreating in wood the tracery of stonework, and he still has the distinction of being the principal exponent in England of the continental classical baroque style.

Photographs in this book have been collected from many different sources. The criterion for their inclusion has not always been the excellence of the carving itself. In many cases, it was the idiosyncratic nature of the carving. While there is some weight of ecclesiastical carving, this is caused inevitably by the fact that England's great age of carving was motivated by church patronage. Later on the pattern changes to royal patronage, and so on to the age which may in the light of history be called the amateur renaissance.

CHAPTER ONE

From the Primitive to the Pattern

THERE are in some churches and buildings throughout the British Isles early carvings which are grotesque and practically unidentifiable as far as their origins are concerned. Some say they were the jests of crude carvers, others claim that they are the links with Celtic and Romano-Celtic Europe, for they feature the emblem of the severed head. As Dr Anne Ross says in *Grotesques and Gargoyles* (David and Charles, 1975), the church in medieval times was a storehouse of the peoples' subconscious, full of bric-a-brac, much of it inherited from earlier times. This may account for the presence of some of the often nightmarish carvings at such widely spaced sites as Winchester Cathedral, Canterbury Cathedral, the church at Lowick, Northumberland, and the series of beam supports at Canterbury, Kent, in which hermaphroditic creatures are carved. The same type of bisexual creature also appears in the carved façade of the Feathers Inn at Ludlow, Shropshire. There is about much of this early carving a demonic and sensuous appeal which is far from accidental.

Any historical study must have a beginning. Scholars start as a rule with the latter part of the 14th century, but this period was not, in fact, the true beginning. In the Introduction mention was made of the pagan Saxons as the first wood carvers in Britain. We have no known examples of their work and the notion that they were carvers at all is based on historical hypothesis. It is now more profitable to move on to the more interesting later medieval period when the European oak frame house with the cruck frame was introduced. This was an inverted V with oak rafters, a timber very plentiful and taken from the great forests which at that time covered the southern areas of the country. An original cruck frame cottage is still in existence at Didbrook, Gloucestershire, with the beams bearing the unmistakeable marks of the adze, a tool which had its origin in ancient Egypt. The

19

timbers of the cruck were put together in such a way as to bear the weight of the infilling material, supplied by the wall builder and consisting of rubble and stone. Although the timbers cannot be said to have been carved in the conventional sense, there is evidence of the craftsman's appreciation of form, because many of the cruck frame beams were finely tapered and fitted together with great precision. Such houses were fairly small by modern standards and while they were added to as the number in the family increased, they were little more than utilitarian dwellings.

In Anglo-Saxon communities, where the sawyer supplied oak and sycamore sawn to exact dimensions for roof building, it was the carpenter who made the mortise and tenon joints, and he also used a system of wooden pegs for additional stability of the structure. His tools consisted of the chisel, in use from Neolithic times, and the auger, originated by the ancient Egyptians and adapted by the Romans. The development of woodworking tools is the story of the growth of woodworking. This is one of the first indications of the professional woodworker being hired to perform tasks which demanded skill and precision. But in those early times, the idea of actually carving the exposed timbers was not considered. Indeed, the best quality building of the time used only the substantial, but unseasoned, heartwood, and it is feasible to assume that carving would have weakened the structure. This was a case of utility triumphing over aesthetics if we can accept that aesthetics existed amongst the house builders of the time.

The carving of house timbers finally occurred almost as an afterthought, and it sprang inevitably from the joiner's trade. Working closely with the timber, cutting and fitting the joints, he became conscious of the possibilities. As the house of the more important people began to move away from the cruck frame, the square-section design, which is still in use, was introduced to provide the inhabitants of the house with more space, and the need for doors was evident. The first internal doors were simple openings cut in the wall, just wide enough to admit one person, later to be widened so that furniture and goods could be moved through them. Separate rooms were set aside for cooking, siderooms served as storerooms and pantries. The openings were framed in wood and doors were introduced. Latches and locks made their appearance, all made of wood. The idea of using wooden frames for exterior and interior doors spread quickly to include civic buildings. There are East Anglian examples of the infill system of building in which the main posts are carved in geometric patterns. The carving itself is what we would now classify as shallow, or light, relief, and it was probably done by the carpenter himself, using the same straight chisels as were employed for normal carpentry work. It is significant that early and middle medieval carving to be found in East Anglia is generally geometrical, suggesting that the carpenter was unconsciously conditioned by the geometry of the building itself. He would be a down to earth man, not given to any flights of fancy and his idea of decoration would necessarily be severely limited. This was the period when mensuration was an established system and the 16ft pole used as a common rule in building operations. Such domestic and civic carving as has come down to us carries all the trammels of this attention to measurement, consisting of formal patterns worked into the square or rectangle. There is no sensuality and no special form, although isolated examples of inspiration can still be found, as exemplified in the roof of the refectory of Bradenshaw Priory, Wiltshire, and now at St Donat's Castle, South Glamorganshire. In this early 14th century piece of carving there is a richly shaped example of the then fashionable ball-flower ornament, taken from tapestry.

One cannot pretend that the carving of this period was anything more than a somewhat coarse and clumsy attempt to lend attraction to plain surfaces. While houses were built on the infill system the carpenter still reigned supreme, constructing the frame of the house so that it formed a strong and rigid framework for the plaster and wattle and, for the wealthy, the occasional use of bricks. But within a few years the building workers were to see a complete *volte face* in which the carpenter was to become a partner of the mason, who specialised in buildings made of stone. This is where the wood carver's true origins can be found, for he acquired his basic skills while working in stone, a material which had no obstinate or troublesome grain and could be cut or shaped in any direction. He later moved into the discipline of the wood which, by its physical structure, laid down different rules and, in due course, dictated the design of carving tools.

Some idea of the longevity of the craft tradition can be gained by looking at the city of York where John Carr, the architect, was born in 1723. He was the son of a mason and quarry owner, and in 1770 became Lord Mayor of York, dying in 1807. His business was profitable, for he had a virtual monopoly and he employed many apprentices. They were taught design, execution, business methods and the discipline of a trade. Within a few years they were able to become craftsmen in their own right.

Peter Atkinson, born 1753, was a carpenter and Carr's assistant. He was in charge of all carpentry. He brought his son, also called Peter, into the trade. In turn the younger Atkinson had two sons, John and William. The family business continued for many years and is, in fact, still in existence, trading today as Brierley, Leckenby and Keighley. From the 16th century to the present day many stone masons and carvers have been trained and they, in turn, have trained others. This is one example of the craft tradition in England. The craftsmen themselves were men of particular character and tenacity, somehow exemplified in the earlier work of a Burgundian worker in stone and wood who was employed to rebuild the burnt-out Canterbury Cathedral after the fire of 1174. After a fall from the scaffolding he was permanently bedridden but still insisted on directing operations for many years.

John Carr and those who followed him were the originators not only of carved wood for churches in the York area but also a by-product. A growth of demand for good decoration created a situation in which demand outpaced supply. Consequently, many of the carved classical ornaments were used as masters to make moulds for plaster castings. It became common for self-employed carvers to spend time carving such masters which they then sold to firms specialising in architectural carvings for town and country houses. The attractions of mass production have parallels in other crafts in the medieval period. Masons operated in similar fashion, working in city shops and creating stereotyped tomb figures in alabaster or marble, all to much the same design, and then loading them on specially built waggons drawn by teams of horses round the countryside where the figures were offered to the gentry in anticipation of a future death in the family. This explains why certain tomb figures bear no resemblance to the occupant of the grave. So it was with the carvers who offered the master carvings for mould making. Needless to say, at least some of their sense of classical design was suffocated by the profit motive.

The period in which the mason was also a carver has from time to time elicited curious comment. For instance, in his *English Church Craftsmanship* (Batsford 1941) the author, F. H. Crossley considers the 14th century and comes to the conclusion that the habit of the mason in copying stonework in wood was both 'wrong headed and wasteful both in labour and time', basing his observation on the screenwork in Chichester Hospital, St Margaret, King's Lynn and others. But Crossley was writing from the standpoint of the antiquary and he did not pause to consider the dual role of mason and carver.

Despite the ability of the provincial carver to work in both stone and wood, there was an earlier long-standing tradition of 'pure' carving with its roots in the 15th century, when seven patent artisans were attached to the central office of the King's Works. They included the Master Mason and the Master Carpenter. In both offices there was scope to create work of quality to which could be added the material security, for each office holder received a wage of one shilling a day plus an appropriate livery or cash equivalent. These offices lapsed, however, with the coming of Henry VIII, to be revived in October 1482 when John Jerveys was appointed Chief Joiner to the Tower of London by Edward IV. His appointment

was confirmed by Richard III, but lapsed in due course. Jerveys' work had two main branches, the first being concerned with ordnance for the campaigns in France and in 1496 for ordnance for the war against the Scots. The second branch developed between 1500 and 1502, when he worked in royal households near London and probably executed a certain amount of carving.

The versatility of men of Jerveys' stamp was not easy to find, but in 1510 Thomas Stockton was selected to become the first of the Tudor Chief Joiners. He was, in fact, mainly a carver with joinery as his second trade. From 1509 he was master carver at King's College, Cambridge, working for the architect, John Wastell. It was Stockton who brought to the fore Ralph Bowman, no more than a name in the contract documents but on the evidence of his work at King's an exceptionally fine carver. Most of Stockton's work was done in the third period of the building of the Chapel, between 1508 and 1515, and there was, consequently, an overlap with his Crown appointment. After his death in 1525 the appointment went to John Ripley. He was mentioned in the Introduction as having carved the King's Beasts for the Privy Orchard at Hampton Court between 1529 and 1530. In the two years, 1531-32 he made a 'bargain in great' for 'the frete of the roufe of the new galarye' at Whitehall, and this entailed the carving of the wainscot. His workshop was outside London, and when the carving was ready in 1531 it was brought to Whitehall 'to be wrought in cealyng for the new galarye'. In the meantime the finishing touches were added at the Tower of London, which then had one of the main carving workshops in the city. The job was done with great speed because construction work on the new gallery at Whitehall was moving towards completion. It was finally finished in 1533, and the Whitehall surveyor was able to submit his bill, which included Ripley's expenses. Ripley's next major job was to do some carving for the royal barge, followed by the payment of £160 5s for carving the stalls in the King's Chapel of Whitehall. On 1 January 1539 he presented a desk and boxes to the King, for which he was paid 6s 8d as a token sum of appreciation.

Ripley was an enthusiastic organiser of carvers, and he travelled widely, seeking out craftsmen who were able to produce work of high quality, including some who had in the past worked for him at Cambridge. While his fees were in accordance with the rates prevailing at the time, he was still able to wield influence. He retired in 1544, but he was not a wealthy man.

Thomas Ware was appointed Chief Joiner to the King's Works in England on 30 May 1544. He died on 28 June 1545, but Ripley still lived on to see his old post occupied by John Manning, once his apprentice. Manning was paid somewhat less than Ripley and Ware, but he did have the advantage of living in the house at

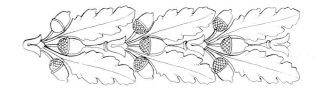

the Tower of London which had, by tradition, been occupied by joiners and carpenters for many years. Yet it was as though the job was fated, for Manning died on 10 July 1551. The next incumbent was Richard Pye, who was joined sometime in March 1568 by Edmund Chapman. Ripley was still alive but there is no record of his death.

A relative of John Ripley, Thomas Ripley (1683-1758), also a carver, married one of Sir Robert Walpole's servants. In April 1715 he was appointed Labourer in Trust at the Savoy, Clerk of Works at the Royal Mews in February 1716, Master Carpenter in September 1721, Comptroller in May 1726 and Keeper of the King's Private Roads in June 1737. After his wife's death he found for himself a Middlesex heiress with a fortune of £40,000. One of his colleagues at official meetings was Vanbrugh, who despised him to such an extent that on seeing notice of Ripley's appointment in a broadsheet he wrote: 'I met with his Name (and Esquire to it) in the News paper; such a laugh came upon me I had like to Beshit my Self . . .' While Ripley was undoubtedly a social climber, he was nevertheless a useful committee man and he attended about 1800 meetings during his years in office. Few craftsmen did as well for themselves as Thomas Ripley.

Some time earlier, on 4 August 1546, Thomas Marcady, joiner and carver, entered Crown service, and he was paid 8d a day and a sum in lieu of livery. French by birth, he had previously worked with his countryman, Robert Sande, on the Hampton Court wainscot, and both men were Ripley's protégés. In this period the Continental carvers were frequent visitors to England, but there is nothing to suggest that they brought with them anything more than their highly developed skills. Certainly, there is no sign of any distinctive Continental design influence in the carving of the time, and it is doubtful whether they even brought their own pattern books across the Channel. Many English carvers carried their own pattern books from job to job, and they were submitted to the master carpenter in charge of the work. He, in turn, consulted the chief architect as to the suitability of design, selecting what seemed to be most suitable. Palaces and state buildings at Whitehall, Oatlands and Nonsuch Palace all had their own pattern books. It was a time of fairly rigid convention as far as carved ornamentation was concerned, and any Continental influences were firmly eschewed.

The joiner-carpenter was not employed solely on the king's works. His terms of employment were such that he was free to develop his business elsewhere. As a general rule, he did very well out of this arrangement, because he could use his connections to advantage in securing outside commissions. In those days the endorsement of the royal warrant meant rather more than it does nowadays. There was another more material stimulant to obtain outside work. This was the system of accounting employed for the king's works. The carver, carpenter and other tradesmen had to submit their intended accounts for payment on a quarterly basis. The accounts were passed round the various establishments for which work had been done. They were dissected and the individual items entered in the ledgers and daybooks, payment being made direct by the paymasters. With the growth of trade in the Middle Ages, the carver's services were much sought after. The crown accounting system appears to have weakened under the strain, and many office holders had to wait for long periods before their bills were paid. Despite widespread dissatisfaction, no changes were made. The situation has changed little, for the modern carver often finds himself in the same position.

In this period carving in England remained 'English' in character and the carvers were forced to accept the narrowness of traditional designs. This continued until Henry VIII came to the throne. The monarch was a thwarted entrepreneur, and it has been said by historians that he tended to think of himself as a Renaissance prince, intent upon the introduction into England of foreign craftsmen and other creative persons. He made a start with the painters, including Antonio Toto (d 1554) and Nicholas Lixard (d 1571), both appointed to the post of Sergeant Painter to the King. Such fanciful titles abounded, for the King was wont to create one post after another simply to accommodate his foreign favourites, but there is no record of a foreign carver achieving any such eminence. Yet all the influences were there. As far as the architects were concerned, this was an excellent opportunity to introduce not only new designs for the state buildings but also a wealth of decorative innovation. Carvers of the traditional artisan establishment found themselves working to many of the King's wild-minded favourites who were in England not so much as architects but as 'devisers of buildings'. Such a man was John Pado, who was paid £36 10s a year. He was very much in the tradition of Leonardo, and came from Padua, bringing with him a reputation as a musician, architect, artificer, engineer and deviser of buildings. His greatest accomplishment lay in the interior decoration of buildings, and he was instrumental in encouraging the more imaginative use of carved wood.

Another craftsman brought to England by Henry VIII was Nicholas of Modena, a designer and carver in the King's service at the same time as Pado. He was largely responsible for the design, construction and decoration of the timber banqueting house in the Privy Garden, and had the then unusual ability to carve slate. He also created the stucco panels for the Nonsuch Palace.

Clearly, this was a time of aesthetic change. Foreign designers and craftsmen mixed with their English contemporaries to work on such ventures as a second timber banqueting house in Hyde Park for the reception of the French ambassadors in 1546. There were also several 'straunge pieces of work', though their exact nature is not known. In these and many other projects the carpenters and the craftsmen were always prominent. Much of their work was ephemeral, created for a specific event and then cast aside or destroyed after use. In a single period of some fifteen years the Crown paid £36,137 3s 1¾d to a multitude of craftsmen for all kinds of work. This comparatively large sum illustrates the extent of patronage provided by royal paymasters. The sum included the elaborate carving of the royal barges and the 'herses' used for royal funerals. The death of Queen Mary created a charge of £16 0s 11d for carvings used at the lying-in-state, including a number of heraldic devices.

If Ripley had been a major figure in his term of office, John Revell was both his equal in stature and highly controversial throughout his service from 25 March 1560 up to his death on 12 December 1563. He was descended from a long line of City of London carpenters. His relative, Nicholas Revell, was a freeman of the Carpenter's Company in 1508. Revell himself was one of the great innovators of woodworking in England, and he had previously been associated with Humphrey Coke, the King's Carpenter and four times warden of the Carpenter's Company. The name of Revell occurs with some regularity in connection with public works throughout the country. Humphrey Revell, for instance, worked at Berwick from 1550 to 1558 as a carpenter and he was also known to Coke, who was then Master Carpenter. Such dynasties were not uncommon amongst the truly gifted craftsmen of the day, and it is to be deplored that this petered out. Sons, brothers, nephews and men who married into the families were automatically absorbed by the respective businesses, and it was expected that they would in turn carry on, one generation following the other.

John Revell unfortunately suffered from one quite useful attribute which was to give him trouble later in his career. He possessed a nose for good timber. In his three and a half years in Crown office he appears to have been on the look out not only for stocks of timber suitable for building and general construction purposes, but also for the carvers from whom he commissioned work in his official capacity. In the summer of 1561 he was to purchase 481 loads from certain merchants. The fact that the bulk of it came from his own relative, James Revell, is purely coincidental. It was the same James who provided northern oak which he obtained from a cathedral committee at Guisborough, Yorkshire. The Queen herself made a gift of timber from Welbeck Manor, Nottinghamshire. One thousand loads were removed under the direction of James Revell, and 48 tons sent to London by sea aboard a chartered Flemish vessel.

Revell's influence on the carving trade was considerable. In the face of

opposition, he introduced new forms of indentures for apprentices, and he also hired carvers by the day to work in shifts on the decoration of Crown buildings. Up to this time it was practically unheard of for the Surveyor-general to sanction the employment of more than one master carver and an appropriate number of apprentices to execute any particular piece of work. Revell did away with this arrangement and created what we would today call a piecework system. In spirit he appears to have been an impatient and impetuous man with little regard for official finances, and after his death a major enquiry was set up to look into his methods of administration and the way he had handled funds. It transpired that he probably diverted the labours of certain carvers to carry out work which was not entirely connected with the State. The carvers themselves would have been unaware of what was going on, being quite satisfied to carve whatever was ordered so long as they were paid for what they did. The real flaw lay in Revell's business methods, which the enquiry ruthlessly revealed. In mitigation, let it be said that there was a weakness in his own terms of employment, which stated that he must cause State works to be carried out 'at reasonable price'. This was imprecise, and because it was imprecise when Revell was under great pressure to produce results, he took advantage of it on many occasions. The sad fact remains, however, that certain discrepancies did come to light following the examination of his accounts. His brother, James, for instance had been paid for 44 days more than he could possibly have worked within a certain period. After John's death James was never again employed on royal contracts and, indeed, the entire Revell ménage of contractors in carpentry and carving practically vanished under the collective embarrassment of implied fraudulent dealing.

The trend of placing men with experience of carving in high office was to continue with the appointment of Lewis Stockett as Surveyor of Works, a post which he held from 12 December 1563 until his death on, or about, 21 February 1579. He took as his wife, Joan Ware, daughter of the Chief Joiner. In his own way Stockett was almost as remarkable as Revell, though for quite different reasons. He was originally a joiner who became a mason and later in life converted himself into a wood carver of distinction. After the disaster of Revell's accounting system and the official enquiry, the terms of reference offered to Stockett did not include the key function of paymaster, this office being delegated to a non-craftsman administrator, who recommended levels of expenditure which were lower than ever. Where Revell had spent an average 7s 11¾d travelling expenses, Stockett was firmly limited to only 4s. Faced with the financial aftermath created by his predecessor, Stockett had no option but to get rid of the many carvers who had, under Revell's administration, been used to accepting one commission after

another. On investigation, it was found that a lot of work had been farmed out. What Stockett decided to do was select six master carvers and give them freedom to hire other carvers on a casual basis and on their own terms, subject to his approval of the standard of their work. Although he was heavily engaged on his official duties, he still made time to execute drawings and designs for the master carvers who had, in Revell's time, been left very much to their own devices. Stockett personally supervised not only the general work but also many of the special carvings made for such royal establishments as Westminster, St James's, Greenwich, Eltham, Richmond, Oatlands, Hatfield, Ampthill, Woodstock, Collyweston, Fotheringhay and New Hall. An examination of his appropriations, estimates and general budget does suggest that he must have been inhibited in his desire to introduce more carved work than before, for he was limited to the annual expenditure of only £100 each for the seventeen royal residences, out of which he had to provide full building maintenance services. Stockett was a man of courage for even attempting the task.

A great deal of purely ephemeral carving was carried out for festivities on the three main annual holidays, Christmas, the Maundy and St George's Day. These carvings were probably executed very roughly, and they consisted of the relief decoration of pillars, the planked platforms with surrounds which served as stages for masques, and the representation of religious and mythological figures to decorate the halls and the outside areas where 'plais, revells and triumphes' were presented.

It is quite obvious in the light of history that Lewis Stockett was unable to be both craftsman and administrator. Throughout the annals of the trades this combination has never met with much success. It is unlikely that he really understood what he was about when it came to handling public money. Whereas Revell created what amounted to an artificial boom for the carving fraternity in London, Stockett somehow could not hold confidence. By the time he died in February 1579 he had run up a number of debts which were outside his remit. Nevertheless, he had many unusual characteristics, bearing in mind the conditions under which he lived and worked. For instance, he trained his second wife, Lucy, to run the business during his many absences on official business. She was not, of course, a working carver, but she did know about the ramifications of the trade and she was well equipped when it came to haggling over prices with the carvers who offered their services. Three years after her husband's death, she was still operating the building business he created.

Carvers were once again prominent in the reign of Elizabeth I. A flourishing business, shared between several carving shops, developed in the carving of heraldic shields under the aegis of the College of Arms. Much of the work was done by carvers who worked not in London but in the country, probably in Buckinghamshire. When the carving was finished, the shield was brought to London for gilding and painting by other specialised craftsmen. This division of skilled labour was not uncommon, and even nowadays it is unusual to find a carver with any great knowledge of surface finishing. In our own time many of the carvings for the College of Arms are executed by Gino Masero, a master carver, whose work hangs in the Royal Chapel at Windsor. As in the reign of Elizabeth I, the painting is carried out by specialists.

After Stockett's death there were no further appointments of carvers to the office of Surveyor-general. The tempo of the carving industry became much slower, and it remained in limbo until Inigo Jones took office as Surveyor on 1 October 1615, continuing until 1643. Like other holders of the position, Inigo Jones almost immediately found himself in financial difficulties. The long history of official debt was without end. Within two years his workmen were 'clamourous' due to arrears of wages. The fault lay not with Inigo Jones himself but with the late Paymaster, Andrew Kyrwyn, who left an unfortunate legacy of £473 18s 5¼d which he alleged was owed to him by the Exchequer. Within a few months the sum increased to £486 12s 0¾d as one account after another fell due for payment. By 1635 Inigo Jones was himself owed two years' salary, while that of Nicholas Stone, the Master Mason and carver, was £59 6s 3d for two years' service.

Stone, a remarkable craftsman, was encouraged by Inigo Jones to develop his craft. The architect had a great fund of ideas, having travelled widely in Italy, visiting such places as Vicenza, Rome, Tivoli and Naples, and he had, moreover, spent ten years of his life designing masques for the theatre. After his successful partnership with Ben Jonson, the playwright, the growing animosity against the plays resulted in parliament suppressing them. As a more sweeping measure, it was decreed that all theatres should be immediately closed down. At the age of 40 Inigo Jones was appointed Surveyor-general to the Crown. What he brought to the position was verve and dash, a sense of the theatrical and, most of all, the Italianate influences which were to inspire Nicholas Stone.

Stone's best work is undoubtedly the figure of Lady Carey at Stowe-Nine-Churches in Northamptonshire. It was executed in marble and black touchstone. But he also worked in wood from time to time, probably using the wooden effigies as maquettes for the final work in stone. He was Master Mason from 1632 up to the time of the Civil War. Born in Exeter some time in 1587, he was apprenticed to the half-Dutch Isaac James, who had workshops in the Southwark district of London. Stone met Hendrik de Keyser in 1606 when the Dutch architect visited London to examine the Royal Exchange with a view to creating a similar structure in Amsterdam. As a result, Stone went with Keyser to the Amsterdam workshop, and in 1613 married Maria, the architect's daughter. When he returned to London it was to start a business in Long Acre which continued to flourish up to 1641. He was imprisoned in the Civil War, and the experience probably contributed to his poor health, for in 1640 he was said to be 'disposed to bee but sickly'. He died in 1647 to be followed in 1648 by Maria and one of their sons. He was buried in St Martins-in-the-Fields where the eldest son, John, erected a mural monument to the memory of his father.

In their heyday the Long Acre workshops were amongst the busiest in London, work being divided almost equally between wood and stone. The premises were more than ample, for Stone owned five houses in the same street and he held a number of leaseholds elsewhere in the district. To them came many carvers and masons, including Francis Carter. He is generally referred to as an architect, but was by trade a carpenter, responsible for making and carving the screen at Trinity College, Cambridge, in 1604. He worked at Cambridge with Andrew Chapman, who originated much of the carved design. Carter's work at Trinity so impressed Stone that he was later able to use his influence to procure for him the post of Clerk of Works under Inigo Jones in the service of Prince Henry. By this time Carter's reputation was such that he commanded high fees for even comparatively minor jobs. In 1612 he was paid 40s by Sir Edward Pytts 'for drawing the upright of the forepart of my house in London'.

Carter was obviously more than a simple carver who happened to have an interest in architecture. He was by nature very ambitious and he certainly found some scope for his talents on his appointment as Clerk of Works with a staff of eight working for him in 1615. But Crown service sapped his energies. From being a practical tradesman he developed into an administrator in a post which was not in itself creative.

There was at this time a top-heavy weight of administration, but even a superficial knowledge of conditions suggests that this was probably necessary. Charles I inherited from his father a plan to restrict the growth of London, which had, within a decade, developed into a vast and ugly spread of ramshackle buildings, many of them representing dangerous fire hazards. The plentiful and cheap supply of wood and the continuing high cost of bricks and stone led to a conglomeration of glorified shed-like buildings in which outbreaks of fire were common. A concerned Charles I instructed Inigo Jones' department to carry out surveys with powers to levy penalties, including imprisonment, on those who refused to improve their buildings.

From time to time during this restless period the names of certain carvers come to the fore. One of them was Zachary Taylor. Inigo Jones became involved in negotiations with Francis Russell, 4th Earl of Bedford, to build 'howses and buildings fitt for the habitations of Gentlemen and men of ability' on some land in Covent Garden owned by the Earl. The grand scheme included the church of St Paul in which Grinling Gibbons was destined to be buried. Zachary Taylor, basically a bricklayer, was hired. In his time he had been a journeyman carver working in various parts of the country. He was joined for the work by John Benson, a tradesman carver, and between them they completed the carving of the pulpit and a reader's pew. Taylor is mentioned at this point for one good and significant reason, it is the first time that history records a bricklayer-carver. Up to this moment it has always been a mason-carver. There is a suggestion that we may have reached the beginning of the period of transition in which the carver was trained as a carver and remained a carver. It is unlikely that a bricklayer would have been able to obtain training in carving, as would a mason in a closely allied trade.

Taylor was to reappear later on in connection with the rebuilding of St Paul's Cathedral under the architect, Sir Christopher Wren. The building was destroyed in 1561 after being struck by lightning. Queen Elizabeth commanded the Lord Mayor and the Archbishop to raise money for the rebuilding, and to set an example she offered to donate a sum of money in addition to some prime timber for fine carving. By the time James I ascended the throne the cathedral remained nothing more than a slum and a scandal. Very little real work had been done and there were apparently no plans for the future. After a series of meetings, plans were made to demolish buildings adjacent to the site to make room for operations. Between 1634 and 1641 there was a renewal of activity, and it was Zachary Taylor who carved a full-scale model of the entablature. No record exists of any payment made to him for his labours. By this time tempers were running high not only among the master carvers and the masons but also the apprentices. Once more there were arrears of wages. Many of the apprentices left when the model of the entablature was only half finished, but Taylor worked on, using whatever labour he could find and despite the lack of suitable timber for the job following the refusal by Hampshire magistrates to contribute to the cost of moving wood from the forests under their control.

It seemed that carving work for the cathedral was doomed. Quantities of half finished and finished carving were stored amongst the stonework which stood about in heaps all over the site. During the Civil War it was hacked to pieces for kindling by soldiers serving under Colonel Jephson, who quartered his horses in the area. Jephson was in a good position to do as he pleased, for he and his men had not been paid for a considerable time.

Under the administration of Inigo Jones carvers and other craftsmen suffered many setbacks. They were barely able to live, and when the Exchequer sank into even deeper waters there was a significant drop in the quality and the quantity of official carving being done. Apprentices were badly treated and left their trade never to return. Any major works were carried out by the few remaining master carvers, many of them ageing by this time and as a result slow to produce acceptable pieces.

Lower down on the trades scale there were the carvers who avoided the well-known uncertainties of working for the Crown. They chose to earn a more humble but certain living in the furniture manufactories of Shoreditch and other areas of London. They were not mass production workshops as we understand the term, but small establishments engaged in making commissioned pieces for the gentry, who brought designs back from travels in France, Germany and Italy.

There was also a comparatively new industry which provided some carvers with a good living, and it consisted of creating carved decoration of what is now called 'cottage furniture' or 'country furniture', the origins of which are interesting. Fashions in furniture originated more often than not in London and, like all fashion, tended to radiate outwards, where the provincial workshops seized on the patterns and set about making credible imitations, usually in oak, which was plentiful, but also in the more exotic mahogany. The clientele for this type of furniture was found mainly amongst the servants of the gentry. The industry was based on snob appeal of a sort. Certain items, such as coffer chests, dressers and tables were produced in great quantities. The carved ornamentation may not have been up to London standards, but it was still passable and had its own naïve charm. Country carvers were soon busy adding appropriate motifs to the furniture. When Charles II returned from exile in Holland, he brought with him a pet obsession for the tulip. After 1660 patterns based on the tulip petal occur in profusion as part of the decoration of country furniture. There is a particularly good example on a chest at Aylesbury Museum, Buckinghamshire, carved with both monogram and date, 16 eh 92. Chests were a speciality of workshops in the Aylesbury area.

Under the Protectorate there was a resurgence of Crown work for carvers, and between 1645 and 1646 the London carvers competed for the opportunity of working on the House of Commons, in which the screen was carved by Zachary Taylor. He also carved the king's arms and supporters, 'to be seene on both sides', a pair of wooden scrolls and an item referred to in contemporary records as a 'frontispiece'. Despite the many extravagant plans for the House of Commons, work was delayed for considerable periods due to an impoverished Exchequer which seemed to be preoccupied with the matter of outstanding debts. At a time when John Embree, Sergeant Plumber, was presenting bills in 1654 for considerable sums, including £12,000 for repairs to the Protector's houses, it seemed highly unlikely that the London wood carvers would make a fortune out of work on the House of Commons.

1   Rural carvers of the late 12th and early 13th centuries had a 'primitive' approach to figure portrayal but displayed a sense of composition, as seen in this corbel at the Bull Inn, Long Melford, Suffolk. The same carving idiosyncrasies can also be seen in American folk carving from 1800 onwards.

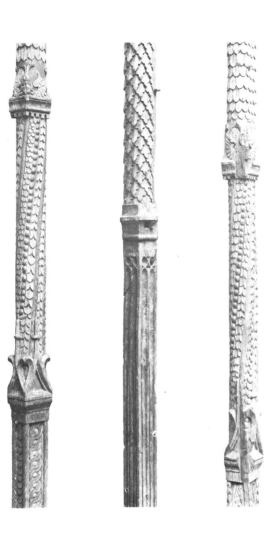

2 Medieval architectural post-carving frequently presents conflicting design motifs. These examples suggest the 'fish-scale' pargetting of Essex in partnership with the major characteristics of Romanesque capitals. In the lower left post there is a hint of the Scandinavian Romanesque.
Victoria and Albert Museum, London.

3 This oak shield with its flamboyant lettering and formalised oak-leaf decoration is not truly heraldic but was probably carved as a recognition or identification piece for a member of the lesser nobility. It can be dated, approximately, by the inclusion of the Norman embattlement, which parallels architectural examples, one of which can be seen at Deeping St James, Lincolnshire, dated 1120.
Victoria and Albert Museum, London.

4 Medieval crucifix, partly restored. The three animals are all symbolic and scrolled, and the angel holds a similar scroll. A feature of this carving is the use of the quatrefoils inside which the carver composed the figures. Taken from stone ornamentation, the quatrefoil formed a frame for much medieval carving.
Victoria and Albert Museum, London.

5 Bench-end at Spaxton, Somerset, illustrates the village carver's aptitude for the ornamentation of a date while avoiding the then sacrilegious embellishment of the Cross. A rough, sturdy example of early rural carving.

6 Medieval door panel suggesting a version in wood of the familiar treatment in stone of the same subject. Done in the Early Gothic style, it is a good example of drapery carving and figure composition which stemmed from the influence of William of Sens, architect of Canterbury Cathedral.
Victoria and Albert Museum, London.

7 Grotesque medieval armrests with designs culled from contemporary bestiaries, such as the 4-volume *Historia Animalium* by Konrad Gesner (1516–1565) and others whose wood blocks continued to be used until well into the 17th century. Gesner's illustrations were reproduced in two zoological volumes on mammals and serpents by the English curate, Edward Topsell, published in 1607 and 1608. The carving is crude but nonetheless effective. Victoria and Albert Museum, London.

9 Arcading used for the ornamentation of walls or furniture. Characteristic of the Romanesque period and carried into the late 16th and 17th centuries, when it was adapted for furniture and the embellishment of chimneypieces. An unusual feature of this example is the addition of the grotesque, animalistic faces, suggesting gargoyles.
Victoria and Albert Museum, London.

8 Cupboard door displaying in the lower panel the medieval carver's aptitude for copying architectural detail. Pillars and arch are strongly reminiscent of aspects of Canterbury Cathedral, though the upper panel is strangely out of character and even alien.
Victoria and Albert Museum, London.

10 Rare example of medieval relief carving showing a lyrical sense of movement and perspective. Originally part of a coffer chest, it has an unusual definition in the treatment of contemporary costume, architecture and plant life. Museum of London.

11 Section of medieval rood screen. They were as a rule divided into bays with pierced openings and a gate. Many had an overhanging cornice with dentil moulding, not shown here. Victoria and Albert Museum, London.

12 Reredos of the Norman period,
1066–1189, in imitation of the Norman French,
developing slowly into a more characteristic
national style. A marked departure from
repetition of the internal quatrefoil decoration
can be seen in this example. The reredos was the
screen covering the wall behind and above the
altar. When made of wood it is, more properly,
called a retablum.
Victoria and Albert Museum, London.

13 A 16th century carver celebrated the
fuller's trade in this bench-end at Spaxton,
Somerset. The detail includes the two-handled
mallet in use on a length of cloth, knife, shears,
weaver's comb, and the three-pronged teasel-
holder. The portrayal of trades relate as a rule
to the industries which in their day contributed
to the wealth of the area.

14   Panel ornamentation of a cupboard carved some time between 1595 and 1698 at Stoke Gregory, Somerset. It shows a woman in contemporary costume tending her garden and holding what appears to be a watering-can. A human note can be found in the slight foreshortening of the woman's head, suggesting that the carver misjudged his dimensions.

16   This Kidlington, Oxon, rebus is a mid 16th century attempt at celebrating the sources of local wealth, including sheep farming. There is also a monogrammed cushion. The source of the fish is unknown.

15   Bench-end at Broomfield, Somerset. This mid 16th century example by Simon Werman with workshops at Taunton, is similar in style and quality to his work at Trull, where his name appears on linenfold panelling and in many village churches in the Taunton area.

17   Top half of a bench-end carved by Simon Werman at his Taunton workshop (see illus. 15). Typical of the Werman style, it shows a clever integration of birds and foliage and a natural frame created by the moulding.

18 A mid 16th century bench-end at Milverton, Somerset. The subject is probably Joshua and Caleb, the spies, coming back from the Promised Land bringing with them a bunch of grapes. Careful characterisation and composition suggest that it was executed by a practised carver with a sure sense of design in the specialised field of relief carving.

19 An outstanding example of misericord carving in which the husband is being vigorously chastised by his wife, who lifts his top garment to reveal a bare backside while he endeavours to wind yarn. Composition in misericord design demanded a skilled eye if all elements were to be included within the dimensions of a triangle.
Westminster Abbey, London.

20 A Beverley Minster, Yorkshire, early 16th century misericord which illustrates the saying 'Putting the cart before the horse.' A further example of the ingenious use of perspective.

21 Few carved medieval trade signs have survived, but they were once common outside premises at a time when illiteracy was defeated by their graphic use. This sign hung outside the premises of a seller of rope and twine. The standard of carving is high and the design forms a natural cartouche.

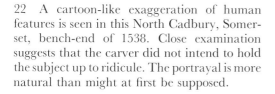

22 A cartoon-like exaggeration of human features is seen in this North Cadbury, Somerset, bench-end of 1538. Close examination suggests that the carver did not intend to hold the subject up to ridicule. The portrayal is more natural than might at first be supposed.

23 Supporter, or side-piece, of a misericord in St George's Chapel, Windsor. One of the major repositories of misericords in the United Kingdom, the chapel contains 96 examples dating from 1477 to 1483, the closing years of the reign of Edward IV. Later misericords were carved between 1786 and 1790 by Henry Emlyn.

24 Late 14th century carving depicting St George in combat with the Dragon. This is one of the outstanding examples of internal quatrefoil composition in which the carver successfully conveyed the essence of the action in near abstract terms. Lincoln Cathedral choir stalls.

25 One of the finest of all elephant carvings. A medieval finial on the bishop's stall at Ripon, North Yorkshire. The carver probably gained his design idea from a bestiary and added to it the howdah, basing the architecture on ecclesiastical forms and adding the heads of personages. His concept was based on the suggestion of the world being carried on the back of the beast.

26 A 15th century interpretation of St Anne, the Blessed Virgin, and her Divine Child, carved in oak with a traditional Gothic treatment of the drapery. The embattled canopy suggests the influence of architecture and the craft of the stone mason at a time when masons were also wood carvers.

27 Detail of one of the finest fully carved pulpits in the United Kingdom at Trull, Somerset. This 16th century masterpiece contains a number of figures in oak, including the Doctors of the Church, shown here. Unlike some figure carving of the same period, this example imbues distinctive personalities and characteristic attitudes to each of the figures.

30 The figure of Jack Blandifer outside Wells Cathedral, Somerset, is part of the clock and dates back to the 14th century. Located above the triforium above the north transept, the figure kicks his heels every quarter of an hour to set two knights in armour striking the bells with their battleaxes outside the walls while small mounted knights gallop on the wall below in the transept. Inside the cathedral are 64 misericords notable for their supporters of oak, vine, rose, marshmallow, ivy, beech and other plants and trees.

28 A fragment from a Nativity carving in Exeter Cathedral, Devon, showing a group of shepherds and their sheep with an angel hovering over the scene. The carving, probably executed between 1238 and 1244, is contemporary with the 50 misericords, representing the oldest complete set in the United Kingdom.

29 One of the late 14th century misericords in Lincoln Cathedral, representative of the carving standard of the total of 92 examples. It is said to show a barbarian king in the centre with his chiefs as supporters. The composition of the king's beard follows the general shape of the seat, above.

CHAPTER TWO

Pre-Renaissance Carvers and Carving

THE methods used by the carvers to obtain commissions from the Crown from 1154 onwards were in their own time as well defined as the modern tendering system is today. There are other parallels between then and now. Some of the records suggest that while the Crown was quick to put work in hand and even to provide ample funds for the initial phases, it often failed in its obligations when the job demanded rather more time than had originally been anticipated. In fairness to the Crown of that time, it should be said that there were several periods when the master craftsmen in charge of work used the time to line their own pockets, a habit not entirely unknown in our own day and age.

English master carvers came from many different parts of the country and they often made a point of keeping in close touch with their home areas. When a royal writ was issued to bring together funds for a particular job, the craft resources would generally be known to a carver in any particular area. The writ itself was inscribed on parchment with the royal seal attached, and the wording was in the following style: 'John, by the grace of God King of England, Lord of Ireland, Duke of Normandy and Aquitaine, and Count of Anjou, to the sherriff of Oxfordshire, greeting. We command you that as soon as you have read these letters you have our houses of Oxford repaired against our coming by the view and testimony of law-worthy men, and the expense shall be allowed to you by the Exchequer. Witness myself at Newbury, the twelfth day of December, in the fifth year of our reign'.

Writs varied only slightly in their texts. On receipt in the area to which it was addressed, the sherriff would issue similar documents to the sherriffs of neighbouring counties, asking them to render due assistance, materials and, above all, craftsmen. It was by this system that the carvers who would otherwise be isolated became known to each other and were able to reach agreements concerning the regulation of their work. It was also necessary to settle in advance the rates to be charged for the work. The same applied to the masons and other craftsmen. In the meantime the sherriffs raised funds for the work by drawing levies from the manors of the county. They also called in overdue debts and applied for grants against central funds.

When estimating for a job, the carver first met the sherriff's finance officers to find out exactly how much work was to be done and how much money was available. If contemporary records are reliable, there seems to have been very little competitive spirit amongst the carvers, and it is doubtful if they felt any great honour at being awarded Crown work. This is understandable when it is understood that carvers living and working outside London generally had business interests, such as landowning and farming. By comparison with London standards, the style and execution of the provincial carver may have lacked metropolitan finesse, but it was acceptable to the contractor.

Disregarding the notorious difficulties of travel at this time, it is interesting to note that the London carvers remained in the city and did not make any attempt to poach work from outlying areas, even when they were well aware of the rewards to be gained. It is possible that there was an unwritten code between craftsmen to prevent this. On the other hand, if a provincial carver elected to go to London to seek work, he would be welcomed by the London master carvers who were conscious of the need to maintain standards. To satisfy them, the provincial carver would carve a specimen piece and carry it to London for examination by the master carvers and, once accepted, the newcomer could count on getting a fair share of whatever work was available. The transition to London was generally dictated by financial considerations and a sense of increased prestige rather than by ambition. As a race of tradesmen carvers have never been exactly forceful. Their satisfaction was, and is, in the work itself rather than self-aggrandisement. This attitude extended towards financial goals, too. Indeed, the entire story of carving suggests that many carvers completed work for which they were only partly paid. Even when the trade was flourishing in England, the departure of apprentices was marked. As far as the apprenticeship system itself is concerned, the trait has continued up to the present day, and it is difficult to find many carving shops in which there is still a firm system of apprenticeship. The trade of the mason is better off, and it is perhaps deplorable that the mason and the carver are no longer synonymous in function. Despite the resurgence of the amateur who produces a remarkably high standard of work, the trade is still unable to attract and hold apprentices. The truth is that in England carving has become a poor trade and it cannot afford the luxury of apprentices, despite a growing problem of succession. On the Continent it is a different story, for the state schools of carving, notably at Oberammergau, have waiting lists, despite the fact that they still follow the same rigorous regimen which has been practised for several hundred years.

From 1154 the English carvers did have apprentices and improvers. A structured work force was necessary in view of the scope of many major works and the time in which they had to be completed. Such work was done very systematically, beginning with the wood coming from the carpenter or sawyer after sizing and squaring up. It was then marked to dimensions under the supervision of the master carver, working to the drawings. The apprentices roughed it out, removing all the surplus wood. On large jobs the tool used for this stage of the work was the short-handled adze which, by its nature, enabled the user to work from many different angles, occasionally standing on top of the piece of wood and working his way downwards on the material beneath his feet. After this phase was completed, the job was then ready for the improvers, who were senior apprentices in their third or fourth year. It was their job to bost-in the shape, cutting the wood down more closely to the original markings and blocking in the internal features. Bosting-in meant working outwards from the marks on the wood, generally to within an inch or two to provide sufficient tolerance for the master carver when he defined the detail. When helping to carve a standing figure, they would also block in the hands, arms, nose, mouth and eyes and hair. This stage was done under the close surveillance of the master carver himself. The improver's tools were gouges and straight chisels, all forged and edged by the smith. The actual choice of tools depended on the scale of the work. Many of the improvers had already acquired their own particular skills and used sets of tools which they would carry with them throughout their working lives. Each man had a personal preference for certain lengths and widths of chisel and gouge and handle, which they made for themselves out of beech wood. At this time the most common handle was octagonal in shape but somewhat longer than the modern type. The dimensions of the work carried out at this time called not only for a well developed aesthetic sense and a knowledge of the properties of the wood but also the controlled muscular development of wrist and arm for which carvers have always been noted. Some jobs involved the carving of figures several feet in height or hundreds of yards of finely carved screen. The most commonly used timber was oak, a tough material with qualities all its own.

The master carver did not work alone. He was assisted by his senior improvers, and one of their tasks was to ensure that the master's tools were kept sharp and in good condition. They were not permitted to execute parts of the final carving, the final shaping and cutting of the finer detail being in the hands of the master himself while witnessed by the improvers who learned their trade in this way.

The actual planning of the work to a time schedule was done by the master carver, who first assessed the nature of the timber supplied to him. From the 10th century onwards it seems that carvers began to explore and understand the nature of wood as a working material. Presumably up to this time carving was done with scant regard for the need to dry and season the wood, and many early carvings consequently developed shakes, or splits, and either fell to pieces beyond retrieval or ended up in the restorer's workshop in later times. With a growth of knowledge of the benefits of air drying timber sections, however, the quality of the carver's material improved. In various parts of England, including Canterbury, Gravesend and London, timber was brought in from the forests, and then cut, trimmed and stacked in yards for years on end. This, in turn, led to the establishment of a new trade which was an offshoot of the mason's yard, where it was possible to see several hundred tons of oak, ash, sycamore and beech drying on racks in an open shed. Attached to these yards were the sawyers who cut the timber to order for the carvers. In many cases the sawyers also worked for the masons, trimming and dressing the stone blocks used for buildings, churches, monuments and fortifications.

When a carving was completed to the satisfaction of the master carver, it was then inspected by representatives of the sherriff and the architect or 'deviser of buildings'. There is some doubt whether any of these worthies actually possessed a very cultivated taste when it came to assessing the worth of a carving, and the inspection ceremony was consequently little more than a formality before the work was passed to the carpenters to fix it in its appointed place. Some notion of the doubtful quality of the persons charged with inspecting and passing finished carvings and other work can be gained when we learn that in 1184 a doctor and a parson were the official viewers at Nottingham Castle, while in London the job fell to one Edward Blund, whose normal function was the purveying of food, wine and clothing to the royal family. It is not hard to imagine the furore which might have occurred had one of these inspectors taken it into his head to object to a carving.

Other systems of employment were available. In one of them the master carver and his apprentices and improvers moved around the country from one job to the next. They were among the elite of the carving trade, being paid regular wages regardless of whether they worked or not. The system evolved as a result of the constant mobility of the Angerin kings. In Norman times the ruler had no permanent home. The Court was always on the move, and a restless and energetic monarch might well traverse the entire length and breadth of his kingdom within a single year. It is recorded that Henry II exhausted his entourage with his comings and goings, while King John never remained in one place for more than a day or two at a time. In some cases the tradesmen, including the carver and his staff, moved with the royal party, but more often than not they travelled ahead to ensure that the castles and other royal residences were in a good state of repair and made ready for the visit.

Carvers who received royal stipends were naturally a cut or two above the provincial and London carvers. Many of them had a long experience of working in both stone and wood, and possessed a good sense of style and design, for they counted among their close colleagues the architects, engineers and *ingeniatores*, the latter being responsible for both civil and military engineering. Court carvers were not as a rule English by birth but came mainly from Normandy, one of the first being Master Elyas of Oxford who, in 1187, was a stonemason but later made a name as a carpenter and carver. In 1195 he worked at Westminster and, later, Rochester, Hastings and Pevensey. From 1200 onwards he worked at Oxford, the Tower of London and Portchester and carried out work for the New Forest hunting lodges. By 1203 he was paid off, but during his tenure he filled many roles, including engineer, designer, mason and carver.

Master Nicholas de Andeli was carpenter and carver in 1207, and he was a man of a different type, for he led a large group of woodworkers, all of them French refugees who came to England after Normandy fell to King Phillip of France. It is assumed that Nicholas de Andeli came from Andeli on the Seine. His craftsmen offered work of the highest quality, and they were quickly granted Crown patronage, working at Finmere in 1207 and then at Gloucester. In 1210 he appeared at Knepp Castle, Sussex, and in the following year travelled to Ireland with King John, but by 1212 he was back in England, carrying out work at Cambridge Castle. His industry and the organisation of his craftsmen were rewarded with a gift of land from the King in addition to a wage of 9d a day with a livery and an annual gift of £5. The actual nature of the work carried out by Nicholas de Andeli's tradesmen is not known, but it probably consisted of ceiling beams, post and supports, heraldry and such, and they also carved the ordnance for military campaigns.

CHAPTER THREE

The Great Works

THE rebuilding of Westminster, which commenced as a result of the initiative of Henry III in 1245, was sufficiently ambitious to call for the services of many carvers in the planning stages, but when the work started far fewer men were employed, due perhaps to the stringent overseership of Master Ode, the Goldsmith, followed later by his son, Edward Henry. The new Westminster was visualised as a vast Gothic edifice in the style of buildings in the Ile de France, Rheims, Amiens and Beauvais. The history of the construction of this almost surrealistic building is not within the scope of the present study, but we should note that the job of carving the lectern was given in 1249 to one John of St Omer, a Flemish carver, and he was instructed to copy the St Albans lectern but make it 'finer and more beautiful'. To study the original, he travelled to St Albans, taking two assistants with him, and he was, rather unaccountably, still there four years later, presumably making drawings and models.

In the 12th and 13th centuries a limited amount of work was available to carvers employed in the King's houses. Edward I inherited 20 houses in 1272 but by 1485 only six were the direct responsibility of the Crown. They were Clarendon, Clipstone, Havering, Windsor, Woodstock and Westminster. Despite a lessening of opportunity some work was available at other houses favoured but not actually owned by the Monarch, including Eltham, King's Langley and Sheen. Many of them had chequered histories, which explains their haphazard patterns of restoration. Some, like Eltham, had large sums of money spent on them only to fall into disrepair within a short time. Yet in their heyday they saw many significant events. Eltham, for instance, was the scene of the reception of the captive King John of France by Edward III in 1363 when John returned to voluntary exile in England. Erasmus dined in the Great Hall in 1500, and it was at that time a gamut of superb carving. It was visited and admired by Leo, King of Armenia, when he came to the court of Richard II. Manuel Paleologus, the Byzantine Emperor was entertained in the Great Hall by Henry IV, and Sigismund, King of the Romans, visited Eltham to discuss ecclesiastical matters with Henry V. Chaucer was robbed of £20 while on a visit in his capacity as Clerk of Works in the reign of Richard II. Yet by 1656 John Evelyn was to write: 'Went to see His Majesty's house at Eltham: both the palace and chapel in miserable ruins, the noble wood and park destroyed by Rich, the Rebel'. Colonel Nathaniel Rich had bought the house and estate for £2,754 some time after the execution of Charles I. There is no trace of what befell the mass of fine carvings. They were probably used as kindling wood for fires.

Many ancient houses in the midlands and south-west were demolished and new ones acquired by the Crown in better favoured parts of the country. As soon as a house was taken over, teams of craftsmen were despatched to make it habitable. This was a period when panelling was finding favour, and buildings made wholly of timber were much in use. Richard II built a portable ornamental summer house with carved timber beams on the Thames near Sheen and furnished it with heavily carved benches and trestle tables.

Fashion in interior decoration changed as rapidly then as now. During the 14th and 15th centuries, when tapestries replaced wall paintings and murals, heraldry was used to embellish walls and doors. Richard II created the vogue by displaying his armorial bearings. Carved and painted emblems were adapted by the carvers who were responsible for embellishing not only the furniture but also panelling, beams and supporting pillars.

In September 1440 Henry VI issued a writ for the building of Eton College, his original intention being to build an institution for secular priests, a small school and almshouse, but he later enlarged the scheme to provide facilities for 70 students instead of the original 25. Funds for the work came largely from the Duchy of Lancaster, supplemented with money from the Principality of Wales and taxes from the sovereign's land holdings. There was an adequate supply of timber for carving and building in the royal woods at Kingswood, Engield, Odiham, Chobham, Wokingham, Foliejohn, Easthamstead and Windsor Park. The master carvers and their assistants worked on the chambers on the east side, the hall and cloister and seven towers and turrets. The work was under the general supervision of the chief carpenter, Robert Whetley, and his account for £252 6s 8d included the construction work and the carving itself.

The same team of carvers worked on the conversion of the nearby parish church which was intended to form part of Eton, and were responsible for the roof-loft and

stalls and the partly-carved screen which was installed between the newly built king's apartment and the chancel.

Eton started out by looking like a rather simple job, but in 1448 the King felt that it lacked ambition and he decided to enlarge it. To say that his new scheme was grandiose is an understatement, for while it had been estimated that the original work would occupy seven years, the new one looked like going on for at least twenty years. Henry subsequently modified his intentions. Nevertheless, the chapel occupied much longer than had been estimated, due to labour difficulties created by the masons, carvers and carpenters, because they were uncertain which direction the work was taking. One plan provided for a choir 103 feet in length and 32 feet in width 'if hit will please the king'. The amount of carving in his construction was more than had been done for any other building, because it was now the practice to carve all exposed wood. Later accounts stated that a new phase of the work would occupy from Michaelmas 1448 to Michaelmas 1449 and 24 carpenters and carvers would be needed 'werking upon the stalles by the hole yere'.

We do not know precisely how much money was paid to the carvers at Eton, but it would seem that there was very little profit in it. Henry's expenditure was in the region of £16,000, but other sums appear in the records, including one for £15,570 2s 4½. Some saving was made by using timber from the royal woodlands, but for all that a large amount was paid for moving the material. Whatever the savings, they were certainly wasted as the work dragged on year after year.

English wood carving was not always firmly rooted in the country itself. In 1347 Edward II captured the strongly defended city of Calais. At Guines, six miles to the south, stood a town and castle, taken in 1352 by a small expeditionary force. The French fled to a nunnery, which they fortified, but this, too, was attacked and taken by the English. It was then decided to reinforce Guines castle. Work went on for ten years or more, in which time many craftsmen were sent to help with the work. With the destruction of many other castles in the area, Guines achieved a certain prominence, and between 1462 and 1474 Edward IV agreed to grant additional funds. Carvers were sent from England to decorate the walls with the shields of the arms of St George, and devices which are referred to in contemporary records as 'the old arms of the castle', consisting in all probability of the former Counts of Guines, also the arms and devices of 'divers lords and magnates'. Some of these were carved in wood, others in stone by John Roger of St Omer, and they were painted by Christopher de Fielde. Roger also carved a wooden lion clutching an iron lance and a weathervane to crown the wellhead which fed a huge cistern designed to provide water in case of fire 'raised by enemies or rebels'.

Carpenters and carvers were sent abroad with the British expeditionary forces to carry out essential works, and they more often than not remained to attend to the houses occupied by the soldiery. These bands of craftsmen were considerable in numbers. In 1415, for instance, Simon Lewys and John Benet organised and enlisted 100 masons and carvers from the counties of Sussex, Surrey, Kent, Essex, Hertfordshire, Buckinghamshire and Middlesex, and assembled them with all their equipment in London on 6 June. They were to work in Normandy as members of Henry V's forces in the campaign to establish a base at Harfleur and later to capture the castles and fortified towns of the Duchy. The pay was 12d a day for master craftsmen and 6d for the rank and file. Among them were William Temple and Thomas Matthew, both master carpenters with carving experience. They travelled with the main forces and, after experience in battle, were engaged in the renovation of captured castles and houses, spending much of their time carving armorial shields for display in banqueting halls and council chambers.

When Rouen fell to the English it was decided to build a royal palace in the area. The master mason was Jehan Salvart, formerly in a post at Rouen Cathedral and, more recently, master mason in charge of the Harfleur fortification against the English. Salvart seems to have worked in harmony with two English master carpenters, William Reyner and his force of 30 carpenters and carvers, and Thomas Matthew, the latter being one of the original members of the expeditionary force and now in charge of his own workforce of 119 carpenters and carvers. After Henry's death the future of work on the palace was in doubt. With the work half finished and a lack of direction, many of the craftsmen drifted away. There is no record of the work actually undertaken, but it does appear that a number of partly-completed carvings were removed, and it is quite possible that they still remain somewhere in the region.

It is common to discover that major works for the Crown fell into abeyance for long periods at a time. The consequence is that the history of craftsmen suffers many chronological gaps. But one scheme did proceed unhindered by indecision. This was the coronation in 1307 of Edward II, an occasion which called for the services not only of carvers but also painters, masons and designers. The fabric of the buildings in Westminster was in a very poor state and the palace itself required attention following a fire which weakened the walls. Due to dry rot and vandalism many areas were littered with fallen masonry and rubbish. The forthcoming celebrations consisted of more than the coronation, for Edward was to marry Isabella in France in February followed on 25 February by the coronation in Westminster. Master Richard of Wytham was put in charge of the essential work, and writs issued without delay to fund the purchase not only of vast quantities of materials but also to pay the wages of craftsmen. So big was the army of crafts-men that they had to be summoned to the site in the morning and dismissed at night by the blowing of a great horn. Even after darkness fell, many men con-tinued working by the light of candles.

Because they had been drawn from different regions of the country, the work of the carvers probably varied, but they nevertheless tackled such enormous and diverse tasks as the embellishment of the huge timber hall in which the coronation was to take place and the decoration of the many outhouses. The hall was more than 500 feet long with pillars, doors and panels heavily carved with the royal arms and heraldic beasts. Carvers and carpenters were also responsible for making good the throne itself after it was found to be in a state of collapse. Some idea of the growing grandeur can be gained when it is learned that a fountain was installed to flow with red and white wine and pimento, a spiced drink. The fountain was crowned with a finely carved canopy. It is possible that the decoration of the huge platform on which the throne rested was carried out by carvers. It was built in the abbey church and stood at such a height that armed men could gallop a troop of horses beneath it with lances at the upright. The coronation ceremony itself was decorated with many splendidly carved objects, including two wooden leopards which were the work of Master Thomas, who also painted them. They were later repositioned on the gables of the Lesser Hall to hold lattern banners bearing the king's arms. The cost of this and other work was high for the times, the final sum being £3000. Everything was accomplished in only a few months.

The building of St Stephens Chapel, on the other hand, went on for 23 years. It was planned, discussed, started, abandoned and then restarted over a total span of 56 years with gestation, so to speak, through the reigns of Edward I, Edward II and Edward III. By 1345 the walls were finished, and it became possible to consider the construction and installation of the roof in which the carvers were to play a major role. The timber was already well seasoned, for it had been stored on site for more than 20 years, as is evidenced by the recurring stock taking which details quantities of great beams, tie beams, lesser beams, 'mountants', 'purlins', 'quarters' and 'corbels'. The annual check by the Clerk of Works and his staff obviously caused feelings to run high due to the extra work which it entailed. One entry in the records states that the quantity of timbers already shaped for the vaulting of the upper chapel 'cannot be counted owing to the number of pieces and the expense which it would entail to move them'. It may be considered that the carving of the beams could have been done more easily and with greater facility at ground level before they were placed in position, but this was not to be the way of it. Master William of Hurley, who was in charge, considered it essential to assemble the entire roof and vault and then determine to what extent the carvers should decorate the surface. Although the timber was of the finest quality, the fact that it was to be carved suggested that it may weaken in the process. Deep carving on a stressed section may well cause the beam to crack. The carvers had to wait for the carpenters to set all the beams in place, but they certainly started carving while the roof was being put on. This meant working on high scaffolding, often at uncomfortable angles, and they may well have been in occasional danger from the work which was going on above them.

At ground level other carvers were working on the king's private pew, or 'closet', situated close to the high altar and jutting out from the south wall of the chapel with an entrance from a gallery connecting the chapel with the Painted Chamber. At one end was a doorway with the jambs carved and painted in squared-off sections to show the arms of England and France.

Other work on the decoration of St Stephens Chapel included the carving of the altar, stalls, screen and statuary, and it went on for fifteen years after the main construction work was completed in 1348. A number of difficulties made progress difficult from time to time. One of the most contentious aspects of the furnishing of the chapel centred on the provision of the pulpitum and stalls, made necessary by Edward III's establishment of a college of canons in 1348. It was an attempt at a late stage to introduce features which were alien to the original design. The carvers went about their work on the pulpitum and stalls under the direction of Master William of Hurley and the warden, William Herland, and the jobs continued until early in 1351. By August of that year the arguments had reached such a pitch that as soon as the carvers had finished their work, half a dozen carpenters were called in to set about 'removing the said stalls, together with their framework in the aforesaid chapel and working on raising various panels for the reredos of the said stalls in order to show and exhibit the form and design of the said stalls to the treasurer and other members of the king's council'. In this context 'reredos' must refer to the woodwork which enclosed the stalls, pulpitum and the screen at the west end of the chapel. In the ensuing confrontation the discomfitted members of the council were forced to give in to the craftsmen, and the finely carved screen was subsequently sold to an order of nuns at Barking for the sum of £33 6s 8d. When the space was cleared, the carpenters and carvers set about making a new and more acceptable one, consisting of timberwork set on a stone foundation.

Very little of the carving in the chapel was carried out without some kind of difficulty. In 1351 Robert Burwell started to carve the seats of the stalls. He was a professional carver with a good reputation, based on his recent work on the stalls in the king's chapel at Windsor. He was able to command 6d more per week at St

Stephens than he had received for his labours at Windsor, and this brought his weekly wage up to 2s 6d. But for some reason still unknown, Burwell's work failed to satisfy his masters, although he laboured hard and long for four years. In 1355 a new carver appeared to replace him in the person of Master Edmund of St Andrew. If Burwell was adequate, Master Edmund was great. A canon in an Augustinian order at Newstead, Nottinghamshire, his wide reputation rested not only on his prowess as a carver but also on recent accomplishments as a mechanic, for he had designed and built an apparatus for raising water. Burwell was forced to stand back and make room for the man who, according to one writer of the time 'had no equal in carver's work in England'. In August 1355 Master Edmund sent word to the Sherriff of Nottingham to bring his tools from Newstead, and he remained at St Stephens for seven years, carving the stalls and eventually being referred to in the work records as 'master of the stalls in the King's chapel'. He presumably had a number of able carvers working under his direction, including John Drax, Robert Warsop and Henry Shirewood, who were in the capacity of foremen.

Elsewhere in St Stephens another carver was at work. He was William of Patrington, a mason who also worked in wood. He created several smaller items, including eleven figures to stand in the chapel stalls.

Work of a domestic but still royal nature continued for many years. Sheen Palace was owned originally by Robert Burnel, Bishop of Bath and Wells, later passing into the hands of Edward III and it was finally destroyed by fire in 1499. Edward carried out some rebuilding and in 1316 it was leased to the Carmelite Friars prior to their move to Oxford. Sheen was owned by Queen Isabella up to the time of her death in 1358, and after it passed to Edward III, work was practically continuous from 1368. The purpose was to revitalise the entire estate and house. Vines were planted in the gardens, a well was dug. But a certain amount of renovation had been going on for some years before 1368. The accounts for 1363 show that £556 was spent. In 1366 and 1367 various objects were brought from London, and extensive work was carried out on the woodwork, including some carving. Edward III had a great affection for the house and grounds, but after his death at Sheen on 21 June 1377 the mansion lay derelict until Henry V built a house in the immediate vicinity, using timber from the Surrey woodlands and stone salvaged from the derelict house. It was decided to call the new building 'Byfleet' because some of the materials were drawn from a demolished residence at Byfleet, a few miles from Weybridge. Although the history of the new Byfleet remains obscure we know of several carved features, including a huge antelope which rested on top of the kitchen. It would seem that somebody on Henry V's

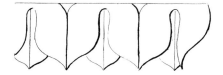

staff had a distinct liking for carved wood, for 80 antelopes and swans were carved at a cost of 20d each by Peter Kervour. It is not known whether he executed any of the other carving, such as the cornices and beams with their cresting of lions and fleur-de-lis or the 240 panels which were carved 'with divers knotts curiously wrought' for the chapel. No expense was spared on the carving or, indeed, on the house itself, for 'the building of the manor of Byfleet next to the said manor of Sheen' cost the then huge sum of £5,815. The end of this fruitful and interesting period came with the death in 1422 of Henry. For nine years only £67 1s 9d was spent on Byfleet, though the storerooms remained packed with carvings and stonework awaiting placement in the manor. Some further work was carried out between 1452 and 1453, but in 1499 the entire edifice went up in flames and was totally destroyed. The same fate befell many great residences due in part to the obvious fire hazards of the time added to the fact that a vast amount of timber was used in their construction.

Other majestic residences died for different reasons. Houses in the south of England periodically went into a state of decay due to lack of money for their upkeep or a diminished interest by their owners. Eltham in Kent was one of the houses consistently favoured, especially in the 14th century, by Edward III who had a good eye for a sound building. With the advent of the Lancastrian and Yorkist kings Eltham was granted substantial funds from the exchequers of Henry IV, Henry VI and Edward IV. Some of this money was used to pay for such carved items as the king's badges, which were placed in the second window of the king's chamber together with the arms of St George. Figures of the Trinity and the Salutation were sited in the third window. Each of the seven windows held fine carvings, and it is likely that they included representations of St John the Baptist, St Thomas, St George, the Salutation of the Virgin Mary, which filled two windows, the Trinity and St John the Evangelist. This was not by any means the full extent of the carving in what must have been an extremely imposing apartment, for the 68 roof bosses were carved with angels and archangels, each bearing escutcheons and scrolls at the positions where the timber intersections formed the ceiling. No details of the cost of this work are extant, although there is a note of £100 paid between 1399 and 1407.

At this point the subject of life-size wooden figures warrants mention. There appears to have been an interim period between the use of stone and marble and metal in which carved wooden figures were used. There is no doubt that in addition to being costly they were also difficult to procure because few carvers worked on such a scale. The records of life-size wooden figures are scanty, but there is a note of a large-scale figure being carved not for a tomb but for the chapel of All Saints at Clarendon, three miles south of Old Sarum in Wiltshire between 1235 and 1236, when Henry II ordered the furnishing of the building. One of the most interesting examples of the full-size recumbent wooden figure can be seen in the church of St John at Little Leighs, Essex. Very little is known about it, but it was brought to the author's attention by Ms Eve Aggiss, a member of a local family. On inspection it was found to be worn smooth on its topside, the timber probably being oak, although it was difficult to be sure due to the surface having been painted white some time in the past. Perhaps the most significant features of the Little Leighs figure is its girth. Other recumbent carved effigies are more slight and delicate, relatively speaking, but this one was obviously carved out of a trunk of prime growth, and the work must have been executed by a craftsman of superhuman strength and ability. There are said to be only about 100 figures in England, all probably dating to the Reformation or earlier. The earliest, dating to the 12th century is of Robert, Duke of Normandy, and it now rests in Gloucester Cathedral. But others are of lesser bulk in comparison with the virtually unknown and undated Little Leighs figure. Examples at the Church of St Mary, Goudhurst, Kent, with the detail in gesso, and coloured, are almost dainty.

Towards the end of the 14th century London saw the work of the Continental carvers who exerted a subtle, if slow-moving, influence on the trade. The Germans and the French had their own hallmarks, while the Flemish displayed a characteristic flamboyance. These and others differed noticeably from the traditional English carving of the day. In many cases it was all the difference between, say, an exotic orchid and the firm but sound and dull cabbage. The Continental styles appealed to only a small but influential number of patrons. Other factors hampered the widespread adoption of Continental styles, including religious bigotry. Many of the new Continental carvers found it very difficult to make anything more than a fairly modest living out of their trade. But of all the nationalities practising trades in London the Flemish carvers did have one great advantage, for they formed part of the strong commercial link between London and Antwerp. Through this avenue of trade came fine fabrics and tapestries and other more basic commodities. Already well established by 1477, the connection was instrumental in bringing the Flemish journeymen and master carvers to England. Among them were Dirike Vangrove, (or van Grove), and Giles van Castell, and the lesser known carvers, including John Duche, John Vanclyffe, Henry Vanshanhale, Garrards Wessell and Meneard de Freseland, all of whom were to leave a legacy in England not only of carving itself but also in the area of design which became integrated into the English style.

Vangrove and Castell executed carvings for Henry VII's chapel in

Westminster. Today this building is regarded as a monument to Henry, but in its original conception it was intended to be an elegant but functional place of worship, a 'sumptoeus and solemne' chapel and a great example of Tudor workmanship. Henry himself played an important part in its design and towards the end of his life he began to lay down his preferences for the interior decoration. Contemporary documents describing the building of the chapel are few, but financial accounts 'for the beleding of the king's new chapel' appeared from October 1502 onwards and it seems that the initial stages of the building were in progress by that year, though the building proper commenced in 1503. The total cost of the construction reached the sum of about £20,000. One of the most interesting documents connected with the building of the chapel was the will of Henry, who died in April 1509. It clearly suggests that he had it in mind not only to create a colourful interior but to provide scope for craftsmen: '. . the said Chapell to be desked and the windowes . . be glazed with stores, ymagies, bagies and cognoisaunts, as is by us redily divised . . and that the walles, doores, windowes, archies and vaults, and ymagies of the same our Chapell, within and without be painted, garnisshed and adorned with our armes, bagies, cognoisaunts . . .' Even while the royal will was being drafted for signature, the decoration of the chapel was in progress. Money for the work was more than ample, and only a few days before his death, the King presented a further £5000 to the fund. Unfortunately, many of his wishes and preferences were not realised, but a great deal of fine stone and wood work did materialise. We know, for instance, that something like 107 stone figures were made, and no less than 95 of them are still with us. In woodwork, the stalls were preserved, being made originally for the use of worshippers who attended the anniversary services made possible by Henry's will. In the 18th century they passed to the Knights of the Order of the Bath when that order was revived. The canopies were carved by Vangrove and Castell, and they were done in the rich Flemish style, presumably with the full approval of the architects. In comparison with carving elsewhere in the chapel, it is evident that the Flemish carvers outdid themselves both in design and execution. The same carvers also created the misericords, the pictorial source of which is now said to be in the woodcuts of Durer and van Meckenen. But carvers of the stature of Vangrove and Castell were not entirely derivative, for they carried their own pattern books from job to job.

Timber and stone vied for supremacy in the 13th and 14th centuries, and it was not until the 15th century that the carver really came into his own. Prior to this he was generally in a subservient role as the craftsman who was called in to embellish furniture and structural timbers. The transition was an odd one. Before the carver

could gain an ascendency he was forced to pass through a lengthy phase in which his craft imitated stonework almost as a mirror to demonstrate its appeal and versatility. There are innumerable examples of this, notably at Stanton Harcourt, Oxfordshire, where the screen comprises trefoil shaped heads painstakingly carved in an exact imitation of fine stonework. Others can be seen at Beverley St Mary, Yorkshire, St Mary, Kirk Ella; also Long Itchington and Ripley in Warwickshire. At Kirk Ella, in particular, imitation in wood of stonework is distinctly marked, for the three columns form an arch with matched mouldings to give the appearance of the conventional church entrance of the period.

One technical aspect of the work in this period was the use of the plank, made possible by the development of the sawyer's trade and the supply of planks sawn and stocked in standard sizes. The carver had them clamped together with iron strapping and carved the piece while it was still held, after which it was unfastened and the individual pieces dowelled together with such close-fitting precision that it is even now difficult to detect the joins in the layers of wood. Dowelling was also employed in the making of many screens, some of which were carved on a 'sandwich' system to achieve size and strength. These screens, many of great height, were carved while flat on the ground on trestles and on completion hoisted into position, the sections being dowelled together piece by piece.

One of the finest effects ever achieved by a carver who worked early in the development of the craft was Master Thomas of Winton. In 1312 he was responsible for the creation of the bishop's throne at Exeter. It had a canopy 60 feet high and six pedestals with the same number of carved figures. He was paid 32s for his work, but it is unlikely that he personally carved the whole of this magnificent piece, for the human head which appears in the canopy was done by Robert Galmeton, who was paid no less than £4 for his contribution. It is possible that he also carved parts of the canopy.

It was in 1370 and later that the carver and the carpenter moved towards an important relationship. There was by now a growing interest in wood as a working material, and it resulted in the carver being more frequently consulted about such matters as ornamentation. Roof beams were now more heavily carved due to improvements in construction techniques which enabled the carver to be more adventurous without fear of seriously weakening the structure. Carving also began to appear on the exteriors of buildings as decoration of doors and porches. Traditionally, however, carving was at its best advantage when displayed in the stalls, especially when the work also embraced the canopies. Examples can be seen at Lincoln, Chester, Nantwich, Whalley, Carlisle, Ripon, Manchester and Beverley, where the stalls are more or less complete. Equally fine stalls were carved

for Vale Royal, Furness, Kirkstall, Fountains, Combermere, Cartmel, Bolton and Byland. The best of all can be found at Lincoln, where the stalls are superior even to those of Henry VII's chapel.

It is always interesting to make a study of comparative regional styles of carving in this period. Such a study will show that the carvers of Yorkshire possessed talents superior to those of their contemporaries in, say, Devon and Somerset. There is a cleanness and a simplicity in the Yorkshire designs and motifs which is not found elsewhere in England, and one could possibly account for this by remembering the incredible lengths to which London carvers went to please their clients by trying to imitate alien styles. While the carving in Henry VII's chapel is undoubtedly fine, it lacks the plain strength of character and integrity which typifies Yorkshire work. Another reason for the Yorkshire supremacy is that the carvers did not have to put up with any strong foreign influences in order to be painfully fashionable. The capital was subject to regular invasions of Continental carvers who, in due course, swayed the London patrons to such an extent that their English counterparts were finally inveigled into believing that they must follow suit. The enforced mating of two different and basically disparate styles produced only a hybrid which must even now cause mixed feelings. There is some irony in the fact that all this occurred at a time when the carver was endeavouring to be true to his material and trying to create an English style.

Again, in comparison with the London carvers, the provincials were more stable and better known and established. One of the reasons for this, at least in the 14th century, was that the guilds were more active outside London. There is still a somewhat imperious ring about their deep rooted traditions. York is just one example. The carving firm of Drawsherd prospered for three generations or more, numbering among its members Thomas Drawsherd who, in accordance with the pattern of history, gained public office and became chamberlain of York in 1501, sheriff in 1505 and 1506, an alderman in 1508, member of parliament in 1511 and 1512, and lord mayor in 1515 and 1523. Few carvers have achieved his prominence either before or since, and yet throughout all these periods of civic service he still remained a working carver, responsible for a large output of all kinds of church furniture in and around York. He also executed the screen for Newark church in 1508 while an alderman of York. He was, incidentally, an unsuccessful contender for the contract carving in Henry VII's chapel.

Elsewhere in the provinces many businesses operated, and they were just as important as the firm of Drawsherd. At Ripon the Bromflet family traded under the revealing name of Carver, and flourished for many years, carrying out work at Bridlington, Flamborough, Jervaulx, Manchester and Wensley. The carving for

Manchester was done in 1506, followed in 1519 by the Bridlington contract, while the work for Beverley was executed between 1520 and 1524. If there is any criticism of the Bromflet brand of carving it may well be that it did nothing to innovate. They worked to set patterns and deviated not at all from beginning to end. There was no whimsy or humour, nothing daring about it. On the other hand, if there is an accolade to be given, it should be presented to Bromflet for the consistently high standards they achieved. In the entire range of examples there is no sign of any falling away or weakening, and the quality is exemplified in the delicately cut grapevine which appears, almost as a trademark, on the stalls and desk standards.

Carvers have always favoured their own designs, and this is nowhere better seen than on the bench ends which in the 14th century represented the flowering of talent in certain parts of England. Some subtle regional differences were expressed. The surmounting poppyhead was not used in the west, where the squared end was preferred. In East Anglia poppys were common, but the bench end itself sometimes developed into a carved fantasy with a free interplay between animals, birds and beasts, representations of buildings, armorial bearings and shields, and fruit and flowers. Even the clumsiest and most primitive bench end carving often displays an unusual degree of imagination and character. For the finer carving we should examine examples at Barningham and Fressingfield in Suffolk, and Wiggenhall and Walsoken in Norfolk.

One of the most curious examples of bench ends occurs at the parish church of St Bartholomew at Corton in Suffolk, work on which commenced soon after the Black Death, the style being Decorated. It was dedicated in 1375. The five bench ends, now positioned on the window ledge on the north side of the nave, are all that remains of the medieval church woodwork. They are typically East Anglian, 15th century poppyheads (derived from *puppis*, a Latin word meaning the stern of a ship) with simple Perpendicular tracery and with grotesques on the arm rests. It is sad that they are so decayed, but a close scrutiny reveals that they are covered with gesso, being a thin layer of plaster of paris which was gilded over after it had hardened. The technique was more usually associated with fonts and screens. The gesso has flaked off here and there, but enough remains to confirm that this church was very rich indeed. Bench ends with gesso do not occur elsewhere in the country and this makes them exceptionally interesting. In 1954 a singular thing happened at Corton. The then vicar received a letter from an archaeologist, making enquiries about the bench ends which were under the tower of the church, and it was proposed that the bench ends be given to the archaeologist on the understanding that he would supply the church with a reconditioned one. The

archaeologist admitted that the bench ends were fine examples of 15th century work and estimated the cost of restoration at £10 each. It was agreed that one bench end should be restored, the intention being to incorporate it in a new pew. In a muddle of a transaction five bench ends disappeared and have not since been seen.

England is particularly rich in carved wood in her parish churches, and it is here that the true heritage can be found. The north-west of Herefordshire has a number of screens, and one of the finest is at Aymestry, dating back to the 16th century. At Eyton there is an earlier example with a loft and a boarded and panelled core and a finely carved frontal beam. At Dilwyn the 15th century screen has a tracery with some carving. In the ruined church at Downton-on-the-Rock there used to be a wooden loft with some rudimentary carving dating back to the 15th or early 16th century. At Monnington-on-Wye there is a chancel screen dated 1679, once crowned with the royal arms, but now removed to the south wall of the nave. In the same area, at Monnington Court, there is an elaborate wooden frieze of the late 16th century, the south front having a moulded oak frame with a shaped head-piece carved to represent two monsters. Leintwardine in north-west Herefordshire should also be mentioned for its stalls, misericords and screen, all of which were originally at Wigmore Abbey but moved in the Dissolution.

The partitioning of churches in the 15th century offered the provincial carver some of his best design opportunities. The standard features of the main screen generally included a rood loft floor with fences on both sides by the gallery fronts. Underneath the loft floor was a cove or fan vault. Examples can be seen at Flamborough, Humberside; Hexham, Northumberland; and Atherington, Devon; with their Welsh counterparts at Llananno, Powys; and Llanrwyst, Gwynedd. Here again, regional differences can be detected. In the south-west the screen was placed across the church practically from wall to wall, while in Wales they were rectangular and low. Actual designs differ, for in some of the Welsh examples there is a display of sheer whimsy not to be found in England. At Llanrwyst the carver shows pigs rooting for acorns. Elsewhere we see the familiar Welsh dragon in a variety of postures, more often than not rebuffing invaders or the Devil. Welsh carvers were obviously inspired by their Celtic heritage. If this is so, then it should be added that English screenwork of the same period has its own more sober virtues, exemplified in the Midlands and the North. Where the Welsh carver eschewed floriation, the English carver working in the Midlands excelled at it.

Certain provincial carving firms have already been mentioned, but sight should not be lost of the individuals who plied for hire. John Crosse worked more or less continuously between 1447 and 1455 on the screen at Yatton, Herefordshire, for which he also carved 69 figures. The screen was later removed and trace has been lost, but it was from all accounts an outstanding piece of work. Other screens fortunately survived and remain in good repair. At Lydd in Kent there is a screen made by carvers employed from 1519 to 1528 by the carpentry firm of Bellamy at Canterbury. The Hackington, Kent screen was carved by John Pares of Devon and by John Dawe who came from Lawhitton in Cornwall.

Screens were as a rule fashioned from timber provided not necessarily by the carpenter or carver but by the church wardens. This apparently arbitrary arrangement was not as unfair to the carver as may at first be imagined, for the wardens were, after all, local men with a good knowledge of supplies and quality, and many of them had the advantage of being able to use their trade connections to ensure that only good timber was supplied for church use. Not all carving wood was obtained locally, however, for knot-free material was being imported from the Baltic to find favour amongst carvers who found English wood full of imperfections. Baltic timber, known as Danske, was comparatively free from such aggravations. Apart from selecting and purchasing the wood, the church wardens also held sway over the nature of the design to be followed, and the carver would as a rule be asked to emulate carving which the wardens had already inspected elsewhere in the area. Taking into account the occasional mixture of English and Continental carving which invaded some of the churches, it now becomes easier to understand exactly how certain styles gained ascendency while others were adulterated or bastardised. There were probably many occasions when the more dogmatic minded carvers were hard pressed to please the wardens, and many a job must have foundered due to divergent opinions.

Despite arguments about design, it was still possible to agree on the main lines of the required carving. For instance, the stereotyped figure of the angel was universally acceptable with the result that the carver peopled the beams with these celestial beings. It is rarely that the angels carved in the 13th and 14th centuries are totally unoccupied, most of them being shown in graceful flight with wings outstretched and expressions of contentment writ large on their unmarred faces, or with wings folded while playing musical instruments or flourishing heraldic devices and missals. There is a long-standing dichotomy of opinion as to the actual sex of many of the angels carved in this period and it has its roots in the wrangles and debates of the theologians. One rarely sees a muscular male or a truly shapely female angel as portrayed by the cautious carver of the 14th and 15th centuries. They are somewhat hermaphroditic in appearance so that the precise sex of the figure is in the eye and the mind of the beholder.

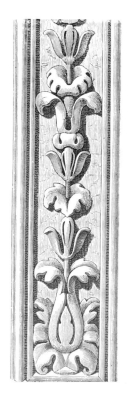

But when it came to the portrayal of everyday life the carver was much more at ease. It is significant that carvings which are other than purely pious tend to be hidden away in many churches and have to be searched out. This hiding of secular subjects was done for a good reason, to prevent worshippers from being distracted from their devotions. As a result, the slyly humorous and versatile carver was able to exercise talents which could not be used in work to be more easily seen.

One of the great paradoxes of 14th century carving was that while it was a period in which the trade expanded, the growth of inspiration apparently lagged far behind. It is quite possible that the humble carver did not even know the meaning of the word inspiration, and was quite content to leave such lofty matters to the great painters. As in misericord carving, the carver often relied upon woodcuts which were, in modern terms, naïve in execution. This naïvety naturally communicated itself to the carvings themselves, for certain works are effectively three dimensional representations of the woodcuts themselves, being cartoons in timber, often vaguely ribald, seldom truly serious, and with an acute observation of human nature. Apart from scenes which include human beings, there are reproductions of single objects, such as the rebus, cooking pots, castles, manor houses. There was, too, the teeming source of mythology, and the carver drew on it for his basic ideas. Once again we see the prevalence of woodcuts for such models as *The Man with his Head in his Belly* and the creatures which were half-bird and half-man. Some carvers consulted the bestiaries, copies of which were common, especially in the libraries of monasteries. These were the source of the carvings of exotic tropical animals, including elephants, examples of which can be seen at Ripon, North Yorkshire, Ottery St Mary, Devon, and in the arms of the city of Coventry. Another common representation was the cat and mouse, dating back to the 13th century and even earlier, examples of which are at Wells and Winchester. Practically all these carvings derive from woodcuts, and it is even possible to date them by comparing certain aspects of the woodcut of the period with the carving itself. If we examine the woodcuts of about 1400 the outlines are broad and flowing without any lines of shading. The figures are long and sinuous, clothed in long mantles which cover the feet, the same mantles used to cover the figure of Christ, the Virgin and Saints. This form of woodcut and carving were common in the first quarter of the fifteenth century. The artists generally made some use of contemporary costume but modified it to give a period appearance. Later on in the same century the men's skirts were gradually shortened and in the second phase, from about 1425 and 1450 the skirts barely pass the hips, while the gowns of the women were more close fitting, leading to grotesque exaggerations of the figure. Here again, the style is mirrored in much of the contemporary carving of the time.

Although Durer has already been mentioned as one possible source of copy material for wood carvers, it is likely that other simpler woodcuts were favoured, including the work of Jerg Haspel, the Continental artist who was responsible for *St Ulrich and St Afra* and the *Agony in the Garden*. Apart from woodcuts printed abroad, there were sources in England, of course, and it is not entirely impossible that carvers were able to consult such publications as the large folio of Lyndewode's *Constitutiones Provinciales*, printed at Oxford by Theodoricus Rood about 1483, which contained a woodcut frontispiece of a monk seated writing at a desk beneath an architectural canopy. Two books published at St Albans may also have produced treasure trove for the carver, for they were rich in illustrations suitable for adaptation. The earliest of these was the *Chronicles of England*, usually known as the *St Albans Chronicle*, and it included a representation of the Tower of Babel. The second publication was the *Book of St Albans* by Juliana Berners, and it appeared in 1486, being full of woodcuts depicting hawking, hunting and the blazoning of arms. Sight should not be lost of the considerable output by the press of Wynkyn de Worde, who came to England with Caxton in 1476 and in 1509 opened a shop in St Paul's Churchyard. Between 1509 and the end of 1534, the year of his death, he was responsible for a great output of illustrated books on such a scale that some at least may have found their way into the hands of the carvers. The standards set by Wynkyn de Worde in typography and book production did not come to an end with his death, for the Wynkyn de Worde Society continues to encourage and actively promote the profession and practice of graphic design from London, the traditional centre of the British publishing industry.

It is notable that the wider spread of printed material led to development in carving techniques. A form of realism asserted itself in which the proportions of human limbs became more correct and and less grotesque while the anatomy of birds and beasts was carefully defined, as exemplified in carvings at Beverley, Wells, Tewkesbury and Ely. Indeed, there was at many places an increased sophistication in the carving of birds. One of the most popular subjects was the *Owl attacked by Small Birds*, depicting wrens and sparrows exacting a revenge on the predator. Elsewhere, notably at Norwich, Stratford, Ugbotough in Devon and at St Cuthberts, Wells, there occurred a curious marriage of ideas in which the revered figures of the Virgin Mary and the Disciples became partly mythological beast and Divine being. By today's standards they may be thought slightly malicious, but at the time of their creation they were products of a society not averse to salacious comment about matters theological. One can sense the very narrow margin which existed between humour and anticlerical sentiments.

31 An example of the carver's boldness in creating a cross between a lion and a man. The composition merges smoothly into the elbow rest of the choir stalls. The late 14th century can best be characterised by a new vigour, exemplified in this type of ornamentation in Lincoln Cathedral.

32 Poppyhead ornamentation in the choir stalls of Lincoln Cathedral depicting the triumph of a saint over the forces of evil. Probably early 15th century, but the decisive figure carving appears to be somewhat later.

33 The distinctive appearance of the panels in this Golant, Cornwall, pulpit is due to the fact that it was made from 16th century bench-ends. Elsewhere, bench-ends have been incorporated in screens and other furniture. The carving of the arch is superior to the relief figures and objects, suggesting that the original bench-ends were carved by more than one craftsman.

34/35 Jacobean pulpit in Wells Cathedral, Somerset, is typical of the mixture of furnishing to be found in ecclesiastical buildings throughout the United Kingdom. Almost confusing in its profusion of detail, it somehow manages to achieve a harmonious aspect.

36 An outstanding example of carving in 1380. The dean's stall end in the choir of Chester Cathedral, showing a hierarchy of costumed figures, all carved with a fine definition, concluding with the symbolic figure in a miniature stall.

37/38 Examples of poppyhead carving on bench-ends at Long Stratton, Norfolk, in the church of St Mary the Virgin. Regional differences between the carving of 'popey' heads are various, and the Norfolk variety follow foliated motifs. Elsewhere, such devices as human figures, animals and allegorical scenes appear.

40 A somewhat uneasy marriage between a 15th century pulpit and the addition of the twelve Apostles, carved in 1868, at Long Sutton, Somerset. The most distinctive detail is the overhanging dentil cornice to a design common on screens.

39 Mid 13th and 14th century carvers sought designs outside the restrictions of architecture. At Beverley Minster, Yorkshire, the carver created a new concept in foliage carving by lifting it away from the parent section and adding gargoyle figures at the intersection.

41   Unusual stem pulpit at Ipplepen, Devon, using to the fullest advantage the carver's interpretation or architectural ornamentation and miniature castellation and geometric patterning on the encircling ribs of the structure.

42/43   Screen, coving and doorway at Llanengan, Dwyfor, Gwynedd, typifies the 15th century carver's work in Wales, where the design was rugged and compact. No great sophistication or imagination was evidenced, but the technique compared favourably with the work of English carvers of the same period.

44   This section of the medieval chancel screen at Bovey Tracey, Devon, is in direct contrast to the Llanengan screen in illus. 42/43. It suggests a superior carving technique, enhanced by the use of colour.

45   13th century angels in the roof of Wells Cathedral, Somerset, act as bearers of heraldry. In some cases the carver omits the hands and uses the armorial shields as vestments. All the figures are polychromed.

72

46   16th century cupboard at Stoke St Gregory, Somerset, variously dated 1595 and 1628, with panels said to depict the five wise virgins. The surmounting crowned angels represent a much higher standard of carving and are by a different craftsman. The doors are carved linenfold.

47   At Cartmel Priory, Lancashire, the choir stalls are 15th century and the screen is 17th century, probably Flemish. A mixture of styles occurred during the restoration in 1618 by George Preston of Holker after the church had stood roofless for 80 years. This carving carries a suggestion of the work done for the churches of S. Maria dei Miracoli at Brescia and Venice.

48   Lincoln Cathedral choir stalls date from
the 13th and 14th centuries when they were
backed by arcaded stone walls. Clergy attended
devotions in a small area enclosed by finely
carved woodwork while the congregation
prayed in the nave.

49   The beginning of the curvilinear floriation
which preceded 17th century English decoration. There is a hint here of the Graeco-Roman
continuous curving meander which finally
manifested itself in the acanthus. St Nicholas
Cole Abbey, Queen Victoria Street, London.

50/51 Gates of screen in King's College Chapel, Cambridge, symbolic of the era of carved magnificence. The chapel was begun in 1446 and completed in 1515. The screen, the earliest timber structure carved in the Renaissance style and costing £12,000, was installed by Henry VIII.

52 Stall canopies in King's College Chapel, Cambridge. A curiosity of the beasts supporting the arms is their Egyptian-style winged ornamentation, first noted, in fact, by archaeologists who accompanied the French expedition to Egypt under Napoleon in 1798. There is no explanation why English or Continental carvers would have been aware of this device at the time of the carving of the canopies.

53 Detail from St George's Chapel, Windsor, depicting a ship against a battlemented coastline with a watcher on horseback. Late medieval carvers were in the habit of including graphic scenes within the curves of arches, almost as a reaction against the formalism of architectural work.

54/55   Secular carving of the Renaissance was highly ornate and significant in its attempt to outdo ecclesiastical forms, as in the Crimson Bedroom at Montacute, Somerset, where the headboard of the bed incorporates not only ten lion heads and four standing figures but also the Royal Arms. Architectural arches are in the English Romanesque style and resemble the triforium arches at Rochester Cathedral, Kent.

56 An unusual use of the cartouche as decoration of the steepled internal porch of the Great Chamber at Montacute, Somerset. The interior of the porch contains fine fan ornamentation and a continuation of the geometric panelled effect.

57 The line moulding of the ogee arch arising from the Early English Gothic presented carvers with opportunities for design equalled only in the world of 10th century Islamic woodcarving. Chester Cathedral.

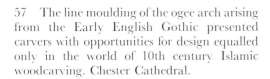

58 A further manifestation of the English Renaissance. In this clockface decoration in the church of St Mildred, Bread Street, London, the true artistry is seen not so much on the supports and quadrant as in the wheat and floriation roundel surrounding the dial.

59/60 A tour-de-force in misericord carving. This example in St George's Chapel, Windsor, suggests an advanced view of perspective in its panoramic representation of a fortified coastal city.

61 The familiar misericord subject of St George and the Dragon portrayed in Lincoln Cathedral with unusual depth and dimension, using the Dragon on both supporters.

62 Misericord carvers constantly exercised their wits in the design of subjects. In this example from Wells Cathedral, Somerset, the mythical wyverne, with origins in Pliny's Natural History, pounces on its prey, using one wing to support the seat. The supporters are synonymous with forest woodland.

63 Representations of the Green Man of archaic English legend are numerous. Portrayed in a Lincoln Cathedral misericord in a malevolent vein, this is one of the more compact compositions, indicating a high degree of carving skill.

64 Refinement of design is evident in this Lincoln Cathedral misericord of the late 13th century. The veins of the oak leaves and the acorn cups are distinctly delineated. Many foliated misericords were destroyed and replaced with moralistic figurative subjects, and by the 15th century foliated ornament had almost completely disappeared.

65/66 Two grotesques showing the Man With His Head In His Stomach at Ripon Cathedral, Yorkshire. They are misericord supporters, probably early 13th century, and suggest that the creative carver had a high degree of bizarre imagination.

67 A glimpse of the role of the medieval jester in a misericord at Beverley Minster, Yorkshire, where the Feast of Fools was held every year. Clergy and acolytes donned costumes and held mock services, following a pagan tradition. The custom was abolished in 1542.

68 Supporter of a St George's Chapel, Windsor, misericord suggests a detail of medieval costume at a time when both men and women wore head cowls. The carving style is entirely naturalistic and well proportioned.

69/71 Construction after 1280 of the Angel
Choir of Lincoln Cathedral demanded furnishings of excellence, made by notable craftsmen,
including the anonymous carver who fashioned
the four heavenly musicians, shown here.

72 Realistic portrayal of a falconer and four cranes in a Lincoln Cathedral misericord. Faced with the problem of depicting a forest, the carver chose to show a single symbolic tree. The graceful positioning of the cranes shows an above-average appreciation of composition.

73 Reflecting on the often strange juxta-position of animal and human bodies in medieval carving, St Bernard of Clairvaux wrote to William, Abbot of St Thierry: 'What mean those ridiculous monstrosities . . . those monstrous centaurs, those half-men?' This example from a misericord in St George's Chapel, Windsor.

CHAPTER FOUR

Grinling Gibbons

WE know a great deal about Grinling Gibbons' accomplishments between the ages of 23 and 60, but there is still good reason to question the quality of some of his work rather than approach his life and work with customary reverence. It is the purpose of this part of the study of English woodcarving, its roots and traditions, to treat Gibbons not in any particular isolation but as part of the development.

Gibbons' name is pre-eminent not necessarily for the quality of design and execution but for his business acumen and the establishment and output of his London workshops. If he is unique, then it is because he is one of the few craftsmen whose work can be readily recognised and is still in a fair state of preservation in such places as the Tower of London; Trinity College Library at Cambridge; the choir of St Paul's Cathedral, London; Blenheim Palace and many more. It is reasonable to suppose that he will continue to hold his place despite the irony that only three carvings can be directly attributed to him. When his style is so easily recognisable and it is appreciated that he was in 1693 appointed Master Carver to the Crown, he cannot fail to hold his place, regardless of whether or not he actually carved the many pieces which are rather dubiously credited to him. In recent years, however, an increasing number of carvings have come to be labelled 'school of Grinling Gibbons', indicating a more discerning attitude.

The popular picture is of Gibbons carving some of the most flamboyant and intricate pieces to be found in the Western Hemisphere. The supposition is entirely false, and anybody even vaguely acquainted with the mechanism of carving must agree. Such a volume of work of varying quality must have demanded more than one pair of hands. In his time Gibbons probably employed dozens of master carvers, apprentices and journeymen not only at his Ludgate Hill, London, workshops but also at different places throughout the country. In his heyday there existed a large reservoir of carving talent from which he would be able to choose. From 1691, when he was retained to execute the work for Kensington Palace, up to 1710, when his talents were engaged on the reredos for the chapel at Hampton Court, he would have been the major employer of carvers in London.

Gibbons' fame rests on two separate foundations. The first was his rich and luxuriant style. The second was the carving technique which he adopted and may even have originated. Up to this time few carvers had the ability to carve so deeply that the finished work became much more flamboyant than ever before, casting the carver in the protagonist's role, whereas he had up to this time played a subservient but still important part. Exactly why this should have been so is both interesting and casts a reflection on human attitudes. Before the coming of Gibbons carvers were required to ornament in an unobtrusive manner rather than assert their own individuality. For centuries they followed the often capricious dictates of wealthy patrons, many of whom believed they knew exactly what was wanted. While many of the London and provincial carvers were technically accomplished, their status was weak because they lacked the kind of alliance which Gibbons formed with England's most accomplished amateur architect, Sir Christopher Wren, whom the diarist, Sir John Evelyn called 'that miracle of a youth'. The combination of Wren, with his groundings in science and academic background, and Gibbons, the carver who emerged from the earthiness of the industrialism of Deptford, seemed unlikely, but it was to develop into a veritable two-man renaissance. There are many remarkable aspects of the liaison. Wren was well educated, socially poised, a former Fellow of All Souls, Oxford, and at the age of only 25 Professor of Astronomy at Gresham College, London, whereas Gibbons remained throughout his life an Englishman born a foreigner who spoke the English language so badly as to be pretty well unintelligible. Wren was an intellectual, Gibbons was at best a superior craftsman. Wren ascended to eminence from the academic life, and Gibbons came from Deptford with all the singlemindedness of the alien determined to make good. It may even have been to his advantage that he understood English so imperfectly that his trade competitors gave up in disgust and left him to pursue his own path. But if we are able to subscribe to the idea that the divine spark of creativity burns only at certain times in certain men, then we must also accept the fact that Gibbons could have worked equally well and received acclaim at any time in history. As it happened, he was, to put it in the modern idiom, in the right place at the right time. Behind the barrier of language he certainly did possess culture of a kind, for it was displayed in his middle and later works as a feeling for nature. He also had a love of music, clearly shown in the carvings which included string and wind instruments and scores. He was also a good showman because he took many chances to attract attention to his work. In the panel which Charles II presented in 1682 to Cosima III, Grand Duke of Tuscany, the foaming detail practically forces itself outside its own boundaries. More important, it contains a relatively large scroll displaying with no modesty whatsoever the signature of Gibbons. Defiantly thrust behind it is a carved quill which appears to signify beyond doubt that the panel was his own work. This was a cheeky gesture, for few carvers of that time would have dared make such a panel into a showcase for their own signature. We can hardly put Gibbons down as a modest man. But then, his fame was not acquired without difficulty. He had singlemindedness thrust upon him, notably by Evelyn, the diarist.

Grinling Gibbons' father was an English draper, James Gibbens (not Gibbons). His mother, daughter of Francis Gorlings, a Rotterdam tobacco merchant, was also English. There has always been some confusion about his parentage, one school of thought saying that he had a Dutch mother and an English father. The other school of thought reverses the parentage. Proof of his English parentage is contained in a horoscope cast for him by Elias Ashmole in 1682, now deposited in the Bodleian Library at Oxford. The date of birth is given as 'Ap 4 1648', the place Rotterdam. At the top of the horoscope are the words 'Mr Grinling Gibbons, the Excellent Carver'.

In the light of Gibbons' later artistic development we come on a curious coincidence. The year of Gibbons' birth saw the stone sculptor, Artus Quellin (1609-1688) at work, creating fantastic devices and elaborate floriation for the Burgerzaal, which is part of the Stadhuys in Amsterdam. Quellin's flights of fancy in stone and marble inflamed discussion, and his critics alleged that he was deliberately flying in the face of national tradition in conjuring up a school of decoration which could not be directly attributed to any particular genre. Some went so far as to call him a heretic, but there was no stopping him as one festoon followed another. He was helped in his work by Artus Quellin (1625-1700), presumably his son. The later Quellin was the father of Arnold Quellin (1653-1688), who became Gibbons' associate in London.

There has for many years been speculation about what has come to be known as the 'Gibbons style'. At the time of its appearance it was as alien to the more conservative English style as the original Quellin's work was to the Burgerzaal. Gibbons' work must have looked like some kind of sculptural freehand with disparate motifs introduced willynilly as scallops, seashells, fruit and flowers and other objects were apparently pushed together almost untidily but in the end forming a dazzling composition. Flowers refused to look neat, they sprang out at odd angles. Stalks of wheat and barley protruded unconventionally and did not form patterns. Any study of Gibbons' style, if it can be called a style, shows that he must have made an intensive study of Quellin, for it burst upon England without any discernable lineage. It was also distinctly separate from Gibbons' formal and often stiff work as a stone carver. We can now safely assert that Gibbons' style was, in fact, an onward flow of Quellin's work which itself had firm historical roots.

The original Quellin went as a young man to Rome to study under François Duquesnoy, the sculptor. It is in the corpus of Duquesnoy's work up to the year 1643 that the basis of Gibbons' style is to be found. The very technique of the cherubim with their musical instruments and the surround of garlands which Duquesnoy carved in stone for the Chapel of the Apostles in Naples is uncannily like Gibbons' treatment. The transmission of the style from Rome to the Netherlands and, eventually, to London began with Quellin absorbing and practising Duquesnoy's style to a point where the work of the two sculptors was practically identical. When Quellin returned to Antwerp he took with him a style which was essentially Italian in character. Almost as soon as his work stood revealed, the new style proliferated throughout the Netherlands. There is no doubt that this, together with the opulence of Rubens, led to the creation of a new school after about 1645. So attractive was it that within a handful of years it was being used at every opportunity not only in the Netherlands but in many other countries in Europe. If Duquesnoy was a creative sculptor, then Quellin was more a tradesman, as was Gibbons himself. One need look only at two aspects to appreciate the sources of Gibbons' style, the flower paintings of the Dutch masters and the combined influences of Duquesnoy and Quellin.

There has always been discussion about Gibbons' treatment of flowers which in his best works are seen clumped together or strewn about hither and thither, but a study of the painting of Rigoulds (1618-1667), van Kessel (1626-1679), Segherds (1580-1661) and other contemporaries suggests a most likely source of design. Gibbons collected paintings, he had a gallery in his own home. One could say, quite rightly, that the entire cornucopiae of ideas was formed by one flower painter being parasitic on the other, modifying and distilling, but always forcing the composition to wider and more extreme limits. When Gibbons' work is examined in any detail, it is all the more remarkable that he made the transition from paint and canvas to wood with such facility. That he was strongly influenced by the vogue for *trompe l'oeil* is undeniable, and the limewood cravat which he later carved for Horace Walpole is generally held up as evidence of this. When seen in profusion the flowers are most convincing, but viewed in isolation they are

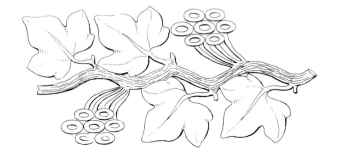

somehow simplistic and even clumsy. Chronological clues tell us that he was often conscious of his limitations, or, more accurately, the limitations imposed upon him by his material. One example is the split pomegranate. The first and probably the last attempt at depicting this symbol of sacrifice was used in the reredos now in St James's Church, Piccadilly, London, but *they are* placed in a minor role in the composition of this large work because they failed to achieve the desired effect. Gibbons often tried out new and experimental arrangements, using commissioned pieces for this purpose. If they were successful, he went on to develop them. If unsuitable, they were dropped from the repertoire, never to appear again. Certain fruits, such as the very familiar nutmeg, had so much similarity that they appeared with great regularity. By this means the pattern of the design became highly selective and the naturalistic work was to dictate the line of future development. But there was nothing restrictive about it, as Horace Walpole observed: 'He gave to wood the loose and airy lightness of flowers, and chained together the various productions of the elements with a free disorder natural to each species'. In 1910, writing in *The Connoisseur*, W. G. Paulson Townsend more acidly commented: 'If these carvings do not reveal any inspired artistic qualities, they are at least marvellous specimens of craftsmanship – there is a truthfulness of imitation which has never been surpassed'. What should be taken into account is the dating of the floral carving. Gibbons was a student of wild flower form, of course, but he also had a deep understanding of cultivated garden flowers. One does not find in his work the immigrant species, such as petunias, dahlias and gloxinias, which were virtually unknown in England at that time. His greatest influence was the flower painters of the Dutch school, coupled with the arrival in England of two carvers. The first was Arnold Quellin, son of Artus Quellin II, and one of the craftsmen responsible for bringing Continental influences to England. The other man was van Ost (1686-1729), who later changed his name to John Nost. In due course Nost was to marry the widow of Quellin.

For more than three centuries there was a sorry lapse in the carving of realistic flowers and foliage in England, and it reached its lowest ebb in the formalised Tudor rose which decorated misericords and other pieces. While the emergence of Gibbons did not represent anything like a one-man renaissance, it did nevertheless bring out the fact that the English carver required only a chance or two in order to demonstrate the fact that he had a dormant lyricism and artistry. To understand why this should have occurred at a certain time in history, it is necessary to understand the circumstances of the lives of the protagonists.

The two most reliable historical sources are Vertue (1684-1756) and Evelyn, the diarist (1620-1706). However, Vertue is not always accurate and Evelyn is windy

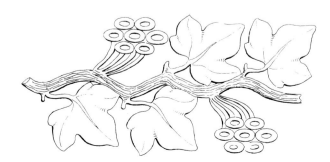

and given to flatulent praise. Here and there, the descriptions of Gibbons and his work might well be criticised for their paucity and lack of detail, but it must be borne in mind that they were commenting, as they thought, on a man of exceptional abilities who was still a comparatively minor figure. This is what Vertue noted: 'Mr Grinlin Gibbons born in Holland of English Parents, came into England about 19 years of Age. Went into Yorkshire where he was first imployd and afterwards came to London with his Family at Deptford and follow'd ship carving. About that time the play house in Dorsett garden called the Dukes house being a building, Mr Betterton finding him an ingenious man imployd him to Carve for him the Ornements and decorations of that house particularly the Capitals cornishes and Eagles, with which Sir Peter Lilly was well pleased and inquiring after the Artist that performed them, Mr Gibbons by his means was recommended to the King Charles 2d who then ordered the beautifying of the Palace of Windsor in which work he was imployd (Bab. May architect etc. recommended him to the King) and first cutt one great Chimney peice of carving in wood which is remaining there, representing a feston of many fishes shells and other ornaments, with which the King being well satisfyd, appointed him to be his Master Carver. Besides this he did all the fine Carvings in the chappell and hall, and without in the great square he made for the equastrian Statue of the King on Horse back in brass with the pedestal of Marble. Many other Statues and works in many places are done by him. His vast reputation in this time procured him a good fortune and a fine collection of picture Models and other Curiosities'.

It is natural that there should be differences of opinion when Vertue's account is compared with that of John Evelyn, who insisted that he and he alone discovered Gibbons in Deptford. But it is interesting to revert to Vertue's mention of Gibbons in Yorkshire. It would appear possible that he was indentured to an architect and carver, William Etty, whose indifferent work unfortunately endures in All Saints church, York. There is something vaguely bizarre in the notion that Gibbons went to the wilds of Yorkshire at all. He was only 19, educated in the Netherlands and speaking even less English than he mastered later in life, when he settled in London to become a ship carver. Exactly how his Yorkshire mentor coped with him, how he lived and established his working relationships, we do not know. If there are lost years in the lives of many great men, then Grinling Gibbons is no exception. Vertue, who took his account of Gibbons' life in part from the portrait painter, Thomas Murray, did not bother to pursue the matter, but if we had a better knowledge of the years in Yorkshire, then we might know more about Gibbons himself. It is not impossible that his indentures or other documents may come to light some day. In view of what happened after Gibbons and his parents came from Yorkshire to settle in Deptford, it is likely that his standard of work was even then very high, although he was still a long way from the Continental classical Baroque style which brought him fame. It was almost fortunate that his inability to express himself other than in Dutch or Flemish forced him to rely on the purely visual. His written work is indicative of this, for in one receipt he signs himself 'Youer ombell obegent Sarvant'. This is practically phonetic and it does not resemble the written style of the period. He possibly picked it up from Etty. It does appear that Etty was acquainted with Gibbons if we can accept what Ralph Thoresby wrote in the middle of 1702: 'Evening sat up too late with a parcel of artists I had got on my hands, Mr Gyles, the famousest painter of glass perhaps in the world, and his nephew Mr Smith, the bell founder . . . Mr Carpenter, the statuary, and Mr Etty, whose father, Mr Etty sen., the architect, the most celebrated Grinlin Gibbons wrought at York, but whether apprenticed with him or not I remember not well. Sate up full late with them'. No doubt the mulled ale had its effect on Thoresby's memory.

It would seem that the Gibbons family travelled by the shortest route from the Low Countries to arrive at York, then a cosmopolitan centre of *émigré* traders, and there they remained for some time. Gibbons may well have been apprenticed to Etty from the age of about nineteen. This would have given him up to five years apprenticeship to the trade of carving. He was in his early twenties when he went to live in the Deptford district of London, which had amongst its working population many tradesmen, including chandlers, carpenters, joiners and metal workers. Ships were brought to Deptford to be refitted and repaired, and vessels were also built there. This maritime district was full of curios, including carved doors, porticos, pillars, brackets and other rambling and unorganised house ornamentation, a visual array without any particular style but ample idio-syncrasy. It was here that a great deal of ships' furniture was made, including the stout brassbound chests, the table fittings, the carved panels for the master's quarters, figureheads, transoms and decklights and, in fact, examples of the artistic fancy that made many sailing ships floating examples of the carver's and carpenter's skill.

It was here that Gibbons had his real start. Fresh from the strict constraints of church and secular carving under the direction of Etty in York, he discovered unlimited possibilities as a journeyman shipcarver, working either for himself or for any carving shop that cared to employ him, and not beholden to any man except his patron of the moment. It is easy to imagine him in his early twenties, a younger and probably leaner version of Kneller's portrait, and no doubt somewhat more scruffy as he went about his work. Whether he spent any time

swilling liquor, like many of his contemporaries we do not know, but it is doubtful, for he must have spent long hours carving a relief copy of the large *Crucifixion* by Tintoretto. It is not clear how he became familiar with this masterpiece, but copies may well have been in circulation at the time. He settled on a size of $56\frac{3}{8}$ in $\times$ $32\frac{1}{4}$ in. The result can now be seen in the Victoria and Albert Museum, London where it is on loan by Lord Stamford of Dunham Massey, Cheshire, but likely to be returned to Dunham Massey, now a National Trust property, in the near future. There is a possibility that Gibbons carved it in order to display it to would-be clients as proof of his carver's skill. The theory may well hold water if we are to believe that the Deptford shipcarvers were so keenly competitive as to force a young newcomer to carve a massive sampler. This is quite unlikely. The Deptford of that time was a busy area with enough business for all except the downright mediocre. The garlanded frame which surrounds the *Crucifixion* is the first indication of Gibbons' aptitude for this form of carving, but it has from time to time come in for some criticism. It is of a different wood from that used for the relief carving. In fact, there are two pieces, a $2\frac{1}{2}$ in. on top of a $1\frac{1}{2}$ in. piece. The floral effect was specifically carved to enclose the *Crucifixion*, consisting of roses and other flowers with a ruched ribbon running through them. True, they do lack the appearance of the later and more typical work of Gibbons, but they were carved according to the limitations of the wood itself, a fact overlooked by some critics. From the practical carving point of view, it is difficult to see what else Gibbons might have done with the frame because he had to fit a lot of floriation into a relatively narrow area.

The *Crucifixion* was a catalyst in Gibbons' career. It was seen, almost by accident, by John Evelyn, who claimed to have discovered the carver working in a broken-down house in a Deptford field. This was Evelyn's parish and he took a keen interest in every aspect of business carried on there. He was also in the habit of taking a stroll round the lanes on the lookout for the unusual and absorbing. He carried trade and other gossip back to London, where he had the ear of the King. Evelyn was a man prone to odd enthusiasms and interests, as his diaries show, and he had an eye for developing genius, using his own money to assist anybody whom he considered to be in need of encouragement. He had already parted with large sums of money to help the gardeners, Wise and London, to gain royal recognition. On discovering Gibbons, his first thought was to bring the young carver to the notice of the court and, hopefully, gain royal patronage. On 18 January 1671 he wrote: 'I this day acquainted his Majestie with that incomparable young man, Gibson (sic) whom I lately found in an Obscure place, and that by meere accident, was I walking neere a poore solitary thatched house in a field in our Parish neere

Says-Court; I found him shut in, but looking into the Window, I perceiv'd him carving that large *Cartoone* or *Crucifix* of Tintorets, a Copy of which I had also my selfe brought from Venice, where the original painting remaines: I asked if I might come in, he opend the doore civily to me, and I saw him about such a work, as for the curiosity of handling, drawing and studious exactness, I never in my life had seene before in all my travells; I asked him why he worked in such an obscure and lonesome place; he told me, it was that he might apply himselfe to his profession without interruption; and wondered not a little how I came to find him out; I asked if he were unwilling to be made knowne to some Greate men; for that I believed it might turne to his profit; he answerd, he was but yet a beginner; but would yet not be sorry off that piece; I asked him the price, he told me 100 pounds. In good earnest the very frame was worth the money, there being nothing in nature so tender and delicate as the flowers and festoones about it, and yet the work was very strong; but in the piece above 100 figures of men etc: I found he was likewise *Musical*, and very Civil, sober and discreete in his discourse. There was onely an old Woman in the house; so desiring leave to visit him sometimes, I tooke my leave: Of this Young *Artist*; altogether with my manner of finding him out, I acquainted the *King*, and beged of his Majestie that he would give me leave to bring him and his Worke to White-hall, for that I would adventure my reputation with his Majestie that he had never seene any thing approach it, and that he would be exceedingly pleased, and employ him: The *King* sayd, he would himself go see him: This was the first notice his Majestie ever had of Mr *Gibbons'*.

Evelyn's attempt to interest the King in Gibbons was not as straightforward as it sounds. In the end Gibbons was persuaded to bring the *Crucifixion* to Whitehall. Prior to this Evelyn conducted Wren, Pepys and others to Deptford to see the carving. In the Evelyn diary for 13 February 1671 this passage occurs: 'This day dined with me Mr Surveyor Dr Chr. Wren, Mr Pepys Cleark of the Acts, two extraordinary and knowing persons and other friends; I carried them to see the piece of Carving which I had recommended to the King'. Next month Evelyn wrote on 1 March: 'I caused Mr Gibbon to bring to *Whitehall* his excellent piece of Carving where being come I advertised his *Majestie* who asked me where it was, I told him in *Sir R. Brownes* (my F. in Laws) Chamber, and that if it pleased his Majestie to appoint whither it should be brought (for 'twas large, and though of wood, yet heavy) I would take care of it: No says the King; show me the Way, Ile go to Sir Richards Chamber; which his Majestie immediate did, walking all along the Enteries after me as far as the Ewrie till he came up into the rome where I also lay; and no sooner was he entred, and cast his eye on the Worke but he was astonish'd at the curiositie of it, and having considred it a long time, and discours'd

91

with Mr Gibbon, whom I broughte to kisse his hand; he commanded it should be immediately carried to the *Queenes* side to shew her Majestie, so it was carried up into her bed-chamber, where she and the King looked on and admired it againe, the King thus leaving us with the Queene, being now caled away, I think to Council, believing that she would have bought it, it being a Crucifix; but when his Majestie was gon, a French pedling woman, one *Madame de boord*, that used to bring petticoates and fanns and baubles out of France to the Ladys, began to find faults with severall things in the worke, which she understood no more than an Asse or Monky; so as in a kind of Indignation, I caused the porters who brought it, to carry it to the Chamber again, finding the Queene so much govern'd by an ignorant french woman; and this incomparable *Artist* (had) the labour onely for his paines, which not a little displeased me; so he was faine to send it downe to his cottage againe, though he not long after sold it for 80 pounds, which was realy (even without the frame) worth a hundred: Sir Geo. Viner buying it of him, as his first Essay, and his Majesties Surveyor *Mr Wren* faithfully promising me to employ him for the future; I having bespoke his *Majestie* also for his Worke at *Windsore* which my friend *Mr May* (the Architect there) was going to alter and repaire universaly; for on the next day I had a faire opportunity of talking to his *Majestie* about it, in the *Lobby* next the Queenes side, where I presented him with some Sheetes of my historie, and thence walked with him thro *St James's* Parke to the *Gardens*, where I both saw and Heard a very familiar discourse between – and *Mrs Nellie* as they cal'd an impudent Comedian, she looking out of her Garden on a Terrace on the top of the Wall and – standing on the greene Walke under it; I was heartily sorry at this scene: Thence the King walked to the *Duches of Cleavelands*, another Lady of Pleasure and curse of our nation: It was on a Council day, and so I went back and on the 4th to my house'.

Sir George Viner, who finally bought the *Crucifixion*, died some months later. His son, Sir Thomas Viner, ended the line in 1663. It is curious that the inventory of Dunham Massey, compiled in 1760, does not attribute the carving to Gibbons. But it is quite possible that the carver's illustrious name was not known at the time.

During his early years in Deptford and a little later on Gibbons attempted to specialise in the carving of relief panels, his works including *The Last Supper*, 20 in. × 24¼ in. in pearwood and now at Burghley House, *The Battle of the Amazons* at Warwick Castle, *The Valley of the Dry Bones* at Deptford Church, and *St Stephen Stoned* in the Victoria and Albert Museum. While all of them have been accepted as being authentic, there has from time to time been a certain amount of controversy, centring on a cipher consisting of the two letters, GG, back-to-back.

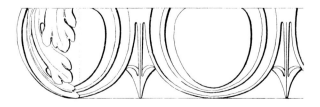

They appear, for instance, at the foot of the ladder in the *Crucifixion*, but cannot be taken too seriously because they might as well be accidental tool scratches as a cipher. When it comes to a satisfactory authentication, we often find ourselves on shifting sands, for there are only three so-called genuine Gibbons in the world, the two panels in Italy, which will be discussed later, and the signed Robert Cotton monument in the church of St Mary at Conington, Cambridgeshire. But, even here, are we absolutely sure that all these works were done from start to finish by Gibbons himself? It is possible that we should devote our attentions more profitably to the 'school of Gibbons' than to the man himself.

The reliefs naturally vary in quality, demonstrating that even Gibbons had his moments. *The Valley of the Dry Bones* is about three inches thick, depicting a veritable tumult of figures, including God with a halo. The carving of the text at the head of the panel is so unlike Gibbons' typographical style as to suggest that the task was delegated to a rather unclever apprentice. It reads AUDITE ARIDA OSSA, VERBUM DOMINUM, HIC DICIT DOMINUS DEUS HIS OSSIBUS INTERMITTAM SPIRITUM MEUM INTER VOS ET VIVENTIS. The work measures 45 in. × 37 in. and is said to have rested, logically enough, over the porch of a charnel house in a churchyard. A relief carving of rather better quality is *St Stephen Stoned*, and here again there is a vast crowd scene containing a total of seventy figures with figures and arches in the background. The carving of the figures is superior to that in *The Valley of the Dry Bones*. This particular work remained in Gibbons' possession for many years and he kept it at his Bow Street house with his collection of pictures or 'models' which he used for reference purposes. It was finally purchased by the Duke of Chandos and lodged at his house at Cannons, near Edgware in Middlesex. In 1747 it passed through the hands of two men, Mr Gore and Mr Rebow, and, after Rebow's death, it was bought by the Victoria and Albert Museum for the sum of £300. For this carving Gibbons used both lime and lancewood, the blocks being bonded together with animal glue to make a piece measuring 6 ft 4½ in. In depth it was about 12 in. The marriage of the two timbers led eventually to the piece developing shakes, or splits, which remain and are virtually irrepairable. The technical execution is good, although the marked disparity of colour between the lime and lancewood does seriously detract from the visual effect. As a sidelight on the style, it is noticeable that when Gibbons used as his model a painting he invariably modified the trees from the space-filling Italian style to the more flattened Flemish style.

In judging Gibbons' relief panels we are not unnaturally influenced by the quality of his better known works, which are of a radically different order. His body of work was in the field of ornamentation. It would be a sorry mistake to

judge the man on the evidence of the panels. They were after all done for a market which appeared promising at the time and, like many craftsmen artists both before and since, he was in the position of having to follow a market rather than attempt to create a new one.

It is doubtful whether he truly appreciated his own capabilities at this early stage in his career, and he was certainly willing to attempt practically any work for which he was sure to be paid. He was still a young man who had to make his own way. What he did have in abundance was faith in himself, as is evidenced in the price of £100 which he put on the *Crucifixion* when Evelyn made his enquiry. In comparison with the pricing of relief carvings of equivalent size by more mature tradesmen, the sum of £100 may have been high and perhaps even exorbitant, despite Evelyn's opinion. Gibbons did not know that Evelyn intended trying to interest the King in buying it. Yet there is still something slightly puzzling about this situation. It does not seem possible that Gibbons offered the panel for £100 simply to enhance its value and his own status as a carver. He may not have wished to dispose of it at all but retain it for some reason best known to himself. This brings us back to the earlier theory that he intended using it as an example of his work in order to attract commissions. The notion hardly holds water when we realise that the market for relief panels of this type was small in comparison with the possibility of making a good living by carving ornamental pieces for the houses of the wealthy. Whatever the reason, it is a mistake to believe that the reliefs are truly a part of the main output of Gibbons. They do display shortcomings in the light of history and are an example of ambition over-reaching ability. If they are representative of anything at all, they demonstrate Gibbons' attention to detail, which was to dominate his later works. Two other reasons for his later success were, of course, his association with Wren and the patronage of Charles II, symbolised by his appointment as Royal Carver, a position not in any way restrictive and similar to that of the medieval carvers engaged on the King's Works who used the recognition to build up substantial private businesses and positions of civic prestige.

His skills at this early stage were better employed in the creation of a series of finely carved small portraits which were apparently produced soon after his arrival in the public eye. They can be classed as *objets de vanité*. In particular, the 7 in. oval plaque which shows Sir Christopher Wren is one of Gibbons' best minor works, although it may well have been flattering and even adulatory to his future patron. It is currently in the care of the Royal Institution of British Architects, London. There is also a portrait in oak of John Evelyn, but it perhaps lacks the elan of the Wren medallion. Vertue noted the occasion of its presentation by writing: 'Gibbons, in gratuity to Mr Evelyn, presented to him his own head carved in wood, by himself, which Mr Evelyn put over his street door at his house in Dover Street, as a signal, where it was for 20 years at least'. It now rests in the National Maritime Museum, Greenwich, London. If, as Vertue claims, it hung for two decades over Evelyn's portico, then it shows remarkably little sign of wear and tear, though it may well have been in a sheltered position. The two final portraits in the series were of Gibbons himself. One of them is at Chatsworth and its shows the carver as a Flemish apprentice, which may be a clue to his very early years in Holland. The other self-portrait is at Modena, Italy, and forms part of the Modena panel which will be discussed later. The portrait itself hangs from a skull and wears a full wig. One other portrait in wood remains. It is somewhat amusing and shows a chubby-faced and seemingly irascible man wearing a finely-carved buttercurl wig. Gibbons may well have disliked the unknown subject, who looks downright cantankerous, but there is some compensation in the beautifully defined forget-me-nots, acanthus and martagon wreath which surround the head.

Gibbons' first involvement in a major job came about in the 1670s when the Earl of Essex retained the services of Hugh May, the architect, to remodel Cassiobury, Hertfordshire. Although May had a free hand, his patron nevertheless had some fixed ideas. A radical approach was adopted and practically the whole house, with the exception of one wing, was rebuilt. The work was left in the hands of builders working under May's direction while the Earl of Essex was absent in Ireland, where he held the post of Lord Deputy. Like so many patrons, he was impatient to get the work done and in June 1675 he wrote in a testy tone: 'I wish you would tell Mr Hugh May that he should hasten the casing of the front of the house at Cassiobury, and the covering of it, and that it be done with all dispatch imaginable, for unless that part of the house be roofed and tiled before I come, I do not know how I shall be able to lie one night there'. In the same year Gibbons and his assistants must have been in more or less constant residence at Cassiobury, following May's builders from one part of the place to the other, and producing a great variety of carved decorations of all kinds, including frames. Other carvers who had no trade connection with Gibbons were also working there. About five years later, on April 18 1680 John Evelyn wrote: 'On the earnest invitation of the Earle of Essex I went with him to his house at Cashioberie in Hertford-shire. It was on Sunday but going early from his house in the square of St James, we arrived by ten o'clock; this he thought too late to go to church and we had prayers in his Chapell. The house is new, a plaine fabric, built by my friend Mr Hugh May. There are divers faire and good rooms, and excellent carving by Gibbons, especially the chimney-piece of ye library'.

Although Cassiobury was again rebuilt in 1800 and finally demolished in 1922 it had the distinction of enabling Gibbons to launch into the Baroque style which he was to develop. The carvings at the house underwent several transitions. Reporting in the Transactions of the Royal Institution of British Architects in 1867 W. R. Rogers commented that many of them were 'covered over and loaded with thick brown paint and heavily varnished'. A certain amount of restoration had been carried out in a hamfisted manner, using plaster and composition rather than recarving the broken pieces. It is, alas, in the way of things that this sort of thing occurs, and it should be said that few carvers have an aptitude for convincingly restoring Gibbons' work.

One of Gibbons' principal pieces at Cassiobury was the library overmantel mentioned by Evelyn and composed in the manner of the French artist, Jean-Baptiste Mannoyer, who settled in London about 1678, where he spent the rest of his life. He was buried in St James's Church, Piccadilly, where Gibbons' reredos is a centrepiece. It was from Mannoyer's style that Gibbons drew many of his ideas for the intertwinings of flowers and vegetation. The overmantel was carved to include the acanthus, floriation and a flute with a musical score for the instrument. A massing of detail was also evident in many of the frames, which featured coats of arms, the eagle and sunflowers, long intertwinings and interloopings of shamrocks, a bunching of cobnuts and gourds. In this glorious profusion Gibbons for the first time achieved the *trompe l'oeil* effect by placing one object almost on top of another.

The Cassiobury carvings have a triumphant history of their own. With the death of the house, a sale was held in June 1922, and the carvings were bought by the Wernher Collection in England and the Hearst Collection in America. The Wernher purchases went eventually to Luton Hoo, Bedfordshire, and they are now in the private dining room, complete with the spreadeagle which Gibbons did originally for the Great Dining Room at Cassiobury. This is one of Gibbons' most adventurous works, depicting the predatory bird with a twig in its beak. Some interesting experiments with naturalistic forms are included, such as tulips which are deliberately out of scale, maize and the inevitable sunflowers. Gibbons was playing about with problems of composition in this, his first major commission, for he also produced the drops which include seashells held together in loops of pearls, strawberry foliage and forget-me-nots which are a direct descendant of those in the wreath encircling the irascible man done earlier. In modern terms the drops are an almost surrealistic example of what a carver could achieve once he immersed himself in the Baroque style.

Some writers naïvely marvel at the fact that Gibbons achieved so much at

74   Grinling Gibbons—the portrait by Sir Godfrey Kneller (1646-1723)

Cassiobury. Of course, he must have had many assistants, perhaps even a few journeymen to help him. The 1922 sale did bring one blessing, and it was a firm identification of the work of Gibbons and the 'school of Gibbons', including the Pierce staircase which was bought for the Metropolitan Museum, New York, for £5000. Up to this time it had often been attributed to Gibbons. Another germane fact is that throughout his lengthy career Gibbons was seldom, if ever, awarded a contract for the entire carved decoration of a single project. He more often than not shared it with other lesser known carvers, and together they created a more or less uniform style. This led inevitably to the creation of so many pieces which are now labelled 'school of Gibbons'. In its own way it was no better and no worse than the habit of the great masters of painting who employed apprentices to provide pieces of detail or cover otherwise tedious acres of canvas with a wooded background. In Gibbons' case, of course, the difference was that no background existed. Everything was to the fore.

There are quite possibly a number of works by Gibbons and his assistants which underwent an enforced dispersal as a result not only of the Cassiobury sale but also the death of other great houses. The fabric of this enriched school of carving will never be completely put together again to form a complete picture. Many pieces are erroneously labelled as being Gibbons, but they can be dismissed out of hand. There are, too, imitations, some of them by Edward Pierce, who was responsible for the Cassiobury staircase, and quite credible they are. Despite this hiatus, it is still worth mentioning new finds, for only examination and research by future scholars will determine the truth. In a letter to the author dated 20 October 1977 the architect-extraordinary, Sir Clough Williams-Ellis CBE MC LLD, who died while the present book was being written, stated that certain doors and a fireplace in the hall at his re-created Italianate village, Portmeirion, on the Cardigan Bay peninsula, Merioneth, were 'in the manner of Grinling Gibbons, and all in panels behind plate glass'. They were, in fact, taken to Portmeirion from the 1851 Great Exhibition held in London and may, or may not, have some association with Cassiobury or Holme Lacy. With greater reservation the same may well apply to what Sir Clough describes as 'a very charming Gibbons-like group in white pine of two cherubs playing on top of a lion, the whole thing being some five feet high. It must have been lurking in some store at Portmeirion for half a century as I cannot now recall where I got it'. There are no examples to suggest that Gibbons ever carved lions and cherubim in conjunction except for the Queen's catafalque in 1695.

Gibbons' methods of base construction are quite frequently just as interesting as the carvings themselves. In the making of the frame at Sudbury, where the closely

allied work of Edward Pierce may also be seen for purposes of comparison, three pieces of lime wood were bonded together. The timber closest to the wall is $\frac{1}{2}$ in. thick, while the two other pieces are 4 in. and 2 in. thick. Although this would be enough for most carving purposes, when the composition of the frame is examined in detail it is evident that the job got out of hand, exuberantly bursting through its own boundaries. As a consequence, additional pieces of wood had to be added to accommodate the projecting parts of the composition. Gibbons was now and then very sketchy when it came to the preliminary planning and, like many carvers, impatient to get to grips with the wood, only to be forced into improvisation once he was well into the job. The Sudbury frame is in doubtful taste, featuring as it does a large peony seen in reverse, cuddled improbably by wheat, roses, a bunch of grapes and the acanthus, which plays its usual role as a visual bond between the different elements. Scarcely content with the incredible visual disturbance which he had created, Gibbons went straight on to include a duck and a cockerel with their heads hanging downwards, plus some game birds, fruit and flower pendants, shells and flowers. As a last flourish he put in a fish held by an eel, the latter then being a gastronomic delicacy. It is indeed difficult to get to grips with the mind of a man who was capable of coercing together all these elements into such a resounding composition, faultless in execution but doubtful in credibility. But then, such comments were also made at one time about many of Beethoven's compositions. Artists of all kinds have been subjected to criticism when they dared to experiment.

The possibility of Gibbons' work being scattered without trace as a result of house demolitions and sales in the last two hundred years has already been mentioned. This applies to the pieces which he carved for Holme Lacy, Hertfordshire shortly after 1674. Completion of the house was planned for 1 August 1675. The builder was Anthony Deane of Uffington, the patron was Lord Scudamore. Hugh May, later to become Crown Paymaster, was the architect. The sale of the contents of Holme Lacy took place in 1910, some of the carvings going first to Beningborough, Yorkshire, but later to a more fitting and permanent home at Kentchurch, near Hereford. While there have in the past been some doubts as to the authenticity of the carvings, they are now nevertheless accepted as being by Gibbons, although they are in a radically different style from his work at Cassiobury. For a change we now have a studied avoidance of the thick and occasionally clumping together of fruit, vegetables and birds. All the over-emphatic brashness has disappeared to be replaced with a sparkling virtuosity. The reason is clear. At Holme Lacy Gibbons clearly had strict instructions to create something of a much more delicate nature, and he accordingly conjured up

the lightness of laurel berries, lilies, roses, shells, pearls and acanthus scrolls. These carvings possess an altogether ethereal touch which matches the nature of the rooms. Here and there in the house Gibbons did return momentarily to his heavier and more masculine style, as though he could not resist depicting the elegance of game birds, which he featured in the frames for the dining room and saloon. The relationship between similar styles at widely spaced periods of his career provides us with some insight into the mind of a man who had an eye to the commercial main chance, for the flowing garlands which he did for Holme Lacy were practically replicas of those in St Mary Abchurch, the small and almost hidden church with the painted dome in Abchurch Lane, London.

Holme Lacy has now become a hospital, but it still contains some fragments of Gibbons' work, including a door architrave with the now well known forget-me-nots and the curled and encircling acanthus. There is a dormitory overmantel with the heads of birds and floriation, palms and two cherubs. Elsewhere in the building is a door top with ivy wreaths. The dining room has a cedar wainscot carved with a frieze of leaves and berries and crossed ruched ribbons. This may be the only example of Gibbons' carving in cedar apart from the screen and lattices in Emmanuel chapel at Trinity, Oxford. A cornice has unfortunately been converted into a chimneypiece with an overbearing acanthus and sidepieces of grapes, tulips, hops and martagons in thick trusses.

Some foreshadowing of Gibbons' aptitude for creating dominant pieces is found in the oak swag which he and his assistants carved for Holme Lacy. It is now at Kentchurch, where it is divided into two sections. In its original composition, it was hung out of doors where it was affected by the weather and developed severe shakes, or splits. It has now been treated and is in no immediate danger of disintegration. Measuring 28 ft across, it includes giant sunflowers and roses, many of them one foot in diameter. Almost monstrous in its dimensions, the swag was one of the biggest carvings of its time. It is a pity that it is now displayed in two sections, because it disjoints the composition. Gibbons was directly influenced here by the style of the stone work in the Stadthuys, Amsterdam, for there are parallels in the treatment of the sunflowers and strong echoes throughout of the Duquesnoy-Quellin school of composition. In the centre of this enormous carving are the arms of the Scudamore family as a final climax. The work can be classified as a *tour de force* or a folly, depending on one's knowledge of Gibbons' development. But there is an over-riding impression that it is an example of a young carver tending to overdo it.

As it happened, the Scudamore commission was to mark the end of Gibbons as the fashionable carver who could be hired to pander to the whims of almost any

private patron. For nearly six years he had been moving steadily upwards. His work was now being noticed and commented upon. The transition which occurred was quite startling. From Cassiobury and Holme Lacy he moved, almost in a single leap, to Windsor Castle itself. One of his champions was Hugh May, appointed in November 1673 to the post of Comptroller of the Windsor Office. At this time Gibbons was also under the guidance of the avuncular John Evelyn and the artist, Sir Peter Lely. May had been responsible for the maintenance of Windsor Castle for some time and drew up many plans for major works which he thought would improve the pile. In 1675 he finally received permission to proceed, and in September of that year he initiated an ambitious rebuilding programme at an annual cost of £23,000. May had spent periods of his life in the Netherlands, and he was greatly influenced by the architecture, including the castellated style which resulted in him being labelled a medieval-revivalist. This was the style which he introduced at Windsor. After two years of intensive work, his stonemasons and carpenters moved out and Gibbons and other tradesmen moved in. They must have worked very quickly indeed, for by Christmas Gibbons was already submitting his first bills: 'Grinling Gibbons and Henry Phillips, Carvers for severall sorts of Carved Workes by them performed upon the Chimney-peeces, Pedestalls, and picture fframes of the Kings Greate and Little Bed Chambers and Presence his Maties Closett, Musicke Roome, Eateing Roome, Withdrawing Roome and Backstaires, the Queenes withdrawing Roome, Bed Chamber and Gallery, and in iii roomes the Dutchesse of Portsmouth's Lodgings – As by Two bills £625 14s.'

The Duchess of Portsmouth was the King's mistress. On the evidence of this bill she must have been in high favour, for her apartment of three rooms received handsome embellishments on a par with those in the King's bedchamber.

A few words here regarding Henry Phillips, whose name appears with that of Gibbons on the first bill. He held the appointment of Master Sculptor in Stone and Master Carver in Wood at Windsor Castle. Gibbons evidently worked under his direction, and Phillips would naturally be jealous of his own position in view of the terms of his warrant of 1661 which stated: 'Whereas the Art of Sculpture of Carving in Wood is an Art peculiar of it Selfe and not practised used or annexed with or in the Names Misteries Art or Occupations of Carpenters Joyners Masons or any other Art of manuall workemanshipp whereof Our Services are Already furnished, but an Art if more excellent Skill and Dexterity for the Adorning and Beautyfying of our Pallaces Castles Manors houses and other Out buildings & workes whatsoever & whereas we have received good Testimony & proofe of the sufficient skill & rare knowledge of Henry Phillips in the aforsaid Art of Sculpture and Carving in wood . . . the Fee or wages to be Eighteenpence by the Day . . . and One Robe yearely of the Suit of other Esquires of our household'.

This was indeed recognition of the carver's art, and it divorced him from the very trades from which he originally sprang, those of the mason and the carpenter and joiner, ensuring him a place as a practitioner of 'an Art of more excellent Skill and Dexterity'. To be granted a Warrant at that time meant that the craftsman had already achieved the stature of Phillips, who was in 1650 a Liveryman of the Joiner's Company. Even so, he had to present certain specimen carvings as proof of his abilities and they were scrutinised not only by experienced craftsmen but also others such as state dignitaries and others with a finely developed taste for such things. The judging was long drawn out while the candidate remained on tenterhooks. The great attraction of the appointment was, of course, the lifelong sinecure followed by a certain amount in monetary patronage, or pension, after retirement. Phillips did retire in 1679, apparently leaving the field clear for Gibbons. The young, ambitious carver from Deptford probably hoped against hope that he would quickly move into Phillips' position to hold the royal warrant. But one thing which he did lack was business experience. If he was a fine carver he still fell short when it came to the money side of his trade. In any case, there were older men working at Windsor who had known Phillips for years, and many of them were better qualified for the appointment. No doubt some kind of nepotism was at work, for Phillips' cousin, William Emmett (1641-1700) eventually took over his uncle's position, though not until Phillips' death in 1693.

Throughout his working life at Windsor Castle Phillips followed the trade custom of imposing his own name on the accounts which were submitted by the carvers who worked under his direction. This meant that he received what amounted to a commission for selecting carvers of quality and distributing work to them, then giving some guidance. In actual practice, it is highly unlikely that he did anything more than simply inspect the work at various stages and give cursory advice to men who were just as accomplished as he himself. For a man of Gibbons' abilities and youth, this must have been galling, for Phillips' presence and patronage did nothing more than draw the glory.

Despite the atmosphere, Gibbons persistently excelled himself. His versatility exploded at Windsor. It was as though he saw his chance to display a unique talent in the noblest of all settings. The phantasmagoric side of his creativity sprouted on a huge scale, like the huge sunflowers which he had been carving in the recent past. The King's Eating Room consequently now contains carvings which marry the magic of wood with the paintings of Verrio, who was employed to decorate the ceiling. He and Gibbons worked together for a time when Verrio's subject was, aptly enough, *The Feast of the Gods*, a triumph of a painting which ran riot all over the ceiling. Gibbons saucily extended the theme of the work by carving lobsters, shells and other marine life. The overmantel, over one foot thick, contains a mass of flowers and fruit, including tulips, here about one foot in width and rivalling the sunflower. When it came to the alcoves, he carved wader birds, woodcock and teal, packed in with fishes of all kinds, some bulbous gourds, rabbits and fruit with flowers. He also practised, not for the first time, the *trompe l'oeil* technique in which a bird was carved on top of a complacent rabbit, and a garland trailed across the bird. Elsewhere he included little quirks of imagination, such as the barley on the duck's plumage. This room imparts one of the major secrets of Gibbons' compositions, namely continuity, which he created by running the now famous ruched ribbon from one section to another, encouraging the eye to move easily. Other carvers may have isolated objects, especially when they had no special inter-relationship, but Gibbons was no believer in isolation. Evidently he shared with Nature an abhorrence of the vacuum, filling any empty space in such a way as to dazzle the eye.

A note here about Verrio, who perhaps influenced Gibbons' ideas about composition. He was well known as a painter of ceilings in 1701. At Windsor his subjects were mainly mythological with Diana and Endymion in the King's Great Bedchamber, Mars and Venus in the Little Bedchamber. Gibbons followed him round the rooms where he painted, and no doubt worked alongside him between 1701 and 1702, when the work was being done on the great staircase. Here the walls were devoted to the subject of Julian the Apostate and the satirical *The Caesars*. Verrio had no position in the Office of Works, but he was a favoured artist and ways and means had to be found to retain him. In 1684 the Chief Painter's post, previously held by Sir Peter Lely, was revived specifically for Verrio's

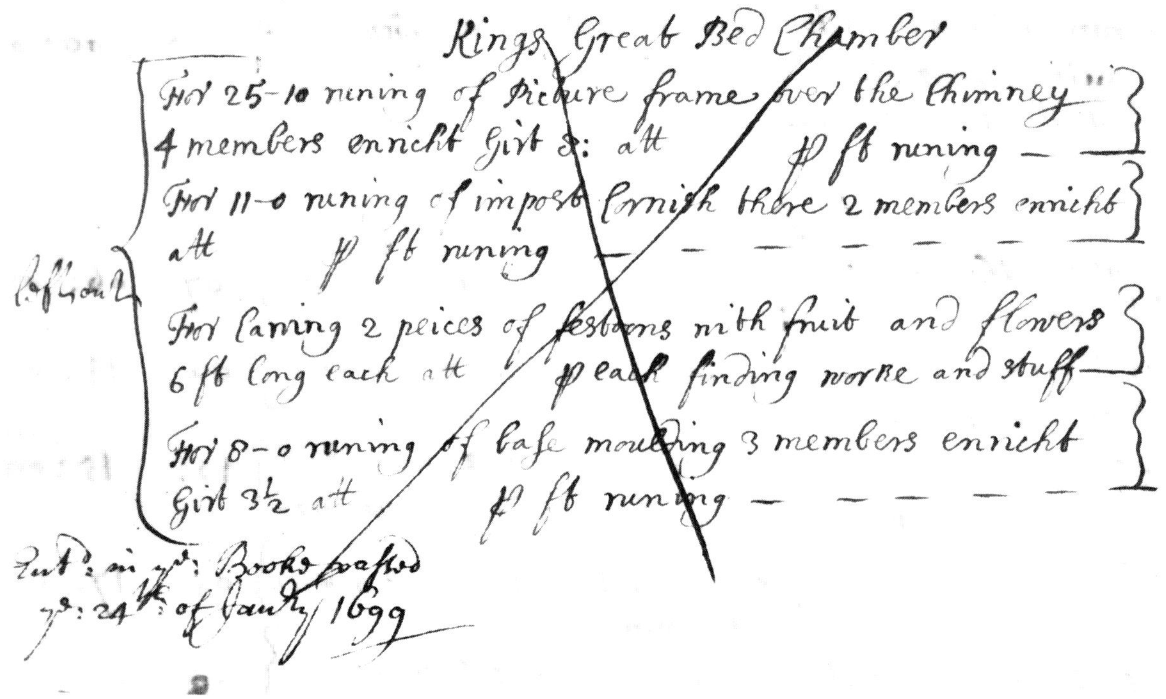

Kings Great Bed Chamber

For 25-10 runing of Picture frame over the Chimney
4 members enricht Girt 8: att   p̸ ft̸ runing _____

For 11-0 runing of impost Cornish there 2 members enricht
att   p̸ ft̸ runing _____

For Carving 2 peices of festoons with fruit and flowers
6 ft long each att   p̸ each finding worke and stuff _____

For 8-0 runing of base moulding 3 members enricht
Girt 3½ att   p̸ ft̸ runing _____

Put: in yr: Bookes pased
yr: 24th of Janry 1699

---

benefit, and he was paid £200 a year by the Treasurer of the Chamber.

The Queen's Audience Chamber, carving for which was carried out in 1677 and 1678, is an example of Gibbons' evident dislike of formal typographical work. Here there is a frame containing a painting of the grotesque beheading of Mary, Queen of Scots. At the head of the frame are the letters MR, carved too large and so boldly that their very size magnifies the faults. But any faults are instantly overlooked at the sight of the carved drops on either side of the frame. Gibbons indulged in rather more than his usual showmanship and included flamboyant sunflowers and martagon lilies, forget-me-nots and, entirely new in his repertoire, peapods, representing his 'trademark'. There are also harebells, reversed poppies and campanulas, all vying for a place. Gibbons remained in an expansive and experimental mood when he worked on the frame for the portrait of William of Orange, for there is an exciting crush of hops, palms and roses and something else not previously seen, willow leaves. But when it came to the frame for the portrait of Frederick of Orange, the results failed to come up to expectation, because he attempted to carve the symbolic oranges which somehow got out of proportion. Here and there in his frame carving Gibbons was obviously ill at ease. He was trying a little too hard, especially when it came to the frames for the Queen's

Presence Chamber. One of them displays an eagle suffering from a painful contortion of the neck, sunflowers with coarse and poorly defined petals, and pears, roses and peonies which somehow lack the tactile quality of much of his other work. In the Gloucester frame, for instance, the acanthus scrolls, which had been included so many times elsewhere, became gross and unlike the usual Gibbons style. Yet the surrounding drop contains maize and lilies which represent the carver at his best. The reason for this lowering of quality is quite unaccountable, but the fact remains that there is a loss of flair. It may well have been due to his employment of assistants who could not reach his exacting standards. But why Gibbons should have tolerated this in the prestigious atmosphere of Windsor Castle is beyond conjecture.

Some time between 1680 and 1682 Gibbons put in a bill: 'For Carving Worke done & laid upon xxvii Seates and Stalls, Carved with Fruit, Flowers, Palmes, Paurells, Pelicans, Pigeons . . . vi Vasses with Thistles, Roses and two Boys, Laurel & other Ornaments in the Front and upon the Topp of the Kings Seate, with Drapery, Fruit, Flowers, Crootesses, Starres, Roses and severall other Ornaments of Carving about the Altar Pews and other places in and about the Kings Chappell. £498 0s 5½d'. By 'crootesses' Gibbons meant cartouches.

Between either working on or supervising his major works at Windsor Castle, Gibbons also executed smaller pieces, including a 'Confession Chaire with 2 Foliage Pannels' and 'a Modell for the Founder to cast the Copper Pipies that Convey water into ye Queens Bathing Cisterne' for which he charged the sum of ten shillings. There was also a mass of other small work to be tackled. Only a few weeks after working with the great Verrio he was asked to carve brackets for three doorways, and he charged one pound each for them. It was unextraordinary work which he would have carried out quickly and expertly, and it shows that he was not above turning his hand to whatever was required. Yet in 1700 he carved the gallery wainscott and charged £122 for it.

Grinling Gibbons Carver for Carving worke done and
laid vpon xxvij:t Seates and Stalls, Carved with ffruite
flowers, Palmes, Laurells Pellicans Pigeons, ye ffoote of
Cornice that has' two members inrich'd with Leaves between
each Seate, Twenty ffoot of framing to every Seat according
to Contract lij xxviij:li Next to him for Carving the Six
Vases with Thistles, Roses' and two Boyes Laurells Palmes
and other Ornaments in the ffront and vpon the Topp of
the Kings' Seate with Drapery ffruite, flowers, frontespeeces
Statues, Roses' and severall other Ornaments of Carving
about the Altar, Pewes and other places in and about the
Kings' Chappell, he finding Timber & Workmanshipp xxx
according to Contract lij iij iiij vonj. v. 0b In both as' by two
bills of the particulars thereof appeares

Gibbons was not alone at Windsor in the heyday of Hugh May's remodelling activities. The throne in St George's Hall was carved by John Vanderstein, who also made the clay models, or maquettes, for the pedestal which formed part of the royal statue. Vanderstein was classed as a sculptor, not a tradesman, and so he was

able to command high fees. He was paid £400 for the throne, but it was Gibbons who supplied the excellent ornamentation which set it off, as we can sense from the mention in the above bill for work done 'upon the Topp of the Kings Seate'. He also executed 'the Garter & Festoones about the two Compass Doores, the two Georges, the upper and lower Rayles on both sides the Pannells & moldings at the Throne . . with severall other Ornaments belonging to the said Throne'.

Of course, Gibbons' lesser works all had their own particular excellence in the field of ornamentation and they belong to all intents and purposes to the world of the sculptor. It was one indication that he was soon to quit the ranks of the tradesmen. He was now carving figures and, typically, making a great success of it. When George Bickham wrote his *Delicaie Britannicae*, published in 1742, he mentioned some of the new work: '. . 4 Wooden Figures beautifully carved and painted, each about 10 feet in Height, who support the gallery and stand in fine Attitudes beinding as it were under their heavy Burthen and representing a father & 3 sons whom the valiant Black Prince had made captives at Leghorn'.

Typically, Evelyn was not quite as restrained as Bickham. After paying a visit to Windsor in 1683 to find out how his prodigy was faring, the diarist practically exploded with enthusiasm: 'Stupendous and beyond description, the incomparable carving of our Gibbons who is without controversie the greatest master both of invention and rareness of work that the world ever had in any age; nor doubt I at all that he will prove as Greate a master in the statuary art'. By this time Gibbons was working not only in wood but also the less tractable stone. It is not the purpose of the present book to examine Gibbons the stone sculptor. Generally speaking, his work in stone is considered less fine than his wood carving. At this time he carved the white marble panels of the pedestal above which Charles II sat on horseback: 'Carving and cutting ye white marble pennells of ye Pedistall of his Maj^ties Statue on horse backe £400 . . and for cutting & carving ye Mouldinges & ornaments for ye pedistall of ye large Diall in ye North Terrace'. This reference is to the dial made by Henry Wynne.

The eventual desecration and loss of much of Gibbons' work at Windsor, May's conversion, and even Verrio's *The Feast of the Gods*, was carried out in 1827 by the monstrous Jeffry Wyatt at the behest of George IV. Little need be said about this fearful catastrophe beyond the fact that Wyatt, like so many 'improvers', was knighted for his expenditure of half a million pounds and the architectural shambles which Windsor Castle eventually became.

Returning to the earlier period, Gibbons was in 1682 awarded a 'Pencion after the rate of £100 per annum for repaireing cleansing and preserving the carved worke in Windsor Castle, according to his Maj^ties Warrant'. Such payment was

more than generous for the time, but may well have been awarded as a result of a financial advisor coming to the well-founded conclusion that Gibbons had already done far too well in hard cash out of his work. It would obviously be much cheaper to retain him on 'pencion' than pay him piece by piece for his artistry. On the other hand, the award of the pension under royal warrant signified that Gibbons had finally made his mark. One of the great hazards in accepting this financial recognition was that he was changed in status and found himself at the behest of the Clerk of Works and his staff, who demanded that he carry out various maintenance tasks, as witness the requisition to 'mend and new make some Pieces that were lost in ye Carving in ye Queenes Bathing Room, mend and alter the carving in ye Queenes Clossett in ye long gallery and make new Pieces for other carved workes by him done'. One can well imagine the position in which Gibbons

was now placed, for this make do and mend position meant that he was precluded from starting any new major works. Putting it bluntly, he was held in thrall to the tune of one hundred pounds a year.

The situation did improve slightly when he received an order for a 'chimnetpiece in Lime Tree with fruit, fflowers & birds and a fframe for a Glasse in ye Queens Dressing Roome, a Cocks Head for ye Dutchesse of Marlboroughs side Board and a Snakes head for ye Basin at ye Queenes Back Stairs'. The order was quite unusual, coming as it did direct from Queen Anne, who was under the baleful influence of the Groom of the Stole, a court dignitary with a strong hatred of all carved wood. History does not tell us why he disliked carvings, but it seems that on this occasion the Queen was able to over-rule her eminence grise.

Despite the volume of work which Gibbons produced at Windsor Castle, this period was not quite the triumph which it ought to have been. He made a brilliant start and, but for the wretched pension, he might well have reached new heights. All that is left at Windsor are three rooms of carvings and various other pieces,

Grinling Gibbons Carver for Carving a Chimney peire in Lime Tree with fruit fflowers and Buds in ye Queens Dressing Roome, Carving bj frames Carving a forks head for ye Dutchesse of Marlboroughs Side Board, and a Snakes head for ye Basin at ye Queens Back Staires, for Carving a fframe for a Glasse in her Ma^{ty} Dressing Roome, and other workes a^o by three Bills

some of which have been badly painted as a prime example of the English attitude to conservation. Yet Gibbons was not overcome by the decline of his scope. He had meanwhile been working quietly on one or two other pieces. Between 1680 and 1682 he drafted and submitted a bill which half-conceals one of his greatest masterpieces. It had nothing whatever to do with his work at Windsor, and the entry itself is tucked away between details of various jobs he had done at the Castle: 'Grinling Gibbons, Carver, for an Extraordinary fine peece of Carved worke made and Carved by him for his Matie & sent by his Matie as a present to the Duke of fflorence £150'. There would seem to be some connection between this carving and the fact that he had in the meantime been introduced by Evelyn to Sir Christopher Wren who 'faithfully promised to employ him for the future'.

The motivation and the inspiration for the unique piece of carving to which the bill casually refers came about in an unusual way. While the carving itself now rests in the Bargello Museum, Florence, it was once an object of importance in an entente cordiale. Cosima III, Grand Duke of Tuscany, grew friendly with Charles II during his 1669 visit to England. Charles provided all kinds of treats for his guest, including a trip by barge down the Thames to Greenwich, the colourful vista of horse racing at Newmarket, and a feast on the royal yacht at Chatham, when salvo after salvo greeted Cosima each time he raised his glass in a toast to Charles. The visit was crowned with a banquet 'protracted to a great length and finally concluded with a most kind wish tendered to his Highness by His Majesty and seconded by all present for the continuation of a sincere friendship and a confirmation of the alliance between the royal family and the Most Serene House of Tuscany'. This effusion of regal goodwill resulted in Gibbons receiving from Charles an order for a carving which must symbolise all the elements of the visit. It was, by any standards, an imposing order, and an analysis of the 5 ft × 3½ ft piece shows how he accomplished it to the satisfaction of the King and the delight of Cosima. It is customary to attempt to read a symbolic message into such presentation pieces, but this is, at best, a tenuous business, and one cannot always be sure how accurate a modern interpretation might be, no matter how studied. The history of symbolism is enwrapt in religion, folklore and heraldry, and in order to create a valid interpretation we require an informed knowledge of the chronology of symbolism, for certain symbols have meant one thing at a certain time and quite the reverse at other times. The swastika, for instance, once had a significance in Christianity. Modern history illustrates its subsequent use. It is safe to assume that the two doves at the head of the Cosima panel symbolise love and accord, although these particular birds are known to be bloodthirsty and given to bullying and general rapaciousness. The lace, which falls immediately below the doves, suggests Charles' predilection for adornment. In fact, he once paid £19 for three cravats. Between the doves and the lace are the famous Gibbons' roses. To create a connecting link on either side are acanthus scrolls, the shells and the pearls. When it came to hinting at the elements of prosperity and the Monarch himself, Gibbons copied the sword and the lions from his earlier works in the First

George Room at Burghley and the Cullen panel. As for the trumpet, this instrument was to herald the two rulers, and from it hangs the medallion with the clever touch of a portrait of Peitro Berrettini, otherwise Pietro da Cortona (1596-1669), a then famous artist in the Leonardo tradition who was not only an architect but also a consummate designer and decorator. He died the year of Cosima's visit to England.

Gibbons' treatment of the crown and the coronet was curious, for he depicted Charles' symbol of authority in the descent while that of Cosima is uppermost and directly opposite. No satisfactory explanation has ever been forthcoming why he carved them in these positions, although he may have intended them as a gentle and even mocking subservience. Because there had been much music making throughout Cosima's visit to England, Gibbons included a highly realistic score and a recorder, the instrument so finely carved that it appeared capable of being picked up and played.

The undoubted glory of the Cosima panel is created by the profusion of detail, but close analysis shows that the effect is gained not so much by the foremost quiver, medallion and chain, the notated score, trumpet, sword, crown and coronet, as by the 'frame' created by the carved fruit, flowers and acanthus scrolls which crowd in to impart a satisfying richness of effect. But other items busily clamour for attention, including jonquils, cyclamen, walnuts almost falling out of their shells, a central sprig of what may well be laurel leaves, and the perfectly formed seashells. The frequent appearance of seashells in Gibbons' carvings suggests that he possessed a collection of such items for reference purposes, including the scallop (*Pecten jacobaeus*) and the complicated *Nautilus pompilius*. Shells were collected and used by artists long before Gibbons' time. Leonardo was interested in their structure, and De Critz in his *John Tradescant and Zythepsa* (1645) depicted a collection of large shells, as did F. H. Francken the Younger in *Cabinet d'Amateur*. Balthasar van der Ast painted *Still Life with Shells* (1656), while Rembrandt made an etching, *The Shell*, depicting in detail *Conus marmoreus* in 1650. The artistic preoccupation with shells by Dutch artists may well have influenced Gibbons' use of them in his compositions.

The passage of the Cosima panel from England to Italy was uneventful, but when it reached the port of Leghorn the authorities decided to impound it on the grounds that it might harbour the plague. At that time the Italians were, as E. Dummer in his *A Voyage into the Mediterranean Seas* of 1865, declared: 'fearful of ye Plague', and so the carving in its specially made deal case, addressed to the British Envoy, Sir Thomas Dereham, remained in enforced isolation until it was rescued and finally presented to the Grand Duke.

Charles' gesture was as infectious as the plague itself, but the results were naturally different. His brother, James II, also commissioned a carving which he intended despatching to Modena, where his eye was set on marriage into the Italian nobility. The subject was a vanitas, incorporating a skull and medallion which showed a miniature of Gibbons himself, wearing a shoulder-length wig. Around the perimeter of the medallion were carved the words

GIBBONS INVENTOR SCULPSIT LONDINA

This panel, now lodged in the Estence Gallery at Modena, was a more diffuse composition than the Cosima presentation piece, and some critics feel that it is the lesser of the two. To some extent this may well be true, for at first glance it is almost unbalanced, the acanthus scrolls to left and right fighting to suggest symmetry, although the downward hanging pair of doves do achieve this feat. Other elements include barley, shells, shamrock, a burst-open peapod, coins and snowdrops, representing one of the most unusual collections of objects which Gibbons ever put together in a single carving. Once more the carver bent a knee to music, to include a wind instrument and a score which shows the chastening poem by James Shirley:

> The Glories of our Blood and State
> are shadows, not substantial things;
> there is no armour against Fate;
> Death lays his icy hand on Kings:
> Septers and Crowns must tumble downe
> and in the dust be equal made
> with the poor crooked Scythe and Spade.

Despite its undoubted virtuosity, the Modena panel did not attract the acclaim accorded to its compact and, let it be admitted, more interesting companion, the Cosima. Even now, it is still to modern eyes the less attractive of the two. While one can appreciate Gibbons' intentions, it nevertheless lacks the elan which illumined his style.

Now at the height of his powers, Gibbons was fast becoming wealthy. He could pick and choose his work, but resolutely remained a craftsman rather than an artist. He had consistently displayed a unique if somewhat erratic genius for composition which was unusual among the carvers of the time, and he had, moreover, been favoured by royal patronage as a result of which his name was better known than that of any other carver. In 1768 he married. There were to be nine children, but none of the sons followed their father's trade. This was unusual at a time when tradesmen's dynasties were the accepted rule. It is not hard to imagine the difficulty which a son, no matter how gifted, might encounter in trying to follow in the footsteps of such a father.

In 1678 the Gibbons' moved into a house in Bow Street, Covent Garden, with Sir Peter Lely, the artist, as neighbour. In common with other well-to-do house owners, Gibbons was able to choose for himself an individual sign and name, which he derived from King's Arms Court, just around the corner. His abode, the King's Arms, quickly became a meeting place for many of the gentry, including John Evelyn, who brought along with him to one soirée not only the Duchess of Grafton, but also Lord and Lady Chamberlain, perhaps in the hope that they would give commissions to his prodigy. With his usual passion for detailed observation Evelyn noted in his diary that the house was 'furnish'd like a Cabinet, not only with his owne worke, but divers excellent Paintings of the best hands'. Gibbons certainly possessed a commercial flair, for he displayed his own work and set it off against oil paintings to impress his guests and friends. He had now moved several rungs up the social ladder of London but he could not afford to let the chance of making more money slip through his fingers. Bow Street represented a great transition from Deptford.

Like a great many of the London properties of the time, the King's Arms was even then ancient and in a ruinous state of repair. It is surprising that Gibbons himself and many of his friends in the profession of architecture and the building trades did not attempt to do anything about it, otherwise the catastrophe of 1702 might well have been averted. A newspaper, *The Postman*, on 24 January 1702, reported: 'On Thursday the house of Mr Gibbons, the famous carver, in Bow Street, Covent Garden, fell down; but by a special Providence none of the family were killed; but 'tis said a young girl which was playing in the court, being missing, is supposed to be buried in the rubbish'.

Apparently not unduly put out or dismayed by what had happened, Gibbons at once ordered that the house should be rebuilt. It was almost the opportunity for which he had been waiting, a blessing in disguise, and the new house contained commodious rooms for the display of the pictures and carvings in addition to a workshop where Gibbons could work in comfort and have his family about him. He had spent practically all his arduous working life on sites which were noisy and dirty and either too hot or too cold for comfort. He engaged domestic servants to run the household under his wife's direction, and he also took in an apprentice, called King, and even a lodger, Madam Titus, who acted as nursemaid.

With its advantage of being in the middle of London, Bow Street suited him for some time, but so much work was now being put his way as a result of his growing reputation that he was able to refuse commissions. The house and workshop were a consolidation. He had spent a large sum of money on the rebuilding and he must now start to recoup it in order to pay off the debts. Acting like any prudent entrepreneur, he decided to expand by taking premises at Belle Sauvage at the lower end of Ludgate Hill, where his apprentices and other members of his staff could live, learn and work. There is an interesting note supplied to Vertue by a man called Stoakes for inclusion in the notebooks: 'Grinlin Gibbons carver (his father a Dutchman) he was born in Spur ally in the Strand he afterwards livd in Bel Savage on Ludgate Hill and there he carvd a flower pot the flowers of light wood so thin that the coaches passing by made them shake surprisingly'. The comments about Gibbons' antecedents are wrong, but the note about the operation at Belle Sauvage underline the fact that Gibbons did have a workshop in the Ludgate Hill area. It was also entered in the Quarterage Books of the Drapers' Company which earlier admitted Gibbons by patrimony on 19 January 1672 and given in 1673 through to 1684 as Ludgate Hill. It would seem that Gibbons had for some time been using the property as a workshop, but when Bow Street became too cramped for comfort he simply shifted the business in its entirety to Ludgate Hill.

The next move was to set up an apprenticeship system to recognise the value of keeping the craft of carving alive in England. He had in the past hired carvers to follow his designs, occasionally with only faint success, but more often than not in the true Gibbons style. He was undoubtedly clever and even cunning when it came to adding his personal touch to the work of those less skilled than himself, and for a man with such a facility with gouge and chisel this would be a rapid process. To perpetuate his style and maintain the commercial success of the business, he set about attracting a corps of apprentices to Ludgate Hill. Arnold Quellin, who had worked on and off with Gibbons at Windsor, was one of the first, followed by another countryman, René Cousin, already a qualified gilder. Cousin brought with him a ménage, including his children, Peter and Mary, and a servant who was also an apprentice gilder. From Windsor came the floral artist, Anthony Montingo, who had worked as the aged Verrio's assistant, and he brought with him Madame Montingo. Then there was Nicholas Lauzellier, a considerable artist in his own right, and John Vanderstein, whom Gibbons had known at Windsor as a stone sculptor, and he, too, had a wife and servant. The term 'servant' can be misleading in this context, for some of these young men were semi-apprentices who already had a loose agreement with Gibbons. They included Anthony Verhuke and Lawrence Vandermuelin. Some came as supporting

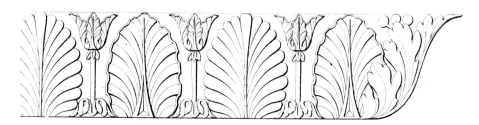

tradesmen to enable Gibbons to provide a full service for the clients. There is still some confusion about Quellin and Gibbons as far as statuary is concerned, and it would seem that Quellin agreed to handle all the work in stone which came Gibbons' way.

The Ludgate Hill establishment, with its predominantly Continental staff, quickly became one of the leading places in London for the commissioning of choice pieces in wood and stone. Gibbons was now all set to enhance his reputation. For good measure he also started a foundry for casting in bronze, thereby adding to the many services available to clients.

One of the first important commissions was work in wood and metal for the Chelsea military hospital, set up originally in 1682 by Charles II, aided by Sir Stephen Fox, the inevitable Evelyn and other influential figures. It was, of course, no mere coincidence that Gibbons should get the business, which he delegated to his associates, William Emmett and William Morgan, both craftsmen and liverymen of the Joiner's Company. By 1687 the Corinthian capitals for the oak altar piece were finished at a cost of £4 each. The accounts also include at £1 each some flowerpots for parapets, and they were probably the items mentioned by Stoakes in Vertue's notebooks, pilaster capitals, medallions and many other items. The altar rails, on which Emmett and Morgan worked together, were one of the most important features. As far as quality goes, the carving of the rails varies from fine to fair, although the standard of the altar rail gates themselves has been compared with that of the carving in the Library of Queen's College, Oxford, and Trinity College, the latter being ascribed to Gibbons on the basis of a note by Celia Fiennes in 1695, in which she stated that it was by the same Gibbons whose work she inspected earlier at Windsor. Although the carving at Chelsea has often been attributed quite wrongly to Gibbons, he did not to the best of our knowledge do anything more than negotiate the financially fat contract and supervise the work. As fine carvers in their own right, Emmett and Morgan did not set out to work in the Gibbons style, although several elaborate pieces, such as Emmett's 'Chimneypiece of Tropheys, painfully wrought' in lime might well be labelled Gibbons.

Like other crafts, wood carving had enjoyed its ascendencies, but it had also suffered at the hands of fashion. Gibbons' bold gesture in setting up the Ludgate Hill workshop was made at a time when carving was very much in favour, stimulated first by Charles and, after his death in 1685, by James II, who was responsible for the first flush of commissions which came through Sir Christopher Wren. The first great order was to build the extension to Whitehall Palace. James had married Mary of Modena, recipient of the Gibbons panel, and one of her

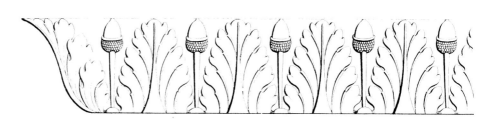

wishes was for a large chapel in which she could make her devotions. Although the bulk of the work favoured stone, there was still scope for Gibbons, exemplified in the pulpit with the four Evangelists, which cost £90, an altar picture frame for £3, a carved throne with 'boyes', and a mass of ornamentation, gilded by René Cousin. And there was also a large side altar, done at a cost of £220. The ornamentation of the organ was done on an extravagant scale with angelic figures triumphantly bearing trumpets. Accounts show that Gibbons, like all other craftsmen engaged on the building and its furnishings, was under intense pressure to meet the deadline for completion under pain of severe financial penalties. Some of the work was done by Gibbons himself, but other pieces were handled by Emmett. Now and then Gibbons was forced to call on Emmett to complete pieces which he had to leave in order to start other commissions elsewhere in the chapel. Somewhere amidst the welter of builders, carpenters and stone masons waited Verrio, now even more fragile than he had been at Windsor, but still impatient to start the painting of the ceiling.

By some standards the chapel for Mary of Modena was a ridiculous royal folly, a sop presented to her by her bridegroom and moreover, a place in which she could practise, as Evelyn disparagingly put it, her 'Popish service'. Whatever the motivation, the work kept Gibbons and his associates fully employed, despite the fact that it was carried out with amazing haste. Consequently, it lacked the studied taste of work done in Charles II's reign. Perhaps this was just as well, for it was used for only two years before being pulled down. The altar was transported first to Hampton Court and later brought back to London, where it was wedded by Wren and Gibbons to the high altar in Westminster Abbey to remain there up to the time of George IV's coronation, after which it was removed.

In 1691 Queen Mary gave the organ to St James's church, Piccadilly, where it still rests, complete with Gibbons' trumpet-blowing angels. The pulpit with its four Evangelists and cascades of flowers and fruit went in 1696 to the Danish church in Wellclose Square. When the church was closed in 1869 the pulpit was sold by auction for £24.

Gibbons was now able to count on trade which came via Wren. Opportunities constantly occurred. If her royal bridegroom lacked taste, Mary herself showed some determination when the time came to decorate her private apartments in Whitehall. Gibbons carved the chimneypiece at a cost of £55, and it took the form of a wooden frame for his own separately costed marble bas relief depicting Goliath. He repeated this piece and it is now at Dalkeith Palace, Midlothian, the 12th century stronghold rebuilt in 1700 by Vanbrugh for the Duchess of Buccleuch. The original Whitehall carving was destroyed in the Whitehall fire.

Elsewhere Gibbons and his workers created for Mary's drawing room a giant overmantel in stone with a carved wood chimneypiece, the woodwork alone costing £60. Seven other chimneypieces were included in a bill for £729 5s 6½d. This stream of work put the Ludgate Hill workshop into a healthy financial position. Wood was always in preparation for future commissions. Joiners 'prepare and glew ye Limetree for the carving of the great Chappell' while others were putting together 'a pannell six footte and five foote high for Mr Gibbons to draw upon'. Here, in two brief statements culled from contemporary records, we gain useful insight into the methods of work at Ludgate Hill. Gibbons ordered wood by size based on the drawings and plans which came from Wren and his associates. When the wood was ready, Gibbons sketched the rough design direct on to the surface, allowing a generous tolerance for the deep cutting and the sinuous shaping which typify his style. Even so, a close examination of many of the major pieces show that sections were added by dowelling or gluing after the main body was carved. A case in point is the reredos at St James's, Piccadilly, claimed as Gibbons' tour de force. Evelyn was characteristically adulatory: 'Dec. 7 1684. I went to see the new church at St James's, elegantly built; the altar was especially adorn'd, the white marble inclosure curiously & richly carved, the flowers & garland about the walls by Mr Gibbons in wood; a pelican with her young at her breast, just over the altar in the carv'd compartment & border, invironing the purple velvet fringed with IHS richly embroider'd, & most notable plate, were given by Sir R. Geere to the value (as was said) of £200. There is no altar any where in England, nor has there been any abroad, more handsomely adorn'd'.

In terms of scale the reredos is almost overpowering with its pendulous bunches of grapes and outbursts of gourds, currants and shells, the large linking floriation, which includes the poppy seedhead, tulips, roses, sunflower and martagon lilies. There is a confident mastery of form and a greater logic of composition here than is found elsewhere in Gibbons' earlier works. If the rest of his carvings were mere practise pieces, this is prime accomplishment. But while St James's has often been called the great showplace of Gibbons' carving, examples just as fine may be seen elsewhere, including the reredos at St Mary Abchurch in Abchurch Lane, which carries many of the same design elements, including the pious pelican which surmounts both. There is, too, a font cover, restored in recent years, and now in All Hallows, Barking-by-the-Tower, which incorporates some of Gibbons' best full length cherubim with a dove at the crest. The cover, for which Gibbons was paid £12, was given to the church in 1681 by a Mr J. Foyle, but for many years it suffered from neglect. It was finally 'improved' by painting. In the *City Press* 30 January 1895, a parishioner, Mr J. T. Page, wrote: '. . . I never walk by the font without wondering how long the coating of white paint will be allowed to veil the glories of the richly-carved cover . . . and it is passing strange that it should ever have been desecrated with paint. Is the cleaning process now a work of impossibility?' In the next 20 years the paint was removed, except for some remnants which remained in the crevices, and the carving was restored to its original appearance. But as time went by the glories of the font cover once more became obscured, this time by an accumulation of dust and grime. In October 1968 the work of cleaning and restoration was undertaken by Mrs Eleanor Goode. The lime wood carving is supported on a circular oak base and attached to a central pylon of triangular section. The carving was made out of a large number of separate pieces, amounting in all to more than 100, which were assembled and fixed in position by the use of steel pins and glue. It was found that many of these joints had become loose or broken through rusting of the pins and disintegration of the glue. Some pieces had been lost, others were detached and their original position was unknown. There had also been some damage. The wings of the dove which surmounts the carving had apparently been broken and although they had been repaired, it seemed that the fragments had been wrongly assembled. Other repairs of an inexpert nature had been carried out.

Due to the great complexity of the carving which comprises about 300 items, including flowers, fruit, leaves and fir cones, and the difficulty of access to some parts of it, the cleaning process was immensely difficult and lengthy. It was found that the use of recommended liquids did not remove all the grime, some of which, together with traces of paint, had penetrated into the surface of the wood, and complete restoration to the original appearance could be achieved only by the use of fine glasspaper.

Loose pieces were removed, cleaned, numbered and stored. Their proper positions were recorded in photographs and drawings. The task of reassembly of these detached pieces on to the main carving was made difficult because many of the pieces had not been made to fit and only touched at points. A gap-filling adhesive, Araldite, was used.

The cherubs, which are the main features of the font cover, are beautiful examples of Gibbons' style. It is not unlikely that the model for these was one of Gibbons' own offspring.

Gibbons was always careful to observe the tenets of religious symbolism in this period, and it would seem that advice was provided by a cleric acquaintance of Wren. While Gibbons was as devout as any man, he remained a simple craftsman rather than a theologian. In his work there is a frequent use of the emblems of the Eucharist, the grapes and wheat, while the pious pelican makes frequent appearances. At St Mary's it has a strange elongation of the bill, while at St Michael's, Cornhill, the bird does not look at all like a pelican but is none the less effective.

Gibbons' command of English did not improve. On 12 May 1686 he wrote: 'Sr. I wold beg the faver from You to send me the 301 (£) due of the olter pees but if the Gentellmen consarnd does not beleave it to be not folle Anof of worck then obleage me to send 301 (£) by this baerer and as soen as I kane kome in toune Agane I will waet one You and sattisfy you Youer desire. Sor I am Youer sarvt Grinling Gibbons'. Despite his long sojourn in England and his friendship with men of letters and culture like John Evelyn, he did not seem able to rid himself of the Netherlands phonetics, exemplified in 'worck', 'baerer' and 'kane kome'. Elsewhere in this note there is the ring of the London craftsman forthrightly demanding what was due to him yet still managing to inject the right note of servility. Any study of Grinling Gibbons cannot help but evoke a sympathy for a prolific genius at the pinnacle of his achievement who still considered himself to be a mere 'sarvt'.

Against a background of political turbulence which ended with the accession of William and Mary, the future of many craftsmen who relied on royal patronage was in the balance. Gibbons was fortunate enough to be sent to work at Kensington Palace, then called Nottingham House, where Wren was supervising the building of the east wing and new state apartments. With Gibbons went Emmett and Nicholas Alcock, who was later to carve the William III head for the Tower of London. Elsewhere, at Hampton Court, about 104 feet of repititious moulding and 942 feet of framing for doors and chimneys were carved for George II's private dressing room and other apartments. This has often been virtually sanctified by having Gibbons' name attached to it, most notably and quite erroneously by the official Department of the Environment guide to Hampton Court Palace by the late G. H. Chettle, with additions by John Charlton and published by Her Majesty's Stationery Office. The truth of the matter is that Emmett took on work which Gibbons might have considered time wasting and boring. The moulding may well be in the style of Gibbons, but little more can be said about it. The pair of chimney pieces for Queen Mary's closet, on the other hand, may be more accurately attributed to Gibbons. The frames for many of the mirrors, featuring 'festoons & foliage & other ornaments' are in the same genre. Only a small amount of the Hampton Court carving is still with us. It is quite puzzling to discover that much of Gibbons' carving appears to have vanished during the last two centuries.

Hampton Court, the most extensive example of Tudor domestic building on a site acquired on lease from the Order of St John of Jerusalem by Cardinal Wolsey in 1514, did not find favour with the later Hanoverians. George III and George IV never, to the best of our knowledge, lived there. The Dukes of Cumberland and York shunned the place, although the Dukes of Gloucester, Kent and Clarence took up residence in the office of Rangers of the park. For a time it was a rabbit warren of grace and favour residences, 'the quality poor house', as William IV called it while it continued to consume large sums of money for its continuous maintenance. It was notorious for its stinking lavatories, the stench from which obliged many high born and ageing ladies to burn frankincense to dispel the overhanging odour of turds and piss. Money funded for its upkeep was spasmodic, but between 1691 and 1696 William 'fix'd upon Hampton Court and it was in his Reign that it put on new Cloaths and being dress'd gay and glorious made the Figure we now see it in'. If it was the King who authorised the expenditure, it was Queen Mary who consulted Wren to discuss the improvements which must be made. Their final conclusions and plans can be divided into three periods, the first from 1689 to 1694, in which year the Queen died. The second period was 1699 to 1702, during which there was a lengthy period of financial stringency, the conclusion of which was marked by the death of the King. The third and final phase was from 1709 to 1711 with the poorly documented refitting of the Chapel Royal as its centrepiece.

In the early stages the Queen assembled her collection of paintings and a large number of pieces of Delft and porcelain in the Water Gallery, a building which later had to be demolished in order to improve the view of the Thames from the south side of the Palace. There is no real evidence to suggest that Gibbons carried out any carving in the Water Gallery, but we know that Emett fashioned some brackets with decorative foliation for which he was paid £5.

Up to this time there were no facilities for tradesmen at Hampton Court, but a commodious temporary workshop was set up for the use of the wood carvers and it was here that Gibbons created the enriched dado, dado-railing and architraves, the panels above the doors for Queen Mary's Closet and the King's Writing Closet, the wooden centrepiece carved with various devices and the Star and Garter, and the initial W for the Guard Room, also the heads of the cherubs which were to be set in the Tudor roof of the Chapel.

In 1693 the King granted recognition to Gibbons in the form of a warrant as Master Carver. On 8 November of that year a document of authorisation was despatched to the Solicitor General, ordering that Gibbons was to be paid 'the usual Fee or Sallary . . . payable from the Feast of St Michael th' Archangel last past'. Once more Gibbons was in the ascendent.

Hampton Court may well have been an exciting place in which to work, but much time was spent considering plans that could never be realised following the deaths of the King and Queen. Gibbons used his working hours making drawings for the Queen's gracious approval, but he could not have realised that he would never see them finished. The end of the dream came suddenly with the death of the Queen from smallpox at the age of 32 on 28 December 1694. The golden period of Hampton Court ended with preparations for a state funeral to take place on 5 March 1695. In the meantime, the Queen's body was embalmed. Wren was naturally involved in the plans for the funeral, as were Gibbons and Nicholas Hawksmoor, chief draughtsman to Wren. The partnership of these three men under the direction of the mourning King resulted in the construction of one of the most elaborate catafalques ever made in England. Some idea of its grandeur can be gained from the bill for only part of the work, prepared by Gibbons himself:

To Gringling Gibbons, Carver

For 3 Boyes 3 ft high in wanscot and the Urne	£14		
For 2 Lyons & 2 Unicornes 3 ft 2 ins high	£16		
For 73 ft of round Cornice 4 members inricht	£9	2	6
For 58 ft 8 ins of Cornice to the pedistalls 3 members inricht	£4	17	9
For 58 ft 8 ins of base molding to the pedistalls all the members	£3	13	4
For 8 great Candlesticks 5 ft 8 ins high	£16		
For 4 hanging on branch Candlesticks with 8 lights to each	£12		
For 16 Shields, Crownes & Leaves on each side the Pedistalls 4 ft square	£20		
For 7 Cartooses	£1	10	
For Carving the Letters on the Qs Coffin	£1		
For Carving the heads of the modell of the Qs charriot			5s
For 2 great Scrowles going to the Choire	£1		
	£99	8	7

The funeral itself was one of the finest seen in England for many a year, as Nahum Tate's verse suggests: 'See where the Royal Shrine erected high, threat'ning the Temple's Roof as that the Sky, with Starry Lamps and Banners blazing round and all the Pageantry of Death crown'd'. The cost was £50,000. The carvers shared a gratuity of £3 4s.

After this sombre event the future of Hampton Court Palace was once more in the balance. It seemed unlikely that there would be any new initiatives, for the King had lost all interest. After his death in 1706 Hampton Court fell from favour. It was not until the reign of Queen Victoria that the State Rooms were opened to the public. The part which it played in Grinling Gibbons' career was marked not necessarily by the work which he did there as by the continuation of royal patronage. If it did nothing else, it enabled him to continue with the development of his Ludgate Hill business. There was one sour note. Although Gibbons got his warrant and an assured 'fee or sallary', Emmett, his fellow carver and close associate, received nothing except steady employment. His standard of work was not far short of Gibbons' yet despite this he had to remain in the shadows and has not until now received any great acclaim. Exactly why he should merit such an injustice is not hard to understand, for Gibbons had, from the beginning, been warmed by the publicity provided both directly and indirectly by Evelyn. One cannot, of course, entirely overlook Gibbons' talents, but it is not too outrageous to claim that he would never have reached eminence without Evelyn's help. After all, he did have some considerable disabilities. He spoke poor English, he was not exactly literate, and he certainly needed a prime mover in the shape of Sir Christopher Wren in order to promote his business. The society in which he lived nourished itself on gossip, on personality cults in the arts and sciences. It was in its attitudes parasitic and circumscribed and given to lionising those whom it made great. A fashion was taken up, and the setter of that fashion could count on fame and fortune. Men of taste, authoritative arbiters, were few and far between. In the light of this interpretation, is should be borne in mind that the refurbishing of Hampton Court was in the hands of Wren, who ruled unimpeded because he could gain royal agreement and the funds that went with it. As for Gibbons' work and all the grandiose plans, much of it turned out to be an echo of what had already been done elsewhere, while the drawings and designs which he did for the Queen could not by any stretch of the imagination be considered wholly original. He was perhaps already learning the truth of the fact that the price of originality came high. Yet again, we have to remember Hampton Court, while appearing to present a great challenge, failed to live up to expectation. From past triumphs and large carvings, he was suddenly in the position of having to devise what amounted to mere titivations for an acquisitive Queen. At best his work would have played second fiddle to the collection of paintings and pottery, whereas it stood in its own right elsewhere. By the time the King was buried, Gibbons' future was very much in the balance. He had to pin his hopes on Wren who, as always, had plenty of commissions to fulfil.

Between 1691 and 1701 there was new activity for Gibbons, necessitating his going from London to the university cities of Oxford and Cambridge. This time he was not the only carver on the scene. Although Wren clearly favoured him, the architect believed in using the provincial carvers, despite their shortcomings in the area of original design. Apart from the provincials there were others at work. Pierce, the staircase carver was there, and so was Emmett, who had previously executed work for the soldier's hospital in Chelsea under the aegis of the Gibbons workshop. But several entirely new names became prominent, including Cornelius Austin, whose work beautifies such Cambridge colleges as Clare, Emmanuel, King's, Pembroke, Queen's and St Catherine's. There was also Frogley and, at Oxford, the Minns brothers. If they were provincial, they were none the worse for it. Certainly, Austin's carving of the fourteen projecting bookcases in Trinity College library to Wren's designs are an outstanding example of enrichment and may be most favourably compared with anything produced by Gibbons. Elsewhere in the library, Gibbons' work, including the swags, was costed at more than £400, complementing, rather than competing with, Austin's work. Rather mischievously, Austin lifted some of Gibbons' motifs and included them in his own designs. It is believed that he did this at the behest of Wren and with Gibbons' agreement. The main Gibbons effort was directed to the carving of the heraldic enrichments, probably amongst his most inspired pieces. These achievement-of-arms, as they are properly called, measure 21 in. × 15 in. and are carved out of blocks of lime, many being laminated to a thickness of about $2\frac{1}{2}$ in. In this context 'achievement-of-arms' is used in the terminology of heraldry, which means that the shield is accompanied by significant external ornaments, including the helm, crest, mantling and supporters. In the plural, it means the insignia of honour carried in funerals and suspended over the monuments of important people, including the crest, shield, tabard, gauntlets and spurs, banners and pennons.

The attributions of the carving of the achievement-of-arms are as follows:

Grinling Gibbons

William Lynnet, D. D.
Humphrey Babington, D. D., Babington quartering Cave
Sir George Chamberlaine
Sir Robert Hildyard, Bt
Sir Thomas Sclater, Bt
The Hon. John Montagu, Montagu quartering Monthermer

123

Isaac Barrow, D. D.
See of Chester impaling John Pearson
See of Lichfield and Coventry impaling John Hackett
Devices of Charles Seymour, 6th Duke of Somerset, Chancellor 1689-1748
Achievement, quarterly of six, the Seymour augmentation, Seymour, Beauchamp
of Hache Esturmy, Macwilliam Prynne, all in a Garter crest with unicorn and
bull supporters
Seymour crest, a demi-phoenix in flames issuing from a coronet
Cyper C. S. in a Garter, coroneted

Cornelius Austin

Robert Drake

The north and south end doorways display oak doorcases with ornamental architraves, and elsewhere in the area are carvings which suggest that Gibbons was now making a return to his past style. The entablature-blocks of the Corinthian columns and the broken segmental pediments are typical. In the pediments are the arms of William III in a garter between trumpets, palm-leaves and wings, the latter carved to perfection with a fine sweep, full of life and spontaneity. Fruit and flowers are carved, somewhat unusually, in the round. It was here that Gibbons came back to the use of his favourite method of giving the design elements of visual continuity by the introduction of flowing straight and ruched ribbons which, in turn, secure the beginnings of the pediment festoons. A new feature were the nails, carved in the neo-realistic style as though hammered in at haphazard angles, seemingly makeshift, to hold the ribbons in place while the design was in the making.

On the bookcases is a series of bust and statues. In their original conception they were intended to be of marble with the two exceptions, the busts of Anacreon and Ben Johnson, which are polychromed and both by Gibbons. Apart from his considerable work as a stone statuary, Gibbons did practically no other busts in wood, and seemed not to bother overmuch with portraiture while in his prime.

Gibbons' influence at Cambridge is everywhere. In the library of Trinity there are the manuscript doors carved with swirls of pierced acanthus, and they are virtual copies of the Gibbons style. For many years they were erroneously attributed to him. In both Cambridge and Oxford it is obvious that the provincial carvers made a keen study of the style used by the King's Carver. Other examples can be found at Queen's College, Oxford, where the library doors were done by the Minns brothers while they were employed by Wren. Of course, if one wished to be censorious, then the famous brothers can be put down as pirates, dexterous in execution but without any actual style of their own. Not content with stealing a few ideas from elsewhere, they removed them wholesale, including the pomegranates, the peaches and the currants, the husks of beech nuts, and throughout this part of their careers they carved them so expertly that they might well have passed muster as having come from the hand of Gibbons. But one main feature which gives the lie to the fact is that the Minns used Norway oak, a wood which lacks the line-holding qualities of the lime so favoured by Gibbons and his school. Norway oak is a hard, tough timber, so recalcitrant as to deter even the most knowledgeable and experienced carver, yet it has to be admitted that the Minns used it and they somehow managed to eclipse all others.

It has already been said that Gibbons was now returning to his former role, but he was also becoming more a designer than a carver, and John Evelyn referred to him on at least one occasion as 'Artist'. When examining this period certain commentators have made disparaging comparisons between the standards of work of Gibbons and Jonathan Mayn. Typical carving by Mayn is to be seen in the Consistory Court Chapel of St Paul's, London. But such comparisons are surely somewhat odious, for the individual carver of any period should be judged entirely in his own right. It is not the place of the writer to say who is best and who is second best. As far as Gibbons is concerned, it can be said that in 1693 he was able to cast aside many restraints and embark on a more unfettered line of development. Mayn, on the other hand, remained the classical master carver with a talent for producing precise mouldings carved in the Gibbons style. This was not Mayn's fault. The clients demanded the seductiveness which Gibbons had introduced.

The Chapel of Trinity College, rebuilt entirely in 1691-94, is a synthesis of the carving of the period with its communion rails in a veneer of *Juniperus bermudiana* and great eruptions of carving in pearwood and lime. The three-way reredos itself, also in juniper veneer, has been called the finest in England with its inset figures and vases, the middle bay being inlaid with geometrical designs around a central star and applied carving on the sides of the panels. These are excellent examples of full relief carving of flowers, foliage, cherub-heads and a vase. In the side bays there are more heads of cherubs with flowers. The rich effect of the carving is in contrast to the darker juniper and is most marked by the amorini, or singing cherubs, and the small scrolls against the Corinthian capitals. The definition of the foliation is extraordinarily deliberate. There is a lack of evidence to suggest that Gibbons carved this piece, for no accounts have ever been found. Such notes as have come down to us mention only two names, Arthur Frogley, the joiner-carver and master carpenter at the Sheldonian, Oxford, who was also responsible for the oak altar rails in the church of St Mary, Oxford, and Jonathan Mayn himself. In the 19th century the carved part of the reredos was painted white but later mercifully restored to its natural state. Nowadays practically no trace of this philistinism is noticeable. Naturally, there has been some research to establish Gibbons as the carver, but such claims as have been made tend to rely solely on the evidence of style, a factor notoriously deceptive in the craft of carving. We know for a fact that the Gibbons workshop in London consistently produced pieces in the Gibbons style, but other pieces were also made which bore no relation to Gibbons' rococo. To obtain a hint of the possible authenticity of the Trinity carving it is perhaps useful to bear in mind that Dr Bathurst, President of Trinity, did make an appeal for funds to pay for the ornamentation of the Chapel. He himself paid for the fabric, but it was John Evelyn and others who eventually offered to meet the cost of much of the carving, and the natural choice of craftsman would, of course, have been Gibbons. If all our suppositions are correct, then there may be a clue in the complex table now resting in Christ Church, Oxford, which he presented to Evelyn. This unique piece of furniture, more a work of art than a utilitarian object, has a walnut top, lime legs and is carved in the rococo style. At the tops of the legs are the putti, or half-boys, composed in continuity with peapods, flowers and some extravagantly shaped fruit. When Evelyn compiled the Inventory of Wotton House, his residence, he noted: 'A table of walnut tree curiously vein'd and varnish'd standing on a frame of lime-tree, incomparably carved with 4 Angels, flowers and frutages by that famous Artist Gibbons, and presented me in acknowledgement of my first Recommending him to K. Charles the Second, before he was scarse known'. This is not, of course, conclusive evidence that Gibbons did carve the Trinity reredos, but it does form part of the chronology of events. On the other hand, the simple explanation may well be that Gibbons now felt that it was time to signify his gratitude to Evelyn for many years of unflagging sponsorship. But for the diarist, he may well have remained an obscure Deptford ship's carver.

Many of Gibbons' later carvings are the subject of almost continuous controversy, and one of the pieces under periodic scrutiny is the frame for the portrait of Elias Ashmole (1617-92), now in the Ashmolean Museum, in which Richard Frogley, brother of Arthur, was master-carpenter. The frame is a piece of heavy flamboyance, not only coated originally with gilding but also painted at a later date with a gold-like composition. It is almost, but not quite, Gibbons, and the same may be said of the nearby frames of the portraits of Charles II and James II. Here, as in so much attribution to Gibbons, earlier research seemed to rely on the fact that the old Ashmolean was the work of Wren, but it was much too traditional for him, and there is nothing to suggest that Wren simply hired Gibbons to carve there. At best, the Ashmolean is simply a good example of late 17th century Renaissance design. That Gibbons might well have done more carving at Cambridge and even Oxford is undeniable, but it is difficult to prove because he was overtaken by events which sent him back to London and kept him there to all intents and purposes for what could have been his greatest triumph, St Paul's Cathedral. Like all monstrous works of its kind, it had built into it many controversies and tragedies.

By the 1690s St Paul's Cathedral was ready for its interior decoration, and it was a wonder that it ever reached this stage. Wren had been associated with the cathedral for a long time. He was advisor in the summer of 1666, after the Great Fire, which left most of the building in ruins, and he had a say in the work of the Commission which in January 1668 decided that a temporary choir containing altar and pulpit, should be built at the west end. But there were numerous catastrophes. Inigo Jones' pre-Great Fire casing of the exterior was badly keyed to the old wall, and during the work done in 1668 a great pillar collapsed. Dean Sancroft wrote to Wren: ' . . . it is the opinion of all men, that we can proceed no further at the West End. What we can do next is the present deliberation, in which you are so absolutely and indispensably necessary to us, that we can do nothing, resolve on nothing, without you. You will think fit, I know, to bring with you those excellent Draughts and Designes you formerly favoured us with'. The outcome was that Wren became responsible to the Dean and Chapter for the reconstruction. Most of the money for the work was drawn from a tax on sea coal introduced by the government. When Wren surveyed the ruins, he realised just how extensive the reconstruction would have to be. The difficulty was money. A vast amount would be needed simply to demolish and clear the ruins, for molten lead had run down the stonework, bonding it into a solid mass. He decided to make a bold move and use gunpowder to bring down what was left of the central tower, but after a serious accident involving some of his workmen, he became more cautious and instead used a battering ram, operated by 30 men.

In 1669 Wren provided the drawings from which William Cleere, a carver and joiner, made the first rather curious-looking model. This was rejected, and in 1673 Wren submitted further drawings, this time suggesting a much grander and perhaps traditional building. Some time between April and September William Cleere was paid £42 2s 6d for a table and frame on which the new model could stand, also two tables on trestles for the use of Wren and his assistant, Edward Woodrofe, in their draughting work. The new model, which alone cost £500, was the work of twelve joiners, and Cleere himself carved 350 capitals, cherubim, festoons and flowers. Grinling Gibbons apparently had a hand in it, and probably carved a number of miniature statues to stand on the parapet of the model. Some past studies claim that it was the first time that Wren and Gibbons were in association, but this is erroneous, for they had already worked together at Cambridge.

In 1696-97 the choir stalls were carved in oak and lime. The result can be said to indicate the fact that Gibbons' career had simply been a preparation for this moment, because they are the finest of his achievements. But there were also the twin towers of the organ case with an adornment of angels, flowers and fruit, and, of course, the great screen. It now seems incredible that the screen was removed by the mid-Victorian improvers in 1860, while the organ was rebuilt in two parts on the sides of the choir.

The thrones of dignitaries on opposite sides of the chancel aisle are also indicative that Gibbons was now at the height of his powers, for it was here that he enjoyed the freedom of his own inventiveness. Close to the Lord Mayor's stall is the epitome of his mature style in the shape of six carvings in lime mounted on oak, four of which consist of the crossed trumpets which were originally conceived as organ tower embellishments. They do not lose a great deal in their dismounted state.

The St Paul's of our time is not, of course, the St Paul's of Wren's time. The onslaught of the improvers has already been mentioned. This happened in its initial phase in the 1860s, but new ravages occurred in 1872. There had for some years been rumblings about the interior of the cathedral, and it was thought that it should be brought into line with the new Victorian notions about architecture. If the Victorians enjoyed the idea of railway stations looking like cathedrals, they were apparently dubious when it came to church buildings. In the next few years much of Wren's work was forcibly ruptured and displaced, and with it went a still unknown amount of Gibbons' carving. Fragments of carving are still to be found in odd corners, isolated and filthy but still stubbornly beautiful. The lyrical amorini have been separated, one of them being kept in a storage room, the other lodged over a side altar at the eastern end of the side aisle, totally desolated. The dead body of this great building is little better nowadays. Dust coats both masonry and woodwork, and practically all that remains of Gibbons' work is devoid of glow, coated as it is with grime.

The tale of St Paul's over the centuries has little joy to it, and yet it started with the best of intentions. When Wren was at work he had a marked preference for employing not only craftsmen whose work was known to him but also his own

relatives, and he was criticised more than once for it. Yet it is easy to understand why he should have strong preferences, because he desired only the best and was determined to have it. Apart from Gibbons, he showed good taste in also employing Mayn, the man who could carve in the Gibbons style. The work of both carvers is now lodged in the chapel of St Michael and St George. It is not, unfortunately, open to the public at the present time. Mayn contributed to the screen, and if there is any criticism of his style here it is that a severe formality inhibits the flow. When Mayn adopted the Gibbons style, he was respectful enough to avoid direct copying, and it is the way the composition is put together rather than the individual components that makes the tyro mistake it for Gibbons. Mayn favoured the bursting horse chestnut, so finely carved that it is practically possible to peer into the recesses of the half-open shell. Then there are the blackberries with the definition of the individual globules, and the tapered lilies of the valley, the poppyheads and cobnuts. Mayn appears to have favoured oak as a carving wood, and a most convincing job he made of it, as can be seen in the 32 acanthus brackets in the library of St Paul's, for which he was paid the high price of £6 10s each. As to the sum total of work carried out by Gibbons and Mayn, this is suggested by the money they were paid. Gibbons earned £2992 11s 4½d while Mayn received £1252 6s 11d. But when it came to settling up time there was a considerable hubbub, summed up in the Minute Book entry for 17 July 1696. The Committee ordered 'that Mr Oliver do compare the measurements set downe in Mr Gibbons' Bill of Carver's work, with his owne measurements thereof, and that Mr Gibbons do then put such Prices to ye same as he does intend to stand by, which he is Ordered to deliver to Mr Dean of St Paul's, who is desired to procure (if he thinks it necessary) some skillful persons in ye same Art to View the Work & report their opinions of the Prices; & it was also Ordered, That no money be paid to the same Mr Gibbons untill the same shall be agreed'.

On 18 September the Minute Book was inscribed: 'Ordered, That it be transferred to Sir Chr. Wren to adjust with Mr Gibbons the Prices of the Carved Capitalls mentioned in his Bill, which could not be agreed on by the Carvers who were appointed to view & examine the Prices of the said Bill, & that he report the same to this Board at their next Meeting'. The chagrin of Gibbons, faced with having his work measured and assessed not only by other carvers but also the architect-administrator, Wren himself, can be imagined. It is not credible to suppose that he was attempting to cheat or defraud, because he had already carried out a large amount of work in the cathedral and his accounts were impeccable. But it is possible that he lost track of many of his commissions in the pressures exerted upon him to get the work done. It is known, for instance, that he carved a number

129

of cherubim and supplied the lime wood from his own stocks rather than delay the work by waiting for the notoriously slow deliveries of materials. Wren and the others were faced with an embarrassing and exacting task. After all, who were they to chide a man of Gibbons' eminence when he charged only a mere £1 for cherub heads? No doubt the questioning of the tradesmen's accounts was in the nature of the committee. Their attitude towards money was thin-lipped to say the least, and in 1697 they even had the effrontery to cut Wren's salary of £200 a year by half. Wren was strong enough to withstand such indignities. In his own sphere he was as great as any of them, shouldering the responsibility for 50 Anglican churches, two big hospitals, a customs house, observatory, academic library and university buildings. He was also in charge of the maintenance of Windsor Castle, the Tower of London, the Houses of Parliament, and many official buildings. The attitude of the cathedral committee was no more than a minor gadfly to him. Committees concerned with building contracts are incapable of change, but their suspicious natures are frequently warranted when the expenditure of public funds is involved.

The basic financing of St Paul's itself was as odd as the behaviour of the committee. It was part of the arrangement that those directly responsible for the actual rebuilding were invited to make various loans to the fund at an interest rate of six per cent. Wren mustered £1000 while Gibbons loaned £1500, which is some indication of their comparative wealth. Others, including the subcontractors, paid lesser sums. It should perhaps be added that this financial structure, built on loans, was Wren's idea, because he believed that the master craftsmen who had a stake in the work would go to great lengths to ensure that they met the contractual obligations with one eye on quality and the other on the stipulated completion dates. The perpetual shortage of money led to disputes and holdups, and even when the loans were combined with the funds provided by the coal tax, there was still insufficient in the exchequer to give any impetus. The coal tax was, in any case, divided between St Paul's and monies which fed the maintenance funds of other city churches. These matters should be pointed out in some mitigation of the attitude of the committee, but there is still a lingering irony in the fact that these men were concerned with building the greatest cathedral in Britain, yet had to spend their time squabbling over minor matters.

Altogether, the building of the new St Paul's cannot be said to have been a very happy or joyous business, carried out as it was in the Late Baroque period. No doubt Wren, who held the Surveyorship of the Office of Works for nearly 50 years, felt profoundly the dichotomy of opinion about how the new edifice should look, and he often became the target of controversy stimulated by the ecclesiastics on the one side and the protestant worshippers on the other. In the years of his personal supervision, he was in almost daily contact not only with Gibbons and Mayn but also an army of other craftsmen. Like them, he was continuously harrassed by the slow delivery of vital materials, but also had to overcome doubts that he would ever get the work finished at all. Nevertheless, after the years 1668 to 1718, in which his enforced retirement occurred, St Paul's was completed and it remained in the same triumphant form until the coming of the mid-Victorian improvers. In due course the bombs of World War Two improved the so-called improvements by almost totally wiping them out of existence.

Wren is worthy of a final comment as it is doubtful whether any other English architect before or since laboured under such difficulties. It was his attitude towards money that led finally to his downfall. Throughout his professional life he was dogged by charges of negligence, inefficiency and even downright corruption. He was savagely attacked by the third Earl of Shaftesbury, who wrote an open letter deploring the state of public architecture 'under the Hand of one Single Court Architect'. Wren's final fault was that he overlooked the necessity to gain Treasury approval for expenditure before actually starting the work. This led to reorganisation and an entirely new structure under which Wren no longer had sole control, and he was ultimately dismissed. His departure marked the end of a period in which men of Gibbons' stature could hope to gain patronage through individual officials. It was the start of an age in which the craftsman saw major Crown commissions dwindle to a trickle.

The completion of St Paul's indicated another phase in Gibbons' career. It is debateable whether he himself knew what the future held. True, his London workshop was still busy and it had recently expanded in line with the growth of his reputation. A number of new commissions arrived, including one for Petworth, the Sussex house which is more famous for its decorated interior than its architectural exterior. He supplied carvings which included flowers, fruit, a violin, cherubs, an exquisite lace handkerchief and a fish. He reverted with vigour to his earlier styles and exuberance after the depression of St Paul's and its constraining financial affairs. The truth of it was that he had to take the Petworth commission in order to recoup some of the losses which he undoubtedly incurred as master carver at the cathedral.

Yet many of his transactions do not suggest high profits in comparison with his other work. One of the difficulties in giving such an opinion is that we cannot always discover the dimensions of work undertaken which has since vanished, because these details do not always appear in the commissions and bills. Proof can be found in the 1692 accounts of the sixth Duke of Somerset. On 26 March this entry was written: 'Re'd of my Lo Duke by a Bill of Mr Alkhorne Ninety Eight Pounds and twenty five pounds in Cash and fifty pounds more to pay of Mr Gibbons for Statues, which said three sumes doth amount to one hundred seventy three pound. I say Recd by mee £173.0.0. John Bowen'. And on 10 December: 'Recd of my Lord Duke by a Bill paid to Mr Gibbons for Carveing one hundred and fifty pounds. I say Recd by mee £150.0.0. John Bowen'. It is possible that about eighteen statues, maybe in wood but more possibly in stone, were sited on the ballustrade at Petworth. They vanished completely some time after the 18th century.

Elsewhere at Petworth there is a tantalising apartment known nowadays as the Carved Room, described by Walpole as being 'gloriously flounced all round the whole length pictures with much the finest carving of Gibbons that ever my eyes beheld. There are birds absolutely feathered: and two antique vases with bas-relieves, as perfect and beautiful as if they were carved by a Grecian master'.

If we are to rely on chronological evidence and accept Walpole as correct in stating that the Carved Room was indeed the work of Gibbons, then it would be as well to remember that he carved the heraldry in the library of Trinity College, Cambridge, in 1690. There is some suggestion of patronage, for the sixth Duke of Somerset, Charles Seymour, was Chancellor of the University of Cambridge at the time, when Gibbons' accounts for the library carving were presented in 1691. The Duke kept Gibbons in mind for the enrichment of his country seat at Petworth.

The Carved Room itself is 60 feet long, 24 feet wide and 20 feet high, and it is beyond doubt one of the most impressive rooms in Britain, presenting a panopoly of carved doves, musical instruments, large baskets of flowers and swooping festoons and tightly bunched trusses. Those who dislike a superabundance of ornamentation may feel that there is perhaps too much of everything, for the overall effect can be overpowering. But this quibble is no more acceptable than an opinion which claims that there are far too many notes in a Beethoven symphony or a Bartok piano concerto. The important factors are harmony and rhythm, both of which are present in the Carved Room. The analogy with music is, in fact, most apt, for the carved surround of the family portrait of Lord and Lady Seymour of Trowbridge includes a musical score with portrait medallions, also a cravat and links of beads. There are, too, the initials, 'G.G.' which may, or may not, suggest the identity of the carver, but as far as we know Gibbons did not use initials to sign a carving. If one is seeking to establish the identity of the man behind the masterpiece, then it must be from the design features alone. It is but a short step from the Cosima panel to the Petworth composition. Of course, we now know that Gibbons' work could be imitated by his contemporaries. It is also known that certain of the original carved flowers were renewed in the 1900s by Henry Hoad, the estate carver at Petworth, and those who know something about it can pick out his wooden blossoms. What was done in Hoad's time could well have been done in Gibbons' lifetime. But there is little doubt that this frame is by Gibbons. Vertue, however, introduces a note which queries the credibility: 'At Petworth . . . in the Carved Room, rich adorn'd with Sculpture of flowers, festoons & fruit, birds & boys etc. by Gibbons, and Seldon who wrought there many Years. This man lost his life by saving the carving from being burnt when the house was on fire'. Seldon, it transpires, was a talented carver responsible for various works executed during his twenty years' service. The house accounts for 1689-90 contain details of his bills. Amongst many other pieces which he carved were a large chimneypiece for the dining rooms, lavishly decorated with fowl, fish and flowers for the sum of £30. He also produced a picture frame decorated with foliage and flowers, amounting in all to 22 feet of work, for which he received £5 10s. Seldon died in the fire which occurred in January 1714 while trying to retrieve some of the carvings. Any study of Seldon's work leads inevitably to a feeling of chronic unsureness. He is known to have made an intensive study of Gibbons, and he no doubt had conversations with him if Gibbons did, indeed, spend time at Petworth. Seldon had, of course, been carving for many years before Gibbons arrived on the scene, and it is quite reasonable to suppose that examples of Seldon's work were in place at Petworth, much of it in the unabashed style of Gibbons. Certain easily identified Seldon pieces fall below Gibbons' standard of work, but they are early in his line of development.

The enigma of the Petworth carvers is further complicated by the appearance in 1815 of Jonathan Ritson. The son of a Whitehaven carpenter, he produced carving of such character and quality that he came within the ken of the Duke of Norfolk, who gave him a start by commissioning some work for Arundel Castle, Sussex. Ritson was a master of the wildlife extravaganza, producing veritable riots of cats pursuing birds, owls attacking mice, fluttering butterflies and moths, aquatic life symbolised by the crayfish struggling about in thickets of water-weed. Ritson was a man with a character which matched his own carved inventions. His portrait shows an elderly individual in a carver's apron with a neckcloth and eyes as sharp as his own chisels and gouges. He was more often than not roaring drunk while working, but this by no means impaired his abilities. No sooner was he ensconced at Petworth than he began to carve one piece after another to fill in all the blank spaces between the carvings by Gibbons and Seldon. There was no holding him in his exposition of nature, and one of his finest works was positioned in a place of honour in the bedroom of Lady Egremont. Here and

133

there in other apartments, his drunken judgement apparently failed him, resulting in carvings which are slightly lopsided.

By any standard, Petworth is a showcase of English fantasy carving, much of it in the tradition of English eccentricity. Unless one is calvinistic in the pursuit of pure Gibbons, it should be accepted for what it is rather than for what it might have been.

In London the Ludgate Hill workshop remained busy, producing carving for the great country houses. Gibbons himself was in charge, but he was satisfied to delegate responsibility. It is likely that he spent his time visiting houses to confer with noble clients and their architects, settling the prices and then returning to London to finalise the details with his senior carvers. Throughout his life he was fortunate in having the benefit of John Evelyn's advice and influence, and when orders did not materialise he was not above jogging Evelyn's elbow. On 23 March 1683 he wrote, as excruciatingly as usual: 'Honred Sr: I wold beg the ffaver wen You see Sir Joseph Willeams agaen You wold be pleasd to speack to him that hee wold get me to Carve his Ladis sons hous my Lord Kildeer ffor I onderstand it will be verry Consedrebell or If You haev Aquantans with my Lord to spaeck to him his Sealf and I shall be for Evre be obleeged to You I wold spaeck to Sir Josef my sealfe but I knouw it wold do better from You. Sr. Youre Most ombell sarvant G. Gibbon'. It is curious that he did not add the final 's' to his surname.

Evelyn was related to the Earl of Kildare. He immediately wrote: 'My Lord, The Bearer Mr Gibbon being so well knowne for what he has done at Winsore and other places, to be the most excellent of his profession not onely in England but in the whole world, needs none of my rhetorick to recommend him to Yr Lp. However, since he believes I may add countenance to his request in be speaking yr Lp's preference for the carving about the house nr Wells which yr Lp s building, I am confident I shall do yr Lp a Service as well as Mr Gibbon, in wishing yr Lp will employ so ingenious and able an artist, who am, My Lord, your most humble and most obliged servant John Evelyn'. The commission did not go to Gibbons, for Lady Kildare died in the first year of her marriage. Nevertheless, these two notes show that Gibbons was not averse to stimulating business, though his pricing methods were, as we know, undeniably odd. When no commissions were forthcoming, he dropped his prices, and this accounts for the relatively low charges which occur now and then. There was, for instance, the sum of £50 for carving at Burghley House, Huntingdonshire, the home of the Cecil and Exeter families for 400 years, and a similar sum for work carried out at Badminton House, Gloucestershire, the Palladian mansion home of the Dukes of Beaufort since the seventeenth century.

True, there must have been many enquiries from the aristocracy for the large-scale carved decoration of their mansions, but Gibbons' estimates were substantial and matched his reputation. Some of the would-be patrons quickly discovered that they could not afford what had by now become something of a luxury. A contributory factor was that many new estates already employed part-time carvers of varying proficiency. While few of them could compete with the great Gibbons, they were, nevertheless, able to create passable work for the enhancement of the mansions. The historical effect has been a fragmentation of Gibbons' work, creating attribution difficulties. For instance, Badminton has a Gibbons frame, a number of overdoors and a pair of drops. The standard of the work is exceptionally high, particularly in the frame which embodies the ducal coronet of 1682, and the Garter which surrounds a cypher around the word 'Beaufort'. As a final flourish Gibbons placed at the lower part two cornucopiae, spilling out fruit and flowers. Whether the frame alone cost £50 or this sum included other pieces, we do not know, but payment was made on 6 July 1683.

Ramsbury in Wiltshire is the resting place of another single frame by Gibbons. It is pear wood with a three-part lamination of $2\frac{1}{2}$ in. each to give depth to a compact composition of cobnuts, barley, flowers, and with the usual ribbon running to the side cascade of leaves and berries. The frame also includes a particularly striking sunflower which seems to be approaching the end of its season of life, for the petals are ragged and sad. The lower section of the frame is typically Gibbons with open peapods, lilies and crocuses. The Ramsbury carving is undocumented and any attribution must depend on the studied analysis of style and technique. But it is generally held to be by Gibbons.

Burghley House, Huntingdonshire, was decorated to the order of the fifth Earl of Exeter. There is little doubt that Gibbons had a great hand in it, although one cannot necessarily rely on Vertue, who wrote: '. . . picture Frames, chimney peices & door Cases carved with Birds, Fruit & Flowers, in the most Beautifull manner, done by Grinlin Gibbons'. The accounts show that on 6 July 1683 Gibbons received £50 from Lord Exeter, followed on 21 December 1685 by a similar sum. His Lordship evidently had a penchant for carving, because he employed both Thomas Young and Jonathan Mayn between 1682 and 1687. Comparatively little is known about Young's life. He was employed at Chatsworth under Samuel Watson, the then carver in residence. It must already have become quite obvious that it is not always a simple matter to distinguish between the work of more than two carvers of the same school when specimens are placed in close juxtaposition. Mayn, the versatile imitator, together with Young and Gibbons,

135

unwittingly created a particularly difficult puzzle for future students. At first sight the Marble Hall overmantel with its burgeoning flowers, shell and fruit is undeniably Gibbons, and for good measure it includes a practically exact replica of the gourd in the St James's, Piccadilly, reredos. Yet the overmantel is oak, and oak was largely Mayn's wood, not Gibbons'. The treatment of the game bird is not quite Gibbons. For instance, the duck with its open bill, hanging by the feet with the barley carved over it is somehow uncharacteristic. Elsewhere in the same piece, with its tumbling tulips, a double poppy, cobnuts and foxgloves, certain features may change the expert's mind. If the *amorini* are pure Gibbons, the ribbonwork is far from his style. It is not beyond the bounds of possibility that more than one carver worked on the creation of the overmantel. The same might be claimed for the overdoor carvings in the First George Room with its Verrio ceiling. In the carving there are multiple echoes everywhere, including a strong reminiscence of the Cosima panel, although the elements here are much more mixed. A study of Young's work shows that he, too, was very fond of including distinctive memorabilia, some of it first cousin to that of Gibbons.

Some hint of how Gibbons was now being successfully copied is gained by the knowledge that at Belton House, Kesteven, near Stamford, Lincolnshire, there is a chimneypiece carved in 1688 by Edmund Carpenter. Belton House was the home of the Brownlow family for 300 years. He received £26 for the work. Its authenticity as a true Gibbons was quite firmly endorsed by a Victorian expert and restorer, Rogers, who airily inferred: 'This light interlacing scrollwork was originated by Gibbons and is met with in most of his important works. It died out with him and no one has successfully attempted to carry it out since his time'.

As one moves from house to house the task of attribution becomes more and more difficult. At Hackwood, in Hampshire, seat of the first Duke of Bolton, there is a virtual repository of carvings brought from another family seat at Abbotstone, Alresford. It is believed that the first Lord Bolton employed Gibbons to carve coronets, festoons, swags which hang from carved nails, pomegranates and flowers. In the library is a cravat of point lace, similar in some respects to the cravat now in the Victoria and Albert Museum, London. Unusually for Gibbons, there are two almost nude females, while the panels feature fettered squirrels eating nuts, scrolls of bay leaves and cornucopiae. One unusual quirk of fancy is that the squirrels are secured by chains looped to nails. Anybody even slightly versed in the Gibbons repertoire may well doubt the authenticity of this work, for the semi-nude female and the squirrels do not appear elsewhere in his work.

Chatsworth is quite different. Although Gibbons had the assistance of other carvers, his influence was dominant. Yet the accounts make no mention of his

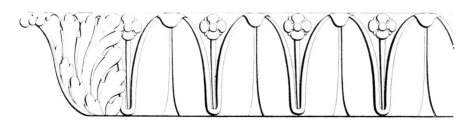

various transactions. The only evidence is a note by Walpole, who wrote: 'When Gibbons had finished his works in that palace he presented the Duke with a point cravat and a medal with his own head all preserved in a glass case in the gallery. I have another cravat by him, the art of which arrives even to deception'. Walpole's collection was sold in 1842, and the limewood cravat was bought by Miss Burdett-Coutts, later Baroness Burdett-Coutts, for a small sum. It was kept in her house at 1 Stratton Street, until her death in 1906, when it was acquired by the late Hercules Read of the British Museum. When his collection was sold in 1928 the cravat was bought by the Hon. Mrs Walter Levy (Mrs Gonides), who gave it to the Victoria and Albert Museum.

There is a strong case for believing that the Chatsworth carving is by Samuel Watson, who served his apprenticeship under Charles Oakley of St Martins-in-the-Fields. Watson was a native of Heanor in Derbyshire, and he remained at Chatsworth until 1715, the year of his death. There was, too, Thomas Young, who worked with Watson, and he could boast the experience of carving with Mayn at Burghley and elsewhere, including Sudbury, Derbyshire, when Pierce was there.

Samuel Watson was a collector of designs. He appears to have spent most of his working life making drawings of other carver's work, including some of the Gibbons' reredos in St James's, Piccadilly. He filled notebook after notebook with drawings in anticipation of being able to satisfy any whim of his employer at Chatsworth. When we come to the matter of the possibility of Gibbons ever having carved at Chatsworth, documents exist to support the claim, including a statement made by Samuel White Watson, the grandson, in which he said that Watson 'assisted Gibbons in the carving of the chapel'. There is a lengthy historical background to this which is of no great moment except to say that Samuel White Watson may well have been tapping the folklore of the family, starting at a point when Walpole embroidered certain of Vertue's writings. None of these is satisfactorily substantiated by accounts or entries in the Chatsworth estate ledgers and archives.

The carving at Chatsworth is fine but not great. Apart from the chapel with part of the altar-piece carved in alabaster by Watson, and *Doubting Thomas* painted by Verrio, there are innumerable swags and drops, but the most striking piece of all is the overmantel which features netted birds. This is situated in the final stateroom. One commentator, Cunningham, author of *The Lives of the Most Eminent British Painters, Sculptors and Architects*, wrote: 'The most marvellous work of all is a net of game; you imagine at first glance that the gamekeeper has hung up his day's sport on the wall and that some of the birds are still in the death flutter'.

The story of Samuel Watson, carver at Chatsworth, has yet to be written. It

137

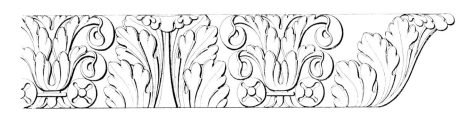

could be as illuminating as that of Gibbons himself. Watson was a man of entirely different character. Apart from his apprenticeship, when he trod the narrow path of conventional carving, he clearly yearned to be elevated to the category of artist, as witness his indefatigable habit of making hundreds of detailed drawings and sketches. One outstanding example of his artistry is the series of carvings in lime wood on a background of cedar in the chapel.

Drumlanrig Castle, Dunfermline, is a mansion built to the design of Sir William Bruce in 1645-88 for William, first Duke of Queensberry. He was so taken aback by the cost of it that he lived there for only one day. It is notable in the present context for housing a remarkable chimneypiece, the upper part apparently carved by Gibbons and the lower part in white marble. The wood is lime with a coronet at the topmost point, held in position by the heads of winged cupids with expressions of great tenderness on their faces. There are fat ears of wheat with links of delicate strawberry leaves, while the drops are richly carved with clusters of cobnuts, the now familiar veined gourd, peapods and oak leaves. The naturalistic atmosphere of the carving is enhanced by representations of birds pecking at berries. It is beyond doubt a Gibbons, for few carvers could achieve so much in such a relatively small space. The carving surrounds a portrait, while the lower surround, in stone, graces a mirror measuring 4 feet 2 in. × 6 ft 3½ in. Here again, there is no documentary proof that Gibbons carved the frame surround, although there is his account for the stone carving. It is not unlikely that he made a hidden charge for the entire surround, both wood and stone.

Elsewhere in Scotland, at Cullen, Banffshire, there is a carved panel which has an uncanny affinity with the Cosima panel, for it contains acanthus scrolls, the now well-known point cravat, music score, quill, the bow of a hunter and a crossed sceptre and sword with the Cosima-type lion hilt. There are two medallions, one of them with a relief of Charles I. Speculation has it that this exceptional piece of carving came from Holme Lacy at the time of the Hereford sale in 1874, but sale catalogues cannot be found for verification.

The whims and stupidities of patrons are part of the history of the trades. When Gibbons was approaching the age of 60 it happened that the fortunes of Sara, Duchess of Marlborough, were to have an effect on the twilight of his career. She was, quite clearly, a philistine. Apropos of her Wimbledon house, she wrote: 'I am determined to have no thing carved . . . my taste having always been to have things plain and clean, from a piece of wainscot to a lady's face'. So much for Gibbons' chances as a carver at Blenheim, where the Duchess exerted her will. True, he did execute a considerable amount of stone carving, but out of a total of £4,135 8s 7d, only £36 10s 2d was for wood carving. The disastrous story of

Blenheim has been told elsewhere and need not be recounted here. Hundreds of bills were left unpaid, the work started and stopped, and finally came to an end. There were the inevitable court cases for small and large sums of money. In the building of the place there was little joy for the many craftsmen, least of all for Gibbons.

The development of Gibbons' career was periodically weakened by numerous requests for items of little or no consequence, most of which have now vanished. He was also diverted from his main purpose as a wood carver by his work as a stone statuary. When it came to stone, he did not excel. In the light of history it is difficult to understand why so many of his patrons commissioned work in stone at all. These comments do not, however, apply to the work which he carried out as a wood carver for the Line of Kings at the Tower of London. The Line as first composed has long disappeared, but the work which Gibbons and other carvers did for it is still with us. In its day it must have been a most majestic sight but, like so many other showpieces, it eventually fell foul of the improvers and the modifiers. It was still in existence up to the end of 1800, and at the present time the remaining mounted and armoured figures on their horses are considered to be amongst the most important examples of wood carving of the 17th and 18th centuries.

The Line of Kings was first established in 1660 as a utilitarian measure because it appeared to be the best way of storing armour. Not all the figures were truly royal, but it did include Prince Henry, Henry VIII, Henry VII, Edward III, Charles I, Edward IV, Henry VI, Earl of Leicester, Charles Brandon and William the Conqueror. Some of them came originally from Greenwich in the 1650s, including eight wooden horses recorded at Greenwich in 1547 in the Henry VIII Inventory. These early examples consisted of well proportioned bodies fitted with straight broomstick legs, suggesting that they were conceived as 'clothes-horses', not fine statuary. Between 1685 and 1690 new wooden horses were made with figures to sit astride them.

Gibbons evidently became involved in the work following a minute dated 4 June 1685, which directed that 'ye Board Contract wt ye best Workmen yt will also work cheapest for his Majs Service to make ye Statue of ye Horse according to ye Draught this day approved at ye Board to make ye for ye mounting of ye Armour in ye Armoury of ye late Kings Charles ye 2nd. And yt Mr Franklin be sent to and spoken wt who he knows to be the fittest man'. Gibbons was granted the contract in addition to an order which directed that a figure be made 'together wt ye sd late Kings face to be placed in ye sd Armour'. The sum involved was £40, and a separate agreement had to be made for the painting of the effigy by another craftsman, because such work was not within Gibbons' province. By 19 December 1685 Gibbons had been paid, and a Mr Valentine Bayly, Painter to the Office of the Ordnance, received £6 17s 0d for his work, including the painting of Charles II's face, burnishing the truncheon and decorating the horse in such a way as to resemble a bay. A further sum of £10 went to Edward White for making the saddle, bridle, breastplate, holsters and crupper, the latter being covered with red velvet and having a white lace fringe.

Although Gibbons did other work for the Line of Kings, he was by no means the only carver. Others included John Nost, who received £20 for a horse, while William Morgan and Thomas Quellin were paid £20 for a horse and a mounted figure. William Emmett carved a horse and figure in March 1689, and Marmaduke Townson made two figures. In March 1690 John Nost carved five figures and horses for which he received £100. By the time the Line was finished it contained no less than 22 mounted figures. The display did not please or satisfy all who saw it. In fact, it riled Dr Samuel Maywick, author of *A Critical Inquiry into Antient Armour* (1820), who angrily pointed out a number of historical anomalies. By way of a sop to his evident expertise, he was invited to rearrange the display, and this he did, incorporating some non-royal figures. Although serious in his intentions, he was, like many 'improvers' a vociferous meddler and should have been sent packing. But like others before him he had his way, probably to the detriment of the Line of Kings.

Precisely how the attribution of the various pieces of individual carvers may be made is still very difficult, but it does appear that the earliest figures were done by Gibbons, and these were Charles I and Charles II, the latter being stripped of paint in the early 1900s. The figure of William II was probably carved by Alcock, and that of Edward III by John Nost or William Emmett.

Attribution of the heads themselves is just as difficult. One theory has it that they were not carved in many cases for the Line of Kings but intended for use on a carousel. In the 17th and 18th centuries it was common for lance bearers to practice on dummy heads mounted on a revolving carousel. It follows that those not directly attributable in the King's Line collection may well have been made for this purpose.

Carving a full-sized horse is a daunting task, and it is done nowadays by bonding pieces of wood together to form the main trunk of the beast. In Gibbons' time it was easy enough to procure large pieces of wood for such a job. Nost, however, adopted the unusual combination of oak and pine, dowelling and gluing the pieces together. The horse of Charles I is made from eight fairly thick planks to form a barrel which is octagonal within. The chest and the rump are carved on wooden plugs pushed into each end of the barrel, while eight pieces of wood are used to form the head, which is later glued in position. The legs are composed of separate pieces of wood, and the tail is separately formed. When the painter got to work all the joints were concealed with gesso, resulting in a highly realistic representation. It is interesting to note that the early roundabout horses were made in much the same way. The dimensions of the Nost horse, which can now be seen in its black and glistening beauty at the Tower of London, were based on the then fashionable battle beast of the period with head forming a high-held extension of the arched neck and a compact formation of the body with shorter legs than the modern counterpart. This proud, sprightly and reliable beast is now being bred anew in the United States and has recently been reintroduced into Britain. It is known as the Morgan horse.

The work of Gibbons and his contemporaries at the Tower of London, one of the traditional workshops for carvers, could not have been regarded as exceptional by the men themselves, and it illustrates once again the fact that while we may tend to reverence them, they were no more than tradesmen, albeit of fine quality. It is only the benediction of history which makes their work seem so outstanding. Gibbons, Nost, Emmett and Bayly, the painter, were ordinary men, not immortals. Their interest would have been in arriving at an acceptable standard for which they would be paid without delay.

A little later, in 1695, Gibbons carved the overmantel for the Board Room of the Admiralty in Whitehall, London. Surrounding a compass by Norden, it is believed to have survived in its entirety, although it has from time to time been renovated. Carved in pear wood, it originally formed a frame for a portrait of the King. The Eye of Glory on sword and sceptre surmounts the composition, and behind it are trumpets and bay leaves with the wings of victory on either side, accompanied by fruit and flower festoons. One quite unusual feature of the carving is the mermen with two tails and the entwined fishes. Mermen do not appear elsewhere in Gibbons' work, and it is interesting to conjecture whether this manifestation was an echo from his days in Deptford, when he may have heard the fables of the sea from on-shore sailors. He also made a major feature of the dolphins which are part of the sea mounts. Below the side drops are some unusual carvings of nautical instruments with flowers and fruit. Once again, Gibbons' attention to detail is prominent, for he included a John Davis backstaff, Outred's ring dial and the astrolabe invented by Gunter, all carved in exquisite detail. The overmantel also contains a profusion of carving amongst which appear such maritime symbols as spars and topmasts, telescopes, globes, charts and logbooks, Mercury's staff against a background of martagons, hops and primroses. It seems very unfortunate that this tour de force is seen by comparatively few people due to its location.

Of much more doubtful lineage but no less interesting is the carving in the Oak Room of the New River Head, Clerkenwell, London, which is now part of a building used by the Metropolitan Water Board. It consists of the arms of William III with his motto *Je Maintiendray*. The decoration includes lobsters and crabs, and there is also a highly realistic creel of fish, a frog, a duck, partridges and peewit and several other birds in a pleasing conjunction with ears of wheat. The Oak Room contains other examples of fine carving, such as wainscot, also a painted ceiling. The entire apartment is said to have been designed by Wren. Due to reconstruction over the years, it is impossible to arrive at any firm conclusion about its origins. While it does date from 1697, there are lingering doubts about the association with Wren and Gibbons, both of whom were more than fully occupied with the rebuilding of St Paul's. It is unlikely that either of the two men would have been diverted from their main purpose, nor could they have spared skilled members of their workforce.

The remaining fifteen years of Gibbons' life were devoted in the main to stone sculpture in the form of monuments, notably in such edifices as York Minster, Westminster Abbey, Nannerch in Wales, and elsewhere. His personal touch is not greatly evident, and it is reasonable to assume that he had by now run his course. He appears to have had a full social life, for in 1709 he served his second term as steward of the St Luke's Club, an association of 'men of the highest character in the arts and gentlemen lovers of art'. It is easy to imagine the now ageing Gibbons in the convivial company of his contemporaries, engaged in raising funds for the club by raffling paintings. As steward it was his duty to provide, and pay for, the annual dinner, and he doubtless played his part in running the annual contests for members who were also sculptors.

Grinling Gibbons died in his house at Bow Street on 3 August 1721, the cause being unknown. He was buried in St Paul's, Covent Garden, in an unmarked grave, where his wife, Elizabeth, had been interred in 1719. His goods, including pictures and carvings, were sold on 15 November 1722 because he died intestate. It is unlikely that he died a wealthy man, but he was far from poor. In the church where he lies there is a small limewood wreath in memory of Gibbons and his wife. It was carved originally for St Paul's Cathedral 244 years ago by Gibbons himself, and restored in 1965 by Mr A. A. Banks before being positioned in the Covent Garden church.

This account of Gibbons does not purport to be a full account of his life and work in material other than wood. Each year a few new attributions are made, for carvings are discovered not only in Britain but also abroad. At Canewden, Essex, there is a particularly striking instance of this in the shape of the pulpit in the Norman church which was rebuilt in the 14th century. The pulpit is richly carved with cherubs, foliage and fruits which cover its panels. It was carried out to Canewden after the Great Fire of London in 1666, and on examination appears to have been carved in Gibbons' workshops. But we cannot be completely sure.

While it is quite true that there may still be a large number of the carvings resting in unknown places, any new discoveries must be treated with extreme caution for the good reason that neither Gibbons nor his extensive workshops could possibly have produced such a tremendous body of work. The same can be said of Gibbons' contemporaries and near-contemporaries, including Jean Tijou, responsible for the ironwork at Hampton Court and St Paul's, Samuel Mearne, bookbinder to Charles II, Tompion and Quare, clockmakers, and Marot, designer of locks and keys. They started at the bench and ascended to the heights from which they directed the work of others.

Carvings attributed to Gibbons or emanating from his workshops may be viewed in London at the following places:

St James's Church, Piccadilly
St Mary Abchurch, Abchurch Lane
St Margaret, Lothbury
St Paul's, Hammersmith
All Hallows, Twickenham
St Bartholomew's, Stamford Hill
All-Hallows-by-the-Tower
Queen's Chapel, St James's Palace
St Alfege, Greenwich
St Paul's, Covent Garden
St Paul's Cathedral
Victoria and Albert Museum
Tower of London

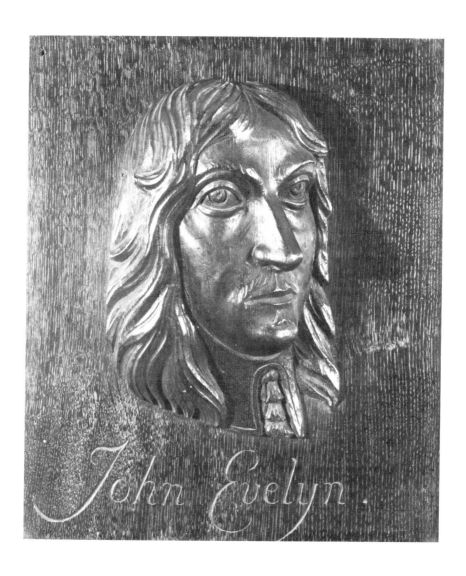

75   One of the 'esteem' carvings made by
Gibbons early in his career, showing a three-
quarter profile of his champion, John Evelyn,
the diarist.

76 Gibbons' relief carving of Tintoretto's *Crucifixion*. A crowded and busy representation in which the drapery is defined in the classical style in addition to a demonstration of equine carving.

76a Detail of frame foreshadowing Gibbons' grasp of composition and delineation of floral subjects. Carved on the curve, the individual blossoms cleverly follow the line of the frame within a limited compass.

76b Detail showing Gibbons' early habit of flattening the Italian tree forms of the original painting to conform to the Netherlands school of painting and sculpture.

77   *The Last Supper* in which the carving is not characteristic of Gibbons, although the work is frequently attributed to him.

148

78 The Cosima panel, commissioned by Charles II for presentation to Cosima III, Grand Duke of Tuscany, following the 1669 visit to England. Signed by Gibbons, it is one of the few positively authenticated carvings with an integrated signature. Gibbons charged £150 for this masterpiece of composition and technical virtuosity.

Details from the Cosima panel, opposite, are arranged to view from the left downwards (78 a-d) and from the right downwards (78 e-h).

78a Musical score and recorder. Realism is created by the curled corner of the score and the overlaying of the wilting plant. The recorder itself is carved, embodying the decoration of the time.

78b A foreshadowing of Gibbons' technique of bunching together foliage and fruit. There is a wealth of carved detail on the hilt of the sword in which lions are featured.

78c An example of the lace carving favoured by Gibbons which followed the patterns of his day with the folds boldly defined.

78d At the height of his career Gibbons elaborated on the acanthus with its origins in Graeco-Roman times and much incorporated in classical architecture. In the carved version there is a marked similarity to the herbaceous perennial known in the United Kingdom as brank-ursine.

78e The crown of Charles II portraying detail which Gibbons may have studied in the original. This is one of the finest pieces of intricate and finely balanced component pieces of the Cosima panel.

78f Accurately carved copies of seashells, suggesting that Gibbons possessed a collection which acted as models.

78g An example of the clustering of foliage to form a natural curve, originating quite possibly as a single drawn line in the draughting stage and used as a guide for the construction and composition.

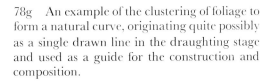

78h Gibbons' carved signature with the quill behind it appears to authenticate the Cosima panel.

79 The Modena panel, commissioned by James II. More widely spaced in its composition than the earlier Cosima panel, it nevertheless contains many of the same natural forms, including the musical instrument and score but with the addition of the human skull.

79a A detail of the Modena panel showing the medallion incorporating Gibbons' self-portrait and the inscription in Latin.

80 Regal heads carved for the Line of Kings at the Tower of London in the 1680s by Gibbons, John Nost and others.

80a The full-size battle horse carved by John Nost in oak and pine, recently restored. Nost's attempt at animation resulted in a portrait of a beast at the height of fury and movement.

82   The point lace cravat carved for Walpole, said to be one of the finest of all Gibbons' accomplishments, but preceded by the example of lace carving in the Cosima panel.

81   Frame of the Ashmole portrait in which Gibbons exercised considerable restraint in composition. Individual components are more widely spaced than in other pieces of the same period. It is unfortunate that this frame is placed against a patterned background.

84   A composition at Petworth House, Sussex, where Gibbons' carvings are mounted around and between the paintings. Again, the lace carving is evident but with a predominance of musical instruments with the score and turned leaf, the ten-stringed lute with its Italian origin, violin and wind instruments. The portrait medallion with its unidentified subject, is offset by the descending link of pearls. An unlikely but still acceptable addition is the sheath of arrows at the head of the composition.

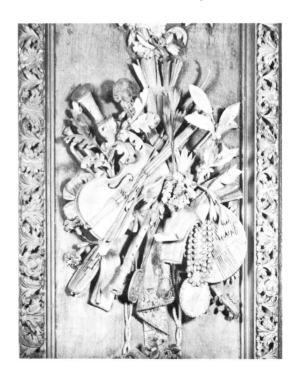

83   The Gibbons heritage, a gilded and more sweeping treatment of the acanthus with cherubs and variety of fruits at Ham House, Surrey, one of the finest examples of the modernisation of the 1670s.

85 Ornamentation of pulpit at the church of St Andrew-by-the-Wardrobe, London. Many such carvings are erroneously attributed to Gibbons. This example is altogether too coarse in treatment and poorly designed in its floriation to have been originated by Gibbons or his workshop.

86 Claydon House, Buckinghamshire, survives in part and contains a wealth of extravagant carving by Luke Lightfoot, who died insane. His work is situated in what have been described as the most amazing suite of rococo rooms in the United Kingdom. Lightfoot's fame rests on his major contribution to 18th century chinoiserie.

86a Lightfoot's habit of giving life to his bird subjects is illustrated in this detail of a frame, but just as important was his technique of cleanly carving the ornamentation.

87 Lyme Park, Cheshire, built to the design of Giacomo Leoni in 1720, contains carvings by an unknown craftsman but often attributed to Gibbons. The carving is nevertheless of a high order and even brilliant in its daring.

88 Sudbury Hall, Derbyshire, was built in the style of the Restoration, and is famous for its internal decoration in a lavish style which includes a staircase by Edward Pearce, now repainted in 17th century style. Elsewhere in the Hall is carving attributed to Gibbons.

89 A Gibbons attribution at Sudbury Hall, Derbyshire. It forms part of the frame ornamentation, and features dead game birds with finely defined plumage, flowers and nuts, all carved in the Gibbons style.

90 St George slaying the Dragon in the centre panel of the back of the stall of the Vice Provost in King's College Chapel, Cambridge, surmounted by the figure of a law-giver. Subjects were carefully chosen to harmonise with the nature of such edifices, hence the choice of England's patron saint.

91 Heraldic panels in the stalls of King's College Chapel, Cambridge. The carving is of such excellence that it should be considered to stand at the heart of the English tradition.

92   The arms of England above the gates of the
screen in King's College Chapel, Cambridge. A
perfect example of carving in the reign of Henry
VIII,   incorporating   architectural   ornamentation.

93   A roundel ornamentation on the side of the
screen in King's College Chapel, Cambridge.
Done in the classical Roman style, it continues
the medieval tradition of composition within
strict spatial limitations.

94 Benthall Hall, Shropshire, was built in the
late 16th century but embellished in the 17th
century. The carving reflects overall decoration
with a profusion of strapwork and scrollwork
with heraldic beasts. The dining room is dated
1610.

95 The staircase of Benthall Hall, Shropshire,
is a fine example of openwork carving with
comparatively shallow carving on the posts.

96 Dunster Castle, Somerset. This detail of the pierced staircase portrays the chase with lean hounds in pursuit. In the centre is a cornucopia from which spill Irish and Scottish coins.

97 Staircase at Dunster Castle, Somerset, one of the finest examples of its kind with vases surmounting the posts. An interesting feature is the manner in which the composition follows the angle of the stair treads.

98 Petworth House, Sussex, contains carvings done by the Gibbons workshop and commissioned by the 6th Duke of Somerset. This display represents one of the most complete settings of Gibbons' work of the period, and includes the portrait surrounds, the drops and acanthus heading, and the picture frames.

157

99   The choir of St Paul's Cathedral, London.
This overall view shows the immensity of the
carving undertaken by the Gibbons workshop
during the surveyship of Sir Christopher Wren.

100   Detail of Gibbons' carving in St Paul's
Cathedral, London, situated on the organ case.
There is a departure from strictly classical
architectural themes to include the head of the
cherub.

101   Detail from the organ case of St Paul's Cathedral, London. A strictly formal piece of carving with little to suggest the flamboyance of Gibbons and his school.

102   Part of the original organ case of St Paul's Cathedral, London, carved in 1697 and embodying a hint of Gibbons in the style of ornamentation.

103   Panel from the original organ case of St Paul's Cathedral, London, now on the north side of the choir stalls. It clearly displays several of the Gibbons motifs, including the musical instruments, flowers and encircling acanthus, and the ruched ribbons.

104   A frieze from the original organ case of St Paul's Cathedral, London, in which Gibbons' composition follows the demands exerted by dimension but still includes a selection of wild and cultivated flowers. Treatment of the cherub wings is cleverly composed in such a way as to avoid clashing with the draped garlands.

105   Empanelled carving in St Paul's Cathedral, London, is in the manner of Gibbons but it hardly parallels his attention to botanical detail. The frame is not contemporaneous.

106   Example of a strongly composed panel in the chapel of St Michael and St George in St Paul's Cathedral, London, probably somewhat later than the period of Sir Christopher Wren's surveyship. The two upper figures with muscular down-reaching arms and hooves form the mainstay of the composition.

107 An inferior example of festoon carving forming the decoration of a pilaster on the west wall of St Paul's Cathedral, London. Executed quite possibly by an apprentice, it lacks the sharp-edged definition which characterises the Gibbons school.

108 The canopy of the Dean's Stall, St Paul's Cathedral, London. A harmonious composition with more than a suggestion of the Gibbons touch, particularly in the formation of the acanthus in the centre.

Font cover, All-Hallows-by-the-Tower, for
which Gibbons was paid £12. It is typified by
the lyrical treatment of the cherubs and the
grouping of the floriation.

CHAPTER FIVE

After Gibbons

THE social flush which lifted Grinling Gibbons to eminence was to die with him. The style was incapable of living on, because it was vested in Gibbons himself and in his contemporaries. The Baroque became démodé. In post-Restoration England a financial rheumatism was to cramp the limbs of the Establishment. The new palaces started originally by Charles II still stood in a half-finished state, and their very spectre-like presence, inhibited the desire to embark on major plans to rebuild Whitehall Palace after the fire of 1698. By the time the auditors had uncovered the scabs of debt and counter-debt, the attitude towards public spending hardened. The Office of Works, once the source of so much encouraging patronage for many carvers and other tradesmen, was overspent in 1666. Between 1675 and 1719 it was in the parlous condition of always owing up to £30,000, and by 1692 the figure had reached £60,000. At the end of the reign of Queen Anne the debt was £80,000 and appeared to be quite out of control. Harsh financial facts like these have a very real bearing on the development of woodcarving in England. There are two underlying considerations. The first is that the Office of Works traditionally devoted part of its expenditure to the maintenance of state buildings, and the second concerned the commissioning of new works. It was in the second category that carving commissions were to be found. And it was here, of course, that the greatest economies had to be made. The view was taken that a plain wall or fireplace was just as good in an unornamented state, and expenditure on carved wood was pointless at such a time. The chilly climate affected not only carvers and tradesmen but also the muralists who followed Verrio. Credit systems had to be introduced to enable the Exchequer to supply funds to the Office of Works, and in this way the Office was able to meet its mounting obligations for the time being. These systems, all inextricably mixed, eventually became known as the National Debt. The raising of basic funds by the Exchequer was not always successful. In the immediate post-Restoration period the sum of £12,000 was needed for running repairs to the palaces. To raise the money a tax was levied against the Welsh counties, but it proved impossible to collect. Other taxes were devised, but they, too, failed, and in the end Hugh May, the Paymaster, had to borrow the money from the London bankers. The process could take years, in which time the palaces continued to moulder and decay. Debt was so common that much business was forced to incorporate allowances for it, thereby creating an early form of national inflation. Craftsmen could go unpaid for months, even years, and the hardest hit were those employed by the Office of Works. The situation seldom improved, and on occasion members of the staff of the Office were invited to lend money to the government. It seems that many ignored the fact that this was simply a form of financial cannibalism and they made the loans in the belief that this would ensure their future prosperity. By 1706 Wren was owed £341 in salary. By 1708 he was in the position of desperately trying to do a deal by agreeing to remit the debt in return to the lease of a house at Hampton Court, where he intended retiring. But by 1718 the Crown was again in his debt. He was not alone in his predicament. Practically all the leading tradesmen were Crown creditors. Charles Hopson, a joiner, was owed the astronomical sum of £10,587 without any hope of receiving settlement. Small wonder that Pepys wrote '. . . no credit, no goods sold to us, nobody will trust us. All we have to do at the office is hear complaints for want of money'. He was, of course, in the front line as one of those responsible for trying to deal with Crown debt. In this financial mess it was the individual craftsman who suffered most of all. A new type of economic reform was needed. Part of this reform, when it manifested itself, was the abolition of ad hoc contracts for tradesmen and the vesting of contract negotiations at agreed rates in the architects. Competitive tendering, still used by government departments, abolished the corruption formerly practised by the Master Mason and the Master Carpenter, and by 1705 a system was drafted but not yet introduced to prevent Crown officers from personally profiting from contracts. Throughout this period Wren continued in office, but he no longer had total control. By 1718 he had been deprived of his title as Surveyor-General, and by 1723 he was dead.

The effect of the financial reform was what one would expect, and for a time it worked to the detriment of fine carving. There was to be a resurgence in due course, but it happened without any credit to the Crown. In his heyday Gibbons and his workshop had without doubt given a new prestige to the trade, although it was still not regarded as anything more than a minor art but classed as ornamental decoration. The single major weakness lay in the nature of the clientele who patronised the great carvers. Practically all their work was undertaken for major projects, e.g. country houses, churches and cathedrals. Everything was done on the grand scale, and there was nothing domestic or intimate about it. It is doubtful whether it exerted any appreciable influence on the lower echelons of the trade. Some faint idea of the state of carving outside the Gibbons circle may be gained from the knowledge that in 1747 a journeyman was paid between £1 10s 0d and £2 a week, although by 1788 a good journeyman chair carver was able to earn as much as £4 a week if he ran a workshop to which jobs could be sent. Contemporary accounts of the character of these carvers vary. One disparaging note had it that the journeyman was generally 'an ignorant besotted fellow who would work hard and drink hard . . . (but) never saved a shilling'. Trade disputes were common, caused generally by allegations that the journeyman was nothing but a profiteer. Pockets of discontent spread rapidly, and carvers were among an estimated 100,000 tradesmen in London who were caught up in the unrest, leading to bloody street riots and fights between the different factions. In 1777 wages were between 18s and 22s a week, and they remained at that level up to 1794. In the 120 years from 1695 and 1815 the country was at war for 63 years, causing prices to inflate. Wages reached 27s by 1802, and by 1810 they were 33s. In 1813 they were 36s.

In the light of the history of unrest brewed by the cycle of war, peace and war, the nagging preoccupation with wages is understandable, and it may well be that the quality of work produced by the carving trade was generally less than good. R. Campbell wrote: 'The carving now used is but the outlines of the art, it consists only in some unmeaning scroll, or a bad representation of some fruit or flowers. The gentry, because it is the mode, will have some sort of carving, but are no judges of the execution of the work: they bargain with the master-builder or architect for something of the kind; he, to make the most of it, employs such hands as can give him a slight flourish for his money, no matter how it is done, therefore it is not necessary to spend much time or money to acquire this superficial kind of carving'. Campbell was, of course, reporting on the trade of house carving. His obvious pessimism might well have turned to optimism had he taken the trouble to look elsewhere at a time when the gentry were demanding fine furniture. From being a simple carver in the late 17th century, the tradesman of the 18th century became both carver and gilder. He gained even more stature as a designer of such items as looking-glass frames, cabinet stands, console tables, candelabra and girandoles. The latter item is of special interest. The word 'girandole' was of Italian origin to describe elaborately carved wall brackets with lights or branched candlesticks. In his diary for 15 November 1684 Evelyn describes the 'girandolas' portrayed in a firework display on the Thames near Whitehall. For some time girandoles were among the most striking examples of the carver's skill, and examples were published in the 1st and 3rd editions of Thomas Chippendale's *The Gentleman and Cabinet Maker's Director* (1754, 1755, 1762) and by the partners, William Ince and John Mayhew in *The Universal System of Household Furniture* (1759-62). By the middle of the 18th century carvers had introduced Gothic and Chinese girandoles which featured arches, temples and pagodas. Carvers with some design aptitude drew on many fantastic sources and freely incorporated classic columns, arcades, balconies and acanthus scrolls. Robert Adam (1728-92) brought back ideas from his travels in Italy from 1754 to 1757 and Dalmatia, and achieved fame as the reinterpreter of the classical style. He was responsible for introducing even more delicate designs to create lighter furniture and house interiors which must have taxed the skill of many a carver.

The period was now struggling out of the doldrums, and the initiative was coming from private entrepreneurs rather than an impoverished Crown. By the time Thomas Sheraton (1751-1806), who trained as a carver and cabinet maker, was writing his book, *The Cabinet Dictionary*, published in 1803, he was able to devote part of his text to a description of the branches of the carver's work within his own industry. He divided carvers into four specialists: '1st. One for architectural work, consisting of the ornamental capitals of the orders, chimney pieces and mouldings. 2d. One for internal decorations in furniture, consisting of pier glasses, windows and bed cornices, &c. connected with gilding in burnished gold and mat. 3d. One for chair work, consisting of flat water and strap leaf work, scrolls and running mouldings, whether for japanning or gilding, applied to chairs, sophas, couches, &c. 4th. One for shipwork, consisting much in mass figures for the heads, and bold foliage for the quarters and sterns of ships'.

That Sheraton held carvers in some esteem is evident from his comment: 'An adept in carving, is no mean person; and in reality requires more to qualify him thoroughly than is generally apprehended; although many in his profession, as in all others, content themselves to know very little. A complete master in carving, ought to be acquainted with architecture, perspective, and, in some degree, with botany; nor should he be ignorant of the true effect of painting nor of the structure of the human body; for unquestionably each of these sciences have something to do with carving. To these should be added an acquaintance with antique ornaments. These, indeed, he is practically concerned with in many branches of carving; and by competent acquaintance with which it is, that the French carvers exceed the English, when they have practised in this country for some time.

Figures, foliage and flowers are the three great subjects of carving; which in the finishing, require a strength or delicacy suited to the height or distance of these objects from the eye. In the proper effect of carving, much depends on a due degree of boldness, or tenderness, answering to local circumstances'. In this passage Sheraton was writing about the philosophy which made Gibbons' work a landmark in the history of English carving.

There was for a time a growth of specialisation among carvers, caused no doubt by the higher rates for work which enhanced certain types of furniture. The 'general' carver had little air of authority, but his contemporary, who was able to provide not only skilled execution but also a design service was now sought after. This evolution was bound to give birth to 'coarse' and 'fine' carving. By 1747 *The London Tradesman* was saying that there was 'a class of carvers who do nothing but carve frames for looking glasses'. The prosperity of many carvers was underlined by J. Collyer in his book, *The Parent's and Guardian's Directory*, a careers guide of its day, which said that owing to the vogue for carving, the practitioners were 'very much wanted and never out of business'. This was doubtless encouraging for the elders in search of profitable vocations for youths at a time when the streets of London were full of beggars and unemployed persons. An apprentice could be bound for a fee of £5, those with a better education could be bound for £15. The attractions of a lucrative career in carving were strong in an era when more than twenty people a week were dying of starvation in London alone. Not that the hours of work for a carver's apprentice were very attractive, for they started at 6 a.m. and worked on until 8 p.m. with few, if any, holidays.

The shops of Georgian London were packed with an amazing selection of finely carved furniture at prices ranging from 5s each for hard-seat chairs ornamented with a flick or two of light carving to monumental pieces like the 'Diana and Minerva' commode made in Chippendale's workshops and sold to Harewood House in 1773 for £86. 'General Description of Trades', published in 1747, said that the shops were '. . . so richly set out that they look more like palaces and their stocks are of exceeding great value'. In the next breath some disparagement sets in. 'But this business seems to consist, as do many others, of two branches, the maker and the vendor, for the shopkeeper does not always make every sort of goods that he deals in, though he bears away the title'. It would have been naïve indeed to believe that all shops had their own workshops, for many of them were served from warehouses where the stocks were topped up by 'small masters' and journeymen who slaved in back streets situated mainly south of the Thames, down Deptford way. Mortimer's *'Universal Director'* of 1763 was a handbook for the use of the nobility and it prided itself on the fact that the recommended establishments

featured only cabinet makers and associated trades 'such as either work themselves, or employ workmen under their direction; and that not one of those numerous warehouses which sell ready-made furniture, bought off the real artist, is to be met with in this work; the plan of which is to direct the merchant and private gentleman to the fountain head of every department.'

Mortimer was no doubt appealing to the snobbery of the Georgians, for the compiler must have known that commercial establishments from the top of the league to the bottom relied almost without exception on the small masters in the cabinet making and carving trades. But there was one exception, described by a German visitor to Britain, Sophie von la Roche, who, in 1786, went to the shop of George Seddon in Aldersgate Street to be suitably dazzled by the contents of the six wings, the fine fabrics and the plain and carved furniture. This great store, perhaps the Harrods of its time, had 400 apprentices on the staff under the tutelage of innumerable master craftsmen. Seddons made practically everything on the premises, using wood drawn from a stock of imported and home-grown timber. But despite the size of the place and the range of stock, Seddon himself was not impregnable. He had many competitors, including Gumley, Grendey, Hallet, Vile, Cobb, Gillow and Tatham. Few of them were able to survive beyond a single generation of entrepreneural activity, so rapidly did tastes change. They also had enemies within the gates, so to speak, for many an ambitious journeyman carver or cabinet maker sought employment with the sole intention of learning the rudiments of the business and then moving on to a competitor or else setting up on his own. The other enemy with whom men like Seddon had to do battle was the customer himself or herself. Practically every furniture business was forced to carry a large amount of unpaid debts, and Chippendale in particular suffered at the hands of his distinguished clientele. In 1770 he wrote personally to Sir Edward Knatchbull of Mercham Hatch, saying that 'it is a time of year when money is much wanted to support credit', whereupon Knatchbull irately replied: 'As I receive my rents once a year, so I pay my tradesmen's bills once a year, which is not reckoned very bad pay as ye world goes'.

Journeymen, on the other hand, were better off, for they were able to claim extra holidays on the eight 'hanging days' every year, and this left them free to watch public executions. The audiences for these base spectacles seem to have consisted mainly of tradesmen, prostitutes who hoped to peddle their wares in the good-humoured hubbub, and a sprinkling of the gentry and foreign visitors.

One special class of carver should be mentioned if only for the reason that its members formed part of the Georgian trades scene for a brief period and yet influenced the pattern of industry at the time. They were known as the 'small masters' or 'working masters', referred to by an anonymous contemporary writer of 1747 as 'those masters who keep no shops nor stocks, but principally follow making, and dispose of their goods as fast as they are finished'. They did, in fact, have their own workshops which were no better than holes in the wall down back alleys, but they employed considerable numbers of apprentices. They had enough initiative to set up on the fringes of the furniture industry at a time when shops needed a variety of stock. In most cases it took only about £50 to start up as a small master, specialising in chair carving and sending finished goods to the warehouses which, in turn, sold to fashionable London emporia, some of which were run by women, who specialised in upholstered chairs, stools and *chaises longues*. The small masters earned their money and survived only by working up to fourteen hours a day. Many of them were former journeymen who saved up for several years to start their own workshops, and some, at least, progressed even further by opening retail premises.

James Pain is a typical figure of the time. His brother-in-law, Francis Place, wrote an unpublished autobiography in 1778, and it is now in the British Museum. In it he stressed that Pain, a journeyman chair carver, was 'a good workman and remarkably swift, he could earn full four pounds a week all the year round, and need never have wanted work, chairs and other small pieces of furniture which were to be carved were sent to his own workshop and he always had much more than he could do'.

Pain must have been remarkably well organised, and he doubtless used the services of apprentices and journeymen, for his income of £4 a week represented a higher than average sum at a time when all work was costed at piece rates. Moderately accomplished craftsmen earned approximately 15s a week, while the journeyman could count on 12s to 15s. Chair carvers were not, as a matter of fact, too highly placed if we are to accept their rating in Kearsley's *Table of Trades*, which referred to their craft as 'laborious'. Despite this, they were conscious of their social class, and the craftsman who worked in the fashionable St Martin's Lane area could expect to earn slightly more than his counterpart who laboured just as diligently in the less salubrious Wapping or Shadwell.

The vogue for fine furniture may well have existed at this time, but carving was now about to go into one of its periodic cycles. Immediately prior to the appearance of Sheraton's book, a slump began which was to continue into the first part of the 19th century, when the entire London trade was represented by only eleven master carvers and some 60 journeymen and even fewer in the provinces. By the time M. J. Wood published his *New Circle of the Mechanical Arts* in 1819 he was able to assert that carving had now relapsed to a position 'long in the

169

background as a branch of the Arts'. Within a few years what had promised to become an exciting development of the carving trade as a sector of the furniture industry had dwindled to practically nothing.

Some idea of the scope which clients expected the carver to offer can be found in eleven design books published between 1740 and 1769 by Matthias Lock, a carver and designer who was largely responsible for the English rococo style. The word 'rococo' was derived from the French *rocaille*, meaning 'rock-work' to describe artificial grottoes and foundations in the gardens of Versailles, and later used in regard to ornate furniture and carving. It began in France with Pierre Le Pantre, a designer and engraver, and was intended to be seen in two dimensions. Later adapted by the French carvers, who brought into play their vibrant energy to incorporate Chinese motifs in their work, it led to the introduction of an asymmetrical design system. They achieved new effects by working in three dimensions to create pieces of elegant complexity, using arrangements of curves. When Chippendale imported rococo into England in the drawings which he included in the *Director*, he modified it so that the designs were less exuberant and more disciplined and conservative. Thomas Johnson, a carver, gilder and designer, who died in 1778, was one of the great exponents of the new style. He opened for business in 1755 at Queen Street, Seven Dials, London, and later continued his establishment at The Golden Boy, Grafton Street, Soho. The start of his business was marked by the publication of *Twelve Girandoles*, a folio of engraved designs. In 1758 he published *The Book of the Carver* with 53 engravings. His influence as an enthusiast of design grew rapidly, and between 1756 and 1785 he was able to start publishing *One Hundred and Fifty New Designs* in monthly parts. His design invention was superior to that of the more reserved Chippendale, but he still remains the lesser known of the two.

The period was not short of propagandists for design. Matthias Lock (birth and death dates unknown), mentioned earlier, was prolific between 1740 and 1756, and the Victoria and Albert Museum, London, has a large collection of his annotated drawings, circa 1740 and 1765, of the pieces which he supplied to the second Earl Poulett of Hinton House, Somerset. They include a carved and gilded mirror frame which is currently deposited in the Victoria and Albert, a side table, a pair of stands and a side table, still to be seen at Hinton House. Lock was for a time in association with Chippendale and he collaborated with his partner, Henry Copland, in making a number of drawings for Chippendale's *Director*. What were perhaps the first drawings for carved neo-classical furniture appeared in *A New Book of Pier Frames* and *A New Book of Foliage*. Lock was a prolific contributor to the library of design and included in his many publications ideas for carved ornaments, shields, sconces and tables in his *A New Drawing Book of Ornaments* published between 1740 and 1765.

This great flood of published design ended the golden age of wood carving in England. Chippendale, Sheraton and others stood at the end of it, the final players in the tragi-comedy which had Grinling Gibbons as its protagonist, the Crown and the Church as stage managers, and the panopoly of the years as scenery. The The curtain is now down. How long it will remain down before the next great production, nobody knows.

109 The only known example of an English
mahogany chandelier of the 18th century.
Made probably between 1768-70, the design
has associations with Robert Adam, and the
carving displays all the precision associated
with a master carver. Overall width 3ft 10in.

110 Detail from the Chevy Chase sideboard, Grosvenor Hotel, Shaftesbury, Dorset. Carved between 1857-63 by Gerrard Robinson of Newcastle-upon-Tyne, it was bought for the hotel in 1919 for £140. The entire piece is covered with carved figures, and there are more than 50 in this section alone. Robinson died a pauper.

111 Modern heraldic carving. The arms of the County of Berkshire, one of a pair now sited on Newbury Court House, and carved by Gino Masero.

112   The Gibbons style of naturalistic carving
continues into our own times in this 1960 clock
executed by Nancy Catford to a design by
J. Rodney Stone for Spillers Limited.

The World of Today's Woodcarver

It is said that the worth of any wood carving lies in the virtuoso performance of the tools that made it. Little importance is placed on the carver's skill, because it is self-evident. There is some truth in this. The wonder is that the fine carving of the 16th and 17th centuries has never been repeated. The reasons are very simple. Firstly, there is no demand for such work. Secondly, the tools needed for the execution of such work no longer exist. Nor, on the other hand, did they exist for Gibbons and his contemporaries or the earlier journeymen who decorated cathedrals and the village carvers who worked on bench ends and misericords for parish churches. The tools had to be made, forged for individual jobs by the metal workers for the carvers. There are no records to suggest that carvers made their own tools, but it is by no means beyond possibility. Towards the end of the 18th century the tools had multiplied to a total of about 300 because the style and nature demanded it. Examine the vast variety of girandoles and realise that such fine work in the Chinoise and Gothic tradition could not have been realised using carving tools as they are today. Many of the miniature temples and grottoes and architectural detail look as though they were carved with microscopic-ended tools and even by tools quite unknown to us. They are altogether too finely detailed to have been in contact with the common gouge or chisel. On the other hand, many medieval misericords and bench ends have a naïve clumsiness which look as though the carving implements were common carpenter's tools, perhaps only slightly adapted for the task.

Regardless of the fineness or the clumsiness of his interpretation, the carver uses two tools in a variety of permutations. They are the chisel and the gouge. In reality, they are one tool, for the gouge is simply a curved chisel. In all likelihood the present range of carving tools is descended from the common chisel. There is, oddly enough, a tendency in the carving trade to employ comparatively few tools for any single job. The working carver will say that he uses only a handful of chisels and gouges to achieve many effects. Everything depends upon his dexterity and the familiarity with implements which he may have been using year after year. It is not necessarily true to claim that the number of tools required by the carver varies in proportion to the nature of the work he is doing. Theoretically, of course, one can make a good case for using up to thirty or forty tools for work of great detail and elaboration, but under actual working conditions this does not prevail. While the different sizes have a wide variance in sweep and edge, the professional carver often makes do with whatever he happens to have to hand, so that it is not uncommon to see a carver using the most minute fraction of the blade of a straight or skew chisel to carve quite small detail. This does not mean that he is an inept tradesman, quite the contrary. What he is doing is making one tool do the work of several. Many carvers can cut a trough using a straight chisel, others can cut a flat area using a gouge, and many gouges have been ground almost flat for this very purpose.

A controversy has gone on for many years about the use of abrasives in carving. True, it is of no great importance to those who appreciate carving purely as an aesthetic pleasure, but it does have a certain importance to those in the carving trade. The purists say that sandpaper should never be employed in carving because it should be possible to use the carving tools to create such a surface. There is much to be said for this point of view, and apprentices were always taught along very strict lines. Yet in our own time mechanical cutters are frequently used to outline the shape. While the controversy continues, certain carving shops do use it and then add the final tooling to impart the marks which fascinate so many people. But this is not true carving. It has no place in the business of learning how to carve.

The teaching of carving is in itself a misnomer, for carving is something which cannot be taught. It can be imparted only by teaching the technique itself. The rest of the knowledge needed by the carver is partly artistic, partly technological. He needs to know how to draw, how to originate the composition unless he is an out and out copyist, which is not progressive and may indeed be downright stultifying. As a technician he must know the properties and the tendencies of the wood he carves. Some wood is useless for carving purposes, other wood seems to have been placed on earth purely for the carver's use and pleasure.

The carver must be able to work in conjunction not only with the tradesman joiner but also the architect with whom he has a traditional alliance. A good carver who is conscious of the antiquity of his trade will cheerfully and tolerantly work with any other tradesman or professional person. It is interesting to conjecture how Gibbons and Wren got on so well together. Gibbons was sufficient of a craftsman to adapt himself to any society in which he happened to find himself. He was not, so far as we know, aloof, nor did he ever pretend to be anything other than a tradesman. In our own time there are some carvers who prefer to call themselves sculptors, though for what reason one cannot tell. It is not a trade in which there is any room for pretension. The mark of the carver is the pace of production and the maintenance of quality.

Speed of carving is often surprising. The carver is truly engrossed in what he is doing, and yet he will more often than not carry on a conversation while working. The master carver himself is sometimes a man of mercurial temperament with many interests, such as heraldry, architecture and history, and he has himself served an apprenticeship to a master carver. Before the First World War it was common for master carvers to be employed on repetition carving of piano legs and furniture ornamentation. This was not by any means assembly line work, it was a true craft and a respected one in which tradesmen earned good wages. As in former times, they had their own apprentices if they were sub-contractors to large firms of manufacturers. If they worked in a firm, they had a number of apprentices allocated to them. They worked rapidly because they were often employed on a piece rate basis. What they taught was sheer technique. Because the repertoire of ornamentation was narrow, the master carver produced hundreds of pieces in a year to strictly standard patterns. It was natural for the apprentices to imbibe the technique of fast and perfect working. This process was, of course, far removed from art as such, it was simply the business of tool handling, and as a result a full generation of conventionally minded wood carvers was produced. There is in all this more than a hint of hard work when we study the scene between 1890 and 1915, when wood carving called for sustained labour, a balanced eye and the determination to finish the job. The same surely applied to Grinling Gibbons, Jonathan Mayn and other carvers in the heyday of the trade.

One of the cardinal rules of the carver's shop is tidiness. It begins with the apprentice diligently sweeping the master carver's work area, collecting the tools and sharpening them in readiness for the morrow's work. He also learns how to read the drawings to which the carver works, and they can be as precise as those of the engineer. If a bracket has to be carved in order to fit into an exact space, then it is necessary to decide in advance the angles at which the wood will be cut and shaped. The moves and working angles are what the apprentice must learn long before he even touches the wood. There is no hint in all this of wild artistic inspiration. Indeed, inspiration as such has no place in wood carving. It is sober work for people who prefer to know what they are about and who have a high

degree of self discipline. Many an apprentice has had a major lesson when facing a rough and large block of wood with the instructions that he must reduce it to chippings of equal length and thickness until it finally disappears altogether. The stipulation in this traditional exercise to learn control of the tools is that only one single chisel or gouge must be used. If he were to reduce twenty blocks of wood to chippings and shavings, using twenty different tools, then he would slowly but surely begin to appreciate the nature of the job.

The aesthetics of wood carving must come later. First, the apprentice must learn many things about the workshop, the tools, the wood. If he spends at least two years getting used to the discipline under the tutelage of the master carver, this will be all to the good. Such strictures may well explain the sorry plight of modern wood carving, for few modern youths are able to adapt to the traditional regimen. As Peter Morton, a leading carver of the Fifties used to say, you must learn the five finger exercises before performing Bach. His views were uncompromising, while his notions of what constituted a suitable apprenticeship would nowadays deter all but the most determined. The world has changed and with it the attitudes of youth. There appears to be some significance in the fact that some of the best amateur modern carvers are women, and so we can only assume that they have greater self discipline and attention to detail coupled with a natural and warm affection for an ancient craft.

To gain a true appreciation of the aesthetics of wood carving, the apprentice should attend art school for one day a week after a two-year service in the shop. The Deed of Apprenticeship of the Master Carver's Association suggests that the field of ornament should be studied in harness with modelling in clay. In addition, lettering, which is the bane of many a young carver, should be included in the syllabus, also the making of pottery in order to gain an appreciation of shape and form. It may well be thought that the apprentice in his second and subsequent years should refrain from frequenting such places as art schools. In fact, it is believed that he is now ready for a widening of outlook in the history and practice of art. There is, of course, the very real risk that he may deviate from the relatively narrow path of carving and elect to become a sculptor or even a painter. It is just as well that this is brought out early, because the purpose of an apprenticeship is to train a tradesman to a certain standard of proficiency. Attendance at art school for one day a week enables him to explore and appreciate. If he draws, makes clay models and works in ceramics, these activities are unlikely to impair his resolve to become a wood carver. It is not too idealistic to believe that the apprentice who serves his full term, eventually to become a proficient carver, will remain in the trade all his life, providing the means exist for him to sell his services and products.

This carries us to a consideration of the state of the trade in this part of the twentieth century. In England there are very few carving shops of any size. Apart from one relatively small professional association, there is practically no liaison between the few remaining master carvers. Some new rural establishments have received financial assistance from government agencies to enable them to employ learners and so promote the craft, other workshops have diversified into other more lucrative lines of work. At the present time the carving trade is sadly decimated. Nevertheless, many individual carvers are still kept busy, carrying out restorations for antique dealers and galleries. There is every sign that carving has finally reached the level of a cottage industry, despite the extremely healthy interest found at an amateur level and manifested mainly in evening classes. Amateur work is far removed from commercial carving, and can more often than not be classed as sculpture rather than traditional carving. It may be wondered why this most venerable of all crafts is not kept alive in England by a state school of carving, such as can be found at Oberammergau. The truth is that it is quite pointless training tradesmen if the outlets for their skills no longer exist.

Carving is a small industry. The word 'small' refers not necessarily to the numbers employed but to its atmosphere. In the entire history of the trade there have never been thousands of carvers. In comparison with other trades the carvers have always been in a minority, working more often than not for others rather than for themselves. On the other hand, there were always some who plied for hire and obtained much of their work on a word-of-mouth recommendation or through the good offices of architects. Since World War Two many of the pre-war carving shops which managed to survive have been forced to go over to the production of plastic facsimiles of carvings. A purist may well shudder at the thought, and small wonder when it is realised that hundreds and perhaps thousands of duplicates can be produced from a single master mould with origins in a single carving by a modern tradesman or a long-dead carver. The making of multiple copies of a carving is in parallel with the early industry when carvings were supplied to workshops which produced plaster copies. There is, of course, a danger of producing sameness and a lack of variety which will, a century hence, bear sour fruit as far as the national heritage is concerned. Yet it is difficult to see how this situation might be improved. We have now reached a time in the history of carving when it is difficult to find a competent carver who will, or can, produce traditional work at an acceptable price. Unless he is a total recluse, he is well aware of the cost of living, and knows that he must cost the job at a profit, even if not a very high one. It would be pointless to suggest that this rare craftsman should be cossetted by being paid a government subsidy, that he should be encouraged to

teach others and so increase the number of carvers. This is a trade which lives on its outlets and the display of its products. The truth of the matter is that the remuneration of a carver is in direct relationship to demand. At the present time, while there is ample admiration of the product no evidence exists of an increase in demand. Modern architecture does not, of course, lend itself to wood carving ornamentation due to the trend in recent years towards the use of metal and stone. Even supposing that a renaissance in carving were to take place, there remains the question of what the apprentice should learn in addition to carving technique itself. In the teaching of art there has been a radical shift away from the classical foundation of the 18th and early 19th centuries. Nowadays the student plunges almost immediately into many forms of self-expression. Like the tyro carver, he is concerned with technique. Only a few art schools now operate on the basis of the traditional syllabus which benefits the apprentice carver. It is difficult to see how the apprentice might fit into such a structure, even on the basis of part-time studies, because carving is by its nature deeply rooted in the field of classical ornament.

One solution may afford a possible line of development for the future. There are still a few master carvers, some approaching retirement, who may be willing to accept students of mature years for the systematic part-time study of the trade and the intricacies of the craft itself. This is far removed from the traditional apprenticeship, of course, and it is highly unlikely that such students would eventually become master carvers. It is, nevertheless, not impossible that the act of casting the bread upon the waters would ensure that the English wood carving tradition does not completely die.

MASTER CARVERS IN ENGLAND 1979

All addresses "LONDON" unless stated otherwise

J. F. Allden, Esq., 'Little Felling', 11 Broad Lane, Lymington, Hants
P. J. Bentham, Stanhope Lodge, Arundel Road, Clapham, Worthing, Sussex
S. F. Brown & Son, Southcourt Road, Worthing, Sussex
H. C. Board & Son Ltd., 2 Merrivale Road, Putney, S.W.15
R. Bridgeman & Sons Ltd., Cathedral Works, Quonians Lane, Lichfield, Staffs
The Crafts & Lettering Centre, 61-65 Borough Road, SE1 1DU
G. Cassia, 31 Sussex Road, Ickenham, Uxbridge, UB10 8PM
V. C. Derham, 83 Troutbeck, Albany Street, N.W.1
W. Dudeney, Woodroffe House, Chiswick Mall, W.4
T. Edgar, 34 Danbury Street, N.1
Fernandes & Marche, 23 Motcomb Street, S.W.1
C. A. F. Griffin, 1a Bouverie Road, N.16
J. B. Graham, 11 Birch Grove, Potters Bar, Herts
B. M. Griss & Longhurst, 122 Petherton Road, N.5
F. Hudson & Son, Rosebury Avenue, High Wycombe, Bucks
House Names & Lantern Co., 10 Royal Parade, Chislehurst, Kent
G. Masero, Battle Farm, Marley Lane, Battle, East Sussex
S. H. Moss, 108 Haybridge Road, Ingatstone, Essex
Norman & Raymond, 122 Stonehouse Street, SW4 6AL
A. Ossowski, 83 Pimlico Road, S.W.1
N. A. Pack, 38 Durham Road, Feltham, Middx
A. R. J. Powell, 18 The Driveway, Shoreham-by-Sea, Sussex
Rattee & Kett, Purbeck Road, Cambridge, CB2 2PG
H. Read, St Sidwell's Art Works, Odams Wharf, Edford, Exeter, EX3 0PB
R. Reid, 3-5 Grape Lane, York, YO1 2HU
W. Thomas Ltd., 1 Warwick Place, Warwick Avenue, W.9
C. Wright, 171 Dawes Road, Fulham, SW6 7QP
G. D. Warder, 14 Hanway Place, Hanway Street, W1P 9DG
A. Wiggins & Sons Ltd., 30-34 Woodfield Place, Harrow Road, W9 2BJ

113 The process of heraldic carving with the design being roughed out as a preliminary to the detailed work.

114 A modern restorer completing work on one of the large relief panels which forms part of the Chevy Chase sideboard (see illus. 110). The restorer must seek to preserve the spirit of the original carving and avoid even the slightest distortion.

115 The carving of a modern quatrefoil screen section in which the workmanship equals the medieval counterpart. The demand for such work is nowadays limited to civic buildings at a time when ecclesiastical work is limited to restoration.

116 Religious figures are still carved for churches and other ecclesiastical institutions, but with a modern interpretation and, as a rule, a simplification of detail.

117 The hands of a carver at work on a section of screenwork for the postwar refurbishing of the House of Commons, London.

118 A profusion of carved sections for the postwar decoration of the House of Commons, London.

119 Assembly of a screen for the House of Commons, London in the postwar years. The method used the traditional system of slotting and clamping the individual pieces.

120 The screen finally set up for inspection before being placed in position in the House of Commons, London, during the postwar years.

121 The arms of England continue to be carved in the grand style. This example is by the modern master carver, Gino Masero, the London craftsman who is well known throughout the world for his heraldic interpretations.

The Woodcarver's Chisels and Gouges

In the trade the tools are commonly referred to as 'chisels', for this is exactly what they are, technically speaking, but in practice they can be divided into chisels proper and gouges, both of which are made in a large number of sizes from $\frac{1}{8}$ inch to 1 inch or more, and patterns which include both straight and bent. The majority have their origins on the Continent and for that reason are measured in millimetres. It is estimated that there were more than 3000 in all, and while the ordinary trade carver may have about 300 to cover his range of work, the majority of carvers use only about 70. Most carving tools are made with a tang which fits tightly into handles made of turned beech, boxwood or rosewood. The handle shape may be plain or octagonal with a slight belly in the middle to facilitate the grip.

During the 19th century carving tools were classified by numbers which corresponded to the cross-section and longitudinal shape. The numbers were the final two digits of the article number in the Sheffield Illustrated List which was published periodically from 1880. Each family of tools with the same shape and cross-section bore the same number, regardless of width. In this same period tools for the carving trade were manufactured predominantly by S. J. Addis and Sons, the firm later changing its name to J. J. Addis and Sons. In 1870 the Addis business was taken over by Messrs. Ward and Payne of Sheffield.

The following are the names of the main tools. Others are variations, sometimes made for specific work and adopted for universal use or, if highly specialised, made in very limited numbers or on demand.

1. Straight chisel
2. Skew, or corner, chisel
3. Straight gouge
4. Curved, or double-bent, gouge
5. Bent chisel (spoon bit: entering chisel)   } used for
6. Bent chisel (front bent spoon bit gouge)   } curved and
7. Back bent gouge (back bent spoon bit gouge)   } undercut detail
8. Straight parting tool } V-shaped
9. Curved parting tool   }
10. Front bent parting tool
11. Unshouldered space chisel
12. Straight macaroni tool (for finishing the sides of recessed sections)
13. Curved macaroni tool (for finishing the sides of concave sections)
14. Straight flutaroni tool (for cutting detail of the acanthus and completing recesses with rounded sides)
15. Bent spoon flutaroni tool
16. Fishtail spade gouge (used mainly for typographical work)
17. Long pod spade chisel (for finishing the carving)
18. Long pod spade gouge (for finishing purposes)
19. Dog leg chisel (for finishing recessed sections)
20. Allongee chisel (used mainly in wood sculpture)
21. Allongee gouge (used in wood sculpture)
22. Side chisel (for working in deep recesses)
23. Fluter   } Gouges with U-shaped channel
24. Veiner   }

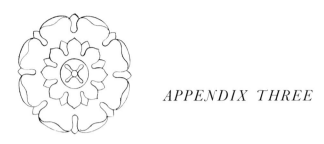

APPENDIX THREE

Research Resources

THE search for information about carvers, their work and conditions of employment is a difficult one, but amongst the most fruitful and well organised sources are the record repositories situated throughout the country. Apart from the collections listed in this Appendix, mention should also be made of the local record offices for which local government authorities are responsible. There are, too, the County Record Offices which can be found in all county towns in England with a growing number in Wales. Here are deposited the papers of private families, including tradesmen. Other research sources include libraries, museums and antiquarian societies, all of which offer facilities for researchers.

ENGLAND

London

Government, Parliamentary, etc., Archives
PUBLIC RECORD OFFICE
Chancery Lane, London, W.C.2.
Tel.: 01-405 0741.
Keeper of Public Records:
H. C. Johnson, C.B.E.
Mon.–Fri. 9.30–5; Sat. 9.30–1.
Museum, Mon.–Fri. 1–4.
Guide to the Contents of the Public Record Office
1963; printed series of *Calendars* and
Lists and Indexes.

CHURCH COMMISSIONERS
1 Millbank, London, S.W.1.
Tel.: 01-930 5444, Ext. 223.
Records Officer: E. J. Robinson, B.A.
Mon.–Fri. 9–5.

DUCHY OF CORNWALL OFFICE
10 Buckingham Gate, London, S.W.1.
Tel.: 01-834 7346.
Secretary and Keeper of the Records:
Sir Patrick Kingsley, K.C.V.O.
Mon.–Fri. 10–5. An appointment should be made for the first visit.

HOUSE OF LORDS RECORD OFFICE
House of Lords, London, S.W.1.
Tel.: 01-930 6240.
Clerk of the Records:
M. F. Bond, O.B.E., M.A., F.S.A.
Mon.–Fri. 10–5.
Guide in preparation; printed series of
Calendars and duplicated *Sectional guides.*
Serves also the House of Commons and
offices within the Palace of Westminster.

IMPERIAL WAR MUSEUM
Department of Libraries and Archives,
Imperial War Museum, Lambeth Road,
London, S.E.1. Tel.: 01-735 8922.
Mon.–Fri. 10–5.

NATIONAL ARMY MUSEUM
Royal Hospital Road, London, S.W.3.
Tel.: 01-730 3477.
Keeper of Books and Archives:
Miss E. D. Paul, M.A.

NATIONAL MARITIME MUSEUM
Greenwich, London S.E.10. Tel.: 01-858 4422.
Mon.–Fri. 10–5.30;
Sat. 10–5.30 (by appointment only).

NATIONAL MONUMENTS RECORD
(attached to the Royal Commission on
Historical Monuments)
Fielden House, 10 Great College Street,
London S.W.1. Tel.: 01-930 6554.
Mon.–Fri. 10–5.30; Sat. 10–12.30.
Measured drawings and photographs of
buildings of architectural and historic interest
in England and Wales.

VICTORIA AND ALBERT MUSEUM LIBRARY
Cromwell Road, London, S.W.7.
Tel.: 01-589 6371.
Mon.–Sat. 10–5.50.

Religious Archives and Libraries
BAPTIST MISSIONARY SOCIETY
93–97 Gloucester Place, London, W.1.
Tel.: 01-935 1482.
Mon.–Fri. 9–5.

CHURCH MISSIONARY SOCIETY
157 Waterloo Road, London, S.E.1.
Tel.: 01-928 8681, Ext. 129.
Mon.–Fri. 9.30–5.
Records are opened to students 50 years after
their date. No photocopying facilities.

LAMBETH PALACE LIBRARY
London, S.E.1. Tel.: 01-928 6222.
Mon.–Sat. 10–5.

ST. PAUL'S CATHEDRAL LIBRARY
St. Paul's Cathedral, London, E.C.4.
Tues.–Fri. 11–12.30, 1.30–3.30.

WESTMINSTER ABBEY MUNIMENT ROOM AND
LIBRARY
The Cloisters, Westminster Abbey,
London, S.W.1. Tel.: 01-222 4233.
Mon.–Fri. 9.30–1, 2–5. Applications should
be made in writing before first visit.

Societies, Colleges, and Institutions
COLLEGE OF ARMS
Queen Victoria Street, London, E.C.4.
Tel.: 01-248 2762.
Mon.–Fri. 10–4; Sat. morning
by appointment.

ROYAL INSTITUTE OF BRITISH ARCHITECTS
The Sir Banister Fletcher Library,
66 Portland Place, London, W1N 4AD.
Tel.: 01-580 5533.
Mon.–Fri. 10–7 (Tues. to 8.30); Sat. 10–5.
Closed 3 weeks, July/August.

ROYAL SOCIETY OF ARTS
8 John Adam Street, London, WC2N 6AJ.
Tel: 01-839 2366.
Mon.–Fri. 9.30–5.30.
Consultation by appointment.

ST. BARTHOLOMEW'S HOSPITAL
Archives Department, St. Bartholomew's
Hospital, Smithfield, London, EC1A 7BE.
Tel.: 01-606 777, Ext. 541, 481.
Mon.–Fri. 10.30–1, 2–6,
Sat. by arrangement.

Post-1850 records may be examined by special permission. The Hospital archives include parish records of St. Bartholomew the Less.

SIR JOHN SOANE'S MUSEUM
13 Lincoln's Inn Field, London, WC2A 3BP.
Tel.: 01-405 2107.
Tues.–Sat. 10–5.

SOCIETY OF ANTIQUARIES OF LONDON
Burlington House, Piccadilly,
London, W1V 0HS.
The Library and collections are not open to the public, but applications to see MSS. for the purpose of historical research may be addressed to the Assistant Secretary.

City of London
CORPORATION OF LONDON RECORDS OFFICE
Guildhall, London, E.C.2. Tel.: 01-606 3030.
Mon.–Fri. 9.30–5;
Sat. morning by appointment only.

GUILDHALL LIBRARY
Basinghall Street, London, E.C.2.
Tel.: 01-606 3030.
Librarian: G. W. Thompson, F.L.A.
Mon.–Sat. 9.30–5.

LIVERY COMPANIES OF THE CITY OF LONDON
Over 60 companies have deposited their records in the Guildhall Library (*q.v.*) where they may be seen. Certain Companies have made special arrangements for access; these are listed below. A list of all Livery Companies, with the names of Clerks, will be found in *Whitaker's Almanack* and in *The City of London Directory and City Livery Companies' Guide*. Application for access to the records should be made in the first instance to the Clerk. Companies' records less than 50 years old are not normally available for inspection.

MERCERS' COMPANY
Mercers' Hall, Ironmonger Lane, London
E.C.2. Tel.: 01-606 2433.
Mon.–Fri. 9.30–5.

GROCERS' COMPANY
Archives transferred to
Guildhall Library, *q.v.*

DRAPERS' COMPANY
Drapers' Hall, London, E.C.2.
Tel.: 01-588 5001.

SKINNERS' COMPANY
Skinners' Hall, 8 Downgate Hill, London,
EC4R 2SP. Tel.: 01-236 5629.

VINTNERS' COMPANY
1 Vintners' Place, Upper Thames Street,
London, EC4V 3BE. Tel.: 01-236 1863.

LEATHERSELLERS' COMPANY
15 St. Helen's Place, London E.C.3.

Greater London
GREATER LONDON RECORD OFFICE
(London Records) County Hall, London,
S.E.1.
Tel.: 01-633 5000, Ext. 8116, 6851 *and* 7808.
Mon.–Fri. 9.45–4.45;
Sat. morning by arrangement.

(Middlesex Records) 1 Queen Anne's Gate
Buildings, Dartmouth Street, London S.W.1.
Tel.: 01-839 7799, Ext. 4430 or 4431.
Mon., Wed., Fri. 9.30–5.30;
Thurs. 9.30–7.30 (prior notice of requirements desirable on Thurs. evening).

London Borough Libraries
BARNET: PUBLIC LIBRARIES
The Burroughs, Hendon, London, N.W.4.
Tel.: 01-202 5625.
Mon.–Fri. 9–8; Sat. 9–6.

BATTERSEA: *see* WANDSWORTH

BERMONDSEY: *see* SOUTHWARK

BETHNAL GREEN: *see* TOWER HAMLETS

BROMLEY: PUBLIC LIBRARIES
Central Library, Bromley, Kent, BR1 1EX.
Tel.: 01-460 9955.
Mon., Thurs. 9–8; Tues., Wed., Fri. 9–6;
Sat. 9–5.

CAMBERWELL: *see* SOUTHWARK

CAMDEN: PUBLIC LIBRARIES
Hampstead Central Library, Swiss Cottage,
London, N.W.3. Tel.: 01-586 0061,
Ext. 67 (Hampstead and St. Pancras).
Holborn Central Library,
32–38 Theobalds Road, London, W.C.2.
Tel.: 01-405 2706 (Holborn).
Mon.–Fri. 9.30–8 (Hampstead); Sat. 9.30–5.

CHELSEA: *see* KENSINGTON AND CHELSEA

CHINGFORD: *see* WALTHAM FOREST

CHISWICK: *see* HOUNSLOW

CLERKENWELL: *see* ISLINGTON

CROYDON: PUBLIC LIBRARY
Central Library, Katharine Street, Croydon,
CR9 1ET. Tel.: 01-688 3627.
Mon.–Fri. 10–7; Sat. 9.30–5.

DEPTFORD: *see* LEWISHAM

EAST HAM: *see* NEWHAM

FINCHLEY: *see* BARNET

FINSBURY: *see* ISLINGTON

FULHAM: *see* HAMMERSMITH

HACKNEY: LIBRARIES DEPARTMENT
Archives Department, Shoreditch Library,
Pitfield Street, London, N1 6EX.
Tel.: 01-739 6981.

HAMMERSMITH: PUBLIC LIBRARIES
Archives Department, Shepherds Bush
Library, Uxbridge Road, London, W.12.

Tel.: 01-743 1522, Ext. 4.
Mon., Fri. 9.15–5; Tues., Thurs. 9.15–8;
Sat. by arrangement.

HAMPSTEAD: *see* CAMDEN

HARINGEY: LIBRARIES, MUSEUMS AND ARTS
DEPARTMENT
Bruce Castle, Lordship Lane,
London, N17 8NU. Tel.: 01-808 8772.
Mon., Tues., Thurs., Fri., Sat. 10–12.30,
1.30–5.

HENDON: *see* BARNET

HOLBORN: *see* CAMDEN

HORNSEY: *see* HARINGEY

HOUNSLOW: PUBLIC LIBRARIES
Chiswick District Library, Duke's Avenue,
London, W.4. Tel.: 01-994 5295.
Hounslow District Library, Treaty Road,
Hounslow, Middlesex. Tel. 01-570 0622.
Mon.–Fri. 9–5. MSS. may be seen by prior
arrangement in the Reference Library until
8 on Mon.–Fri., Sat. 9–5.30.

ISLINGTON: PUBLIC LIBRARIES
Central Library, 68 Holloway Road, Luton,
N7 8JN. Tel.: 01-607 4038.
The Finsbury Library, 245 St. John Street,
London, E.C.1. Tel.: 01-837 4161.
Mon.–Fri. 9–8; Sat. 9–5.

KENSINGTON AND CHELSEA:
PUBLIC LIBRARIES
Central Library, Hornton Street, London,
W.8. Tel.: 01-937 2542.
Chelsea Library, Manresa Road,
London, S.W.3. Tel.: 01-352 6056.
Mon., Tues., Thurs., Fri. 10–8; Wed., Sat.
10–5.

KINGSTON UPON THAMES:
CORPORATION MUNIMENT ROOM
Guildhall, Kingston upon Thames.
Tel.: 01-546 2121.
Mon.–Fri. 9–5.15.

KINGSTON UPON THAMES, Surrey Record
Office: *see* SURREY

LAMBETH: PUBLIC LIBRARIES
Minet Library, 52 Knatchbull Road,
London, S.E.5. Tel.: 01-733 3279.
Mon.–Fri. 9.30–8; Sat. 9.30–5.

LEWISHAM: LIBRARIES DEPARTMENT
Archives and Local History Department,
The Manor House, Old Road, Lee,
London, S.E.13. Tel.: 01-852 5050.
Mon., Sat., 9.30–5; Tues., Thurs., Fri.
9.30–8; Wed. 9.30–1.

LEYTON: *see* WALTHAM FOREST

NEWHAM: PUBLIC LIBRARIES
Stratford Reference Library, Water Lane,
London, E.15. Tel.: 01-534 4545, Ext. 334.
Mon.–Fri. 9–8; Sat. 9–5.

PADDINGTON: *see* WESTMINSTER

POPLAR: *see* TOWER HAMLETS

ST. MARYLEBONE: *see* WESTMINSTER

ST. PANCRAS: *see* CAMDEN

SHOREDITCH: *see* HACKNEY

SOUTHWARK: PUBLIC LIBRARIES
Newington District Library, Walworth Road,
London S.E.17. Tel.: 01-703 3324, 5529,
6514.
The archives may be seen by appointment
only.

STEPNEY: *see* TOWER HAMLETS

STOKE NEWINGTON: *see* HACKNEY

TOTTENHAM: *see* HARINGEY

TOWER HAMLETS: LOCAL HISTORY LIBRARY
Central Library, Bancroft Road,
London, E1 4DA. Tel.: 01-980 4366.
Mon.–Fri. 9–8; Sat. 9–5.

WALTHAM FOREST
Leyton Library, High Road, Leyton,
London, E10 5QH. Tel.: 01-539 3650,
Ext. 137.
Walthamstow Museum of Local History,
Vestry House, Vestry Road, Walthamstow,
London, E.17. Tel.: 01-527 5544, Ext. 391.
Mon., Tues., Thurs., Fri. 10–8;
Sat. 10–5.30 (Leyton);
Mon.–Sat. 10–12, 1–5; Mon. and Wed. till 8
(Walthamstow).

WALTHAMSTOW: *see* WALTHAM FOREST.

WANDSWORTH: PUBLIC LIBRARIES
Battersea District Library,
265 Lavender Hill, London, S.W.11.
Tel.: 01-228 3474 *and* 8899.
Mon.–Fri. 10–9; Sat. 9–5; Sun. 2–6.

WEST HAM: *see* NEWHAM

WESTMINSTER: PUBLIC LIBRARIES
Archives Department, Buckingham Palace
Road, London, S.W.1. Tel.:
01-730 0446, Ext. 23.
Local History Library, Marylebone Road,
NW1 5PS. Tel.: 01–935 7766, Ext. 137.

WOOD GREEN: *see* HARINGEY

Bedfordshire

BEDFORD COUNTY RECORD OFFICE
County Hall, Bedford.
Tel.: Bedford (0234), 63222, Ext. 276.
Mon.–Fri. 9.15–1, 2–5; Sat. mornings by
appointment only.

Berkshire

BERKSHIRE RECORD OFFICE
Shire Hall, Reading, RG1 3EY.
Tel.: Reading (0734) 55981, Ext. 230.
Mon., Tues., Wed., Fri. 9–1, 2.15–5.30,
Thurs. 9–1, 2.15–7.30.

BRACKNELL: METEOROLOGICAL OFFICE
ARCHIVES
Meteorological Office, London Road,
Bracknell, RG12 2SZ.
Tel.: Bracknell (0344) 20242, Ext. 521.
Mon.–Thurs. 8.30–5; Fri. 8.30–4.30.

READING: CORPORATION ARCHIVES
DEPARTMENT
Central Public Library, Blagrave Street,
Reading, RG1 1QL.
Tel.: Reading (0734) 55911.
Mon.–Fri. 9.30–7; Sat. 9.30–5.30.

READING UNIVERSITY LIBRARY
Whiteknights, Reading, RG2 2AH.
Tel.: Reading (0734) 84331.
Mon.–Fri. 9–10.15; Sat., Sun. 2–6 (term);
Mon.–Fri. 9–5; Sat. 9–1 (vacation).

WINDSOR: THE AERARY
Dean's Cloister, St. George's Chapel,
Windsor Castle.

Buckinghamshire

BUCKINGHAMSHIRE RECORD OFFICE
County Offices, Aylesbury. Tel.: Aylesbury
(0296) 5000, Ext. 586-588.
Mon.–Fri. 9.15–5.30.

AYLESBURY: BUCKINGHAMSHIRE
ARCHAEOLOGICAL SOCIETY
The County Museum, Church Street,
Aylesbury.
Wed. 9.30–5, and by appointment.

ETON COLLEGE RECORDS
Penzance, Eton College, Windsor, SL4 6DB.
Tel.: Windsor (95) 66438, 68635.
By appointment, preferably in writing.

Cambridgeshire

COUNTY RECORD OFFICE
Shire Hall, Castle Hill, Cambridge, CB3
0AP. Tel.: Cambridge (0223) 58811,
Ext. 281.
Mon.–Fri. 9–1, 1.30–5.15.

CAMBRIDGE: UNIVERSITY LIBRARY
West Road, Cambridge, CB3 9DR.
Tel.: Cambridge (0223) 61441.
Mon.–Fri. 9–10 (term), 9–7 (vacation); Sat.
9–1.

CAMBRIDGE: UNIVERSITY ARCHIVES
The Old Schools, Cambridge, CB2 1TN.
Tel.: Cambridge (0223) 58933, Ext. 227.

HUNTINGDONSHIRE RECORD OFFICE
County Buildings, Huntingdon.
Tel.: Huntingdon (0480) 2181, Ext. 136.
Mon.–Fri. 9–1, 2–5.

HUNTINGDON: CROMWELL MUSEUM
County Offices, Huntingdon.
Tel.: Huntingdon (0480) 2181, Ext. 136
(Weekends 2861).
Tues.–Sat. 11–1, 2–5; Sun. 2–4.

Cheshire

CHESHIRE RECORD OFFICE
The Castle, Chester, CH1 2DN.
Tel.: Chester (0224) 24678.
Mon. 9–9, Tues.–Fri. 9–5.30; Sat. 9–12.30.

BIRKENHEAD: PUBLIC LIBRARY
Central Library, Borough Road, Birkenhead,
L41 2XB. Tel.: CLAughton (051 652) 6106.
Mon., Wed., Thurs., Fri. 9–8; Tues. 9–1;
Sat. 9–5.

CHESTER: CITY RECORD OFFICE
Town Hall, Chester, CH1 2HJ.
Tel.: Chester (0244) 40144, Ext. 2.
Mon.–Fri. 9–1, 2.15–5.15.

Cornwall

CORNWALL COUNTY RECORD OFFICE
County Hall, Truro.
Tel.: Truro (0872) 3698.
Mon.–Fri. 9–1, 2.15–5; Sat. 9–12.30.

193

TRURO: ROYAL INSTITUTION OF CORNWALL
River Street, Truro.
Tel.: Truro (0872) 2205.
Mon.–Sat. 10–5.

Cumbria

CUMBERLAND, WESTMORLAND, AND
CARLISLE RECORD OFFICE
The Castle, Carlisle, CA3 8UR.
Tel.: Carlisle (0228) 24248;
and County Hall, Kendal.
Tel.: Kendal 21000.
Mon.–Fri. 9–5; on Saturdays MSS. may be
seen by arrangement at either The Castle,
Carlisle, or County Hall, Kendal. Records of
the Leconfield estate, Cockermouth Castle,
available at the Record Office, Carlisle, upon
one week's notice.

CARLISLE: CATHEDRAL LIBRARY
The Fratry, Carlisle Cathedral.
Tel.: Carlisle (0228) 21614 (Librarian).

Derby

DERBYSHIRE RECORD OFFICE
County Offices, Matlock, DE4 3AG.
Tel.: Matlock(0629) 3411, Ext. 288.
Mon.–Fri. 9.30–1, 2–5.

CHESTERFIELD: PUBLIC LIBRARY
Corporation Street, Chesterfield.
Tel.: Chesterfield (0246) 2047 *and* 2661.
Mon., Tues., Thurs., Fri. 10–7; Wed.
10–5.30; Sat. 9–1.

DERBY: CENTRAL LIBRARY
Wardwick, Derby, DE1 1HS.
Tel.: Derby (0332) 31111, Ext. 306.
Mon.–Fri. 9–8; Sat. 9–5. Appointments are
advisable for Saturday and evening visits.

Devon

DEVON RECORD OFFICE
County Hall Topsham Road,
Exeter, EX2 4QD.

Tel.: Exeter (0392) 77977, Ext. 463
(Enquiries).
Mon.–Fri. 9.15–12.30, 1.45–5.15; first and
third Sat. of each month 9–12 (excluding
Bank Holiday weekends).

EXETER: CITY RECORD OFFICE
City Library, Castle Street, Exeter,
EX4 3PQ. Tel.: Exeter (0392) 73047/8.
Mon.–Fri. 10–5.30; Sat. 9.30–12.30.

EXETER: CATHEDRAL LIBRARY
The Bishop's Palace, Exeter, EX1 1HX.
Tel.: Exeter (0392) 72894.
Mon.–Fri. 2–5 (Mon.–Fri. mornings by
special arrangement); closed Bank Holidays
(Christmas plus three days).

PLYMOUTH: CITY LIBRARY
Central Library, Drake Circus, Plymouth,
PL4 8AL. Tel.: Plymouth (0752) 68000.
Mon.–Fri. 9.30–5.30; Sat. 9.30–12.

DORSET RECORD OFFICE
County Hall, Dorchester. Tel.: Dorchester
(0305) 3131.
Mon.–Fri. 9–1, 2–5.

Durham

DURHAM COUNTY RECORD OFFICE
County Hall, Durham. Tel.: Durham (0385)
4411, Ext. 576.
Mon. 8.45–5.15, Tues.–Fri. 8.45–4.45;
evenings by arrangement.

DURHAM: THE PRIOR'S KITCHEN
The Prior's Kitchen, The College, Durham.
Tel.: Durham (0385) 4561.
Mon.–Fri. 10–1, 2–5; Sat. 10–1. Closed for a
few days at Christmas and Easter and a
month during summer.
(Contains records of the Dean and Chapter,
the Halmote Court, the Palatinate and
Bishopric, the Consistory Court (probate
records) and the Grey of Howick MSS.)

DURHAM: DEAN AND CHAPTER LIBRARY
The College, Durham.
Tel.: Durham (0385) 4561.
Mon.–Fri. 9–1, 2.15–5; Sat. 9–1.

DURHAM: UNIVERSITY LIBRARY
Palace Green, Durham.
Tel.: Durham (0385) 61262.
By prior arrangement.

GATESHEAD: PUBLIC LIBRARIES
Central Library and Borough Record Office,
Prince Consort Road, Gateshead, NE8 4LN.
Tel.: Gateshead (0632) 73478.
Mon., Tues., Thurs., Fri. 10–8; Wed. and
Sat. 10–5.

Essex

ESSEX RECORD OFFICE
County Hall, Chelmsford, CM1 1LX.
Tel.: Chelmsford (0245) 53233, Ext. 2104.
Tues.–Fri. 9.15–5.15; Mon. 9.15–8.45.

COLCHESTER: PUBLIC LIBRARY
Shewell Road, Colchester.
Tel.: Colchester (0206) 70378.
Mon., Tues., Wed., Fri. 9–8; Thurs., Sat.
9–5.30. (24 hours' notice required for access
to archives).

SOUTHEND-ON-SEA: PUBLIC LIBRARY
Central Library, Victoria Avenue,
Southend-on-Sea, SS2 6EX.
Tel.: Southend-on-Sea (0702) 49451,
Ext. 540.
Mon.–Fri. 9–7; Sat. 9–5.

Gloucestershire

GLOUCESTERSHIRE RECORDS OFFICE
Shire Hall, Gloucester, GL1 2TG.
Tel.: Gloucester (0452) 21444.
Mon.–Fri. 9–5.

BRISTOL: BRISTOL ARCHIVES OFFICE
Council House, Bristol, BS1 5TR.
Tel.: Bristol (0272) 26031, Ext. 440, 441.
Mon., Tues. 8.45–5; Wed.–Fri. 8.45–4.45;
Sat. 9–12.

GLOUCESTER: CITY LIBRARIES
Brunswick Road, Gloucester, GL1 1HT.
Tel.: Gloucester (0452) 20020 and 20684.

GLOUCESTER: CATHEDRAL LIBRARY
The Cathedral, Gloucester.
By appointment only.

Greater Manchester

BRADFORD: CITY LIBRARIES
Central Library, Prince's Way, Bradford,
BD1 1NN. Tel.: Bradford (0274) 33081.
Mon.–Fri. 9–9; Sat. 9–6.

Hampshire

HAMPSHIRE RECORD OFFICE
The Castle, Winchester.
Tel.: Winchester (0962) 4411, Ext. 7143.

PORTSMOUTH: CITY RECORD OFFICE.
Guildhall, Portsmouth, PO1 2AL.
Tel.: Portsmouth (0705) 21771, Ext. 7.

SOUTHAMPTON: CIVIC RECORD OFFICE
Civic Centre, Southampton, SO9 4XL.
Tel.: Southampton (0703) 23855, Ext. 248.
Mon.–Fri. 9–1, 2.15–5.

SOUTHAMPTON: UNIVERSITY LIBRARY
Southampton, SO9 5NH. Tel.: Southampton
(0703) 56331.
Mon.–Fri. 9–10 (Term); 9–5 (Vacation);
Sat. 9–12.30.

WINCHESTER: CITY RECORD OFFICE
Guildhall, Winchester.
Tel.: Winchester (0962) 3361.
Tues., Wed. 9.30–12.30, 2–5; documents
may be consulted at the City Library by
special arrangement.

WINCHESTER: CATHEDRAL LIBRARY
The Cathedral, Winchester.
Tues. 10–12; Wed., Sat. 10.30–12.30,
2.30–4.30; others times by arrangement.

WINCHESTER COLLEGE MUNIMENTS
Winchester College, Winchester.
Tel.: Winchester (0962) 2107.
By appointment only, Mon.–Fri. 10–5; visits
at other hours and on Sat. can be arranged.

Herefordshire

HEREFORD COUNTY RECORD OFFICE
The Old Barracks, Harold Street, Hereford.
Tel.: Hereford (0432) 5441.
Mon.–Fri. 9.15–5.

HEREFORD: CITY LIBRARY
Broad Street, Hereford.
Tel.: Hereford (0432) 2456.
Mon.–Wed. 9–6; Thurs., Sat. 9–5; Fri. 9–8.

HEREFORD: CATHEDRAL LIBRARY AND
MUNIMENT ROOM
The Cathedral, Hereford.
Tel.: Hereford (0432) 66193.

HEREFORD: DIOCESAN ARCHIVES
The Cathedral Muniment Room, Hereford
and The Palace Muniment Room, Hereford.
MSS. may be seen by appointment.

Hertfordshire

HERTFORDSHIRE COUNTY RECORD OFFICE
County Hall, Hertford.
Tel.: Hertford (433) 4242.
Mon.–Fri. 9.15–5.15.

BARNET: PUBLIC LIBRARIES: *see* LONDON

Humberside

EAST RIDING COUNTY RECORD OFFICE
County Hall, Beverley. Tel.: Beverley (0482)
881281, Ext. 65.
Mon.–Fri. 9–1, 2–5.15.

HULL: CITY RECORD OFFICE
Record Section, Town Clerk's Department,
Guildhall, Alfred Gelder Street, Kingston
upon Hull, HU2 2AA.
Tel.: Hull (0482) 36880.
Mon.–Fri. 8.30–12.45, 2.15–5.15.

HULL: UNIVERSITY LIBRARY
The Brynmor Jones Library, The
University, Hull. Tel.: Hull (0482) 408960.
Mon.–Fri. 9–10; Sat. 9–1 (term); Mon.–Fri.
9–5.30; Sat. 9–1 (vacation).

EAST RIDING REGISTRY OF DEEDS
Beverley. Tel.: Beverley (0482) 881281,
Ext. 123.
Mon.–Fri. 9.15–4.

Isle of Wight

ISLE OF WIGHT COUNTY RECORD OFFICE
County Hall, Newport.
Tel.: Newport (0983 81) 4031, Ext. 302.
Mon.–Fri. 10–12.30, 1.30–4.

Kent

KENT ARCHIVES OFFICE
County Hall, Maidstone.
Tel.: Maidstone (0622) 54321.
Mon.–Fri. 9–5.15.

BECKENHAM: THE BETHLEM ROYAL
HOSPITAL AND THE MAUDSLEY HOSPITAL:
see LONDON

BROMLEY PUBLIC LIBRARY: *see* LONDON

CANTERBURY: CATHEDRAL LIBRARY and
CITY RECORD OFFICE
The Precincts, Canterbury.
By appointment only.

HYTHE: MUSEUM AND ARCHIVES
DEPARTMENT
Municipal Offices, Oaklands, Stade Street,
Hythe. Tel.: Hythe (0303) 66565.

Mon. and Fri. 10–12.30, 2–6; Tues.
10–12.30; Wed., Thurs., Sat., 10–12.30,
2–4.30. MSS. may be seen by appointment.

MAIDSTONE: THE MUSEUM
Faith Street, Maidstone.
Tel.: Maidstone (0622) 4497.
Mon.–Sat. 10–5.30.

ROCHESTER: DIOCESAN REGISTRY and
CATHEDRAL LIBRARY
c/o Messrs. Arnold, Tuff, and Grimwade,
The Precincts, Rochester.
Tel.: Medway (0634) 43231–2, 47067.

SEVENOAKS: PUBLIC LIBRARY
The Drive, Sevenoaks, Kent.
Tel.: Sevenoaks (0732) 53118.
Mon.–Sat. 9–5.30.

Lancashire

LANCASHIRE RECORD OFFICE
Sessions House, Lancaster Road, Preston,
PR1 2RE. Tel.: Preston (0772) 51950.
Mon.–Fri. 9–5.

BARROW-IN-FURNESS PUBLIC LIBRARY
Ramsden Square, Barrow-in-Furness.
Tel.: Barrow 20650.
Mon.–Fri. 9–7, Sat. 9–5.

LANCASTER PUBLIC LIBRARIES
Central Library, Market Square, Lancaster.
Tel.: Lancaster (0524) 2800.
Mon., Tues., Thurs., Fri. 9–7; Wed., Sat.
9–5.

LIVERPOOL RECORD OFFICE
City Libraries, William Brown Street,
Liverpool, L3 8EW. Tel.: 051-207 2147.
Mon.–Fri. 9–9; Sat. 9–5.

LIVERPOOL: UNIVERSITY ARCHIVES
The University, Senate House, Abercromby
Square, P.O. Box 147, Liverpool, L69 3BX.
Tel.: 051-709 6022, Ext. 735.

LIVERPOOL: UNIVERSITY LIBRARY
The University, P.O. Box 123,
Liverpool, L69 3DA. Tel.: 051-709 6022.
Weekdays 9–5.

MANCHESTER: CENTRAL LIBRARY
St. Peter's Square, Manchester, M2 5PD.
Tel.: 061-236 7401, Ext. 42.
Mon.–Fri. 9–12, 1–5.

MANCHESTER: CHETHAM'S LIBRARY
Manchester M3 1SB. Tel.: 061-834 7961.
Mon.–Fri. 9.30–5; Sat. 9.30–12.

MANCHESTER: JOHN RYLANDS LIBRARY
Deansgate, Manchester, M3 3EH.
Tel.: 061-834 5343.
Mon.–Fri. 10–6; Sat. 10–2.

MANCHESTER: UNIVERSITY LIBRARY
The University, Manchester, M13 9PL.
Tel.: 061–273 3333.
Mon.–Fri. 9–9.30; Sat. 9–1 (term);
Mon.–Fri. 9.30–5.30; Sat. 9.30–1 (vacation).

ST. HELENS: CENTRAL LIBRARY
The Gamble Institute, Victoria Square, St.
Helens. Tel.: St. Helens (0744) 24061.
Mon.–Sat. 9–7.

WARRINGTON: PUBLIC LIBRARY
Museum Street, Warrington.
Tel.: Warrington (0925) 31873.
Mon.–Fri. 9–7.30; Sat. 9–5.

WIGAN RECORD OFFICE
Central Library, Rodney Street, Wigan.
Tel.: Wigan (0942) 41387, Ext. 9.
Mon.–Fri. 9.30–8; Sat. 9.30–5 (notify in
advance by post).

Leicestershire

LEICESTERSHIRE RECORD OFFICE
57 New Walk, Leicester, LE1 7JB.
Tel.: Leicester (0533) 57121.
Mon.–Fri. 8.30–5.
Also includes some Rutland material.

LEICESTER MUSEUMS, DEPARTMENT OF
ARCHIVES
The Museum and Art Gallery, New Walk,
Leicester, LE1 6TD.
Tel.: Leicester (0533) 26832.
Mon.–Fri. 10–1, 2–5; Sat. 10–12.
(Acts as City Record Office for Leicester.)

Lincolnshire

LINCOLNSHIRE ARCHIVES OFFICE
The Castle, Lincoln.
Tel.: Lincoln (0522) 25158.
Mon.–Fri. 10–1, 2–5 (by arrangement during
lunch hour); Sat. 10–1; advance notice of
intended visits is requested. Closed for a
fortnight in October.

GRIMSBY: BOROUGH ARCHIVES OFFICE
Central Library, Town Hall Square,
Grimsby. Tel.: Grimsby (0472) 56012,
Ext. 20.

LINCOLN: PUBLIC LIBRARY
Free School Lane, Lincoln. Tel.: Lincoln
(0522) 28621.
Mon.–Fri. 9–7.30; Sat. 9–6.

SPALDING: GENTLEMEN'S SOCIETY
The Museum, Broad Street, Spalding.
Tel.: Spalding (0775) 4646 (Librarian);
Spalding (0775) 4658 (Caretaker).

Middlesex: *see* GREATER LONDON RECORD
OFFICE (MIDDLESEX RECORDS) *and* various
London boroughs.

Norfolk

NORFOLK AND NORWICH RECORD OFFICE
Central Library, Norwich, NOR 57E.
Tel.: Norwich (0603) 22233.
Mon.–Fri. 9–5; Sat. 9–12. Evenings and Sat.
afternoons by arrangement.

NORWICH: MUNIMENT ROOM OF THE DEAN
AND CHAPTER
The Cathedral, Norwich.
Cathedral Librarian: The Rev. Canon
Martin Kaye, M.A., 26 The Close,
Norwich, NOR 16P.

GREAT YARMOUTH: BOROUGH RECORDS
Archives transferred to the Norfolk and
Norwich Record Office, except the borough
charters and Assembly Books which are
available for consultation at the Town Hall,
Great Yarmouth on Wed. 2–5, or at the
Norfolk and Norwich Record Office by
appointment.

Northamptonshire

NORTHAMPTONSHIRE RECORD OFFICE
Delapré Abbey, Northampton, NN4 9AW.
Tel. Northampton (0604) 62129.
Mon., Tues., Wed., Fri. 9.15–1, 2–4.45;
Thurs. 9.15–2–7.45; Sat. 9.15–12.15.
Contains also the records of the Soke of
Peterborough to 1889.

NORTHAMPTON: PUBLIC LIBRARY
Central Library, Abington Street,
Northampton, NN1 2BA.
Tel.: Northampton (0604) 35651 and
(office hours) 34881.
Mon.–Fri. 9–8; Sat. 9–5.30.

North Yorkshire

HARROGATE: PUBLIC LIBRARY
Victoria Avenue, Harrogate, Yorks.
Tel.: Harrogate (0423) 2744.
Mon.–Wed., Fri. 10–7; Sat. 10–5.

MIDDLESBOROUGH CENTRAL LIBRARY: *see*
TEESSIDE PUBLIC LIBRARIES

NORTH RIDING COUNTY RECORD OFFICE
County Hall, Northallerton.
Tel.: Northallerton (0609) 3123, Ext. 306.
Mon.–Fri. 9–1, 2–5.

NORTH RIDING REGISTRY OF DEEDS
Racecourse Lane, Northallerton. Tel.:
Northallerton (0609) 2123, Ext. 126.
Mon.–Fri. 10–1, 2–4.

TEESSIDE PUBLIC LIBRARIES
Reference Department, Central Library,
Victoria Square, Middlesborough, Teesside,
TS1 2AY. Tel.: Middlesbrough (0642)
45294–5.
Mon.–Fri. 9.30–8; Sat. 9.30–6.

YORK: BORTHWICK INSTITUTE OF
HISTORICAL RESEARCH
St. Anthony's Hall, Peaseholme Green, York,
YO1 2PW. Tel.: York (0904) 59861,
Ext. 274.
Mon.–Fri. 9.30–1, 2–5. Closed for a short
period at Christmas and Easter and week
beginning the first Monday in October.

YORK: CITY ARCHIVES DEPARTMENT
City Library, Museum Street, York,
YO1 2DS. Tel.: York (0904) 55631.
Mon.–Fri. 9–12.30, 2–6. MSS. may also be
consulted in the Reference Library,
Mon.–Fri. 9–9; Sat. 9–5.

YORK: MINSTER LIBRARY
Dean's Park, York, YO1 2JD.
Tel.: York (0904) 25308.
Mon.–Fri. 9–5.

Nottinghamshire

NOTTINGHAMSHIRE RECORD OFFICE
County House, High Pavement, Nottingham,
NG1 1HR. Tel.: Nottingham (0602) 54524.
Mon., Wed., Thurs., Fri. 9–5; Tues. 9–7.30;
1st and 3rd Sat. in each month 9.30–12.30.

NOTTINGHAM: CITY LIBRARIES
South Sherwood Street, Nottingham,
NG1 4DA. Tel.: Nottingham (0602) 43591.
Mon.–Fri. 9–5.30. MSS. may be consulted
from 5.30–8 and on Sats. by previous
appointment.
Acts as City Record Office for Nottingham.

NOTTINGHAM GUILDHALL MUNIMENT
ROOM: *see* NOTTINGHAM CITY LIBRARIES

NOTTINGHAM UNIVERSITY: MANUSCRIPTS
DEPARTMENT
University of Nottingham Library,
University Park, Nottingham, NG7 2RD.
Tel.: Nottingham (0602) 56101.
Mon.–Fri. 9–5; Sat. 9–12.30 (by
appointment).

SOUTHWELL: DIOCESAN REGISTRY
Church House, Park Row, Nottingham,
NG1 6GT. Tel.: Nottingham (0602) 44934.
MSS. may be seen by appointment
Mon.–Fri. 9.30–5.

SOUTHWELL: MINSTER LIBRARY
Southwell, Notts.
MSS. may be seen by appointment only.

Oxfordshire

OXFORDSHIRE COUNTY RECORD OFFICE
County Hall, New Road, Oxford,
OX1 1ND. Tel.: Oxford (0092) 49861,
Ext. 202.
Mon.–Fri. 9–1, 2–5.

OXFORD: BODLEIAN LIBRARY
Oxford OX1 3BG.
Tel.: Oxford (0092) 44675.
Mon.–Fri. 9–7 (10 in full term); Sat. 9–1.

OXFORD: UNIVERSITY ARCHIVES
Bodleian Library, Oxford, OX1 3BG.
Tel.: Oxford (0092) 44675.
Mon.–Fri. 9–10 (term), 9–7 (vacation);
Sat. 9–1.

Peterborough, Soke of
See NORTHAMPTONSHIRE RECORD OFFICE

Shropshire

SALOP RECORD OFFICE
Shirehall, Abbey Foregate, Shrewsbury,
SY2 6ND. Tel.: Shrewsbury (0743) 52211.
Mon.–Fri. 9–5.

SHREWSBURY: BOROUGH ARCHIVES
Guildhall, Dogpole, Shrewsbury, SY1 1ER.
Tel.: Shrewsbury (0743) 52255 *and* Borough
Library.
Mon.–Fri. 9–5.15.

SHREWSBURY: BOROUGH LIBRARY
Castle Gates, Shrewsbury, SY1 2AS. Tel.:
Shrewsbury (0743) 54876.
Mon.–Fri. 9.30–8; Sat. 9.30–5.

Somerset

SOMERSET RECORD OFFICE
Obridge Road, Taunton.
Tel.: Taunton (0823) 7600.
Mon.–Fri. 9–1.15, 1.45–5; Sat. 9.15–12.15.

BATH: GUILDHALL
Guildhall, Bath, BA1 5AW.
Tel.: Bath (0225) 5423, Ext. 702.
Mon.–Fri. 8.45–5.30.

BATH: VICTORIA ART GALLERY AND
MUNICIPAL LIBRARIES
18 Queen Square, Bath, BA1 2HP.
Tel.: Bath (0225) 24747.
Mon.–Fri. 10–8; Sat. 9.30–6.

South Yorkshire

DONCASTER: SOUTH YORKSHIRE
INDUSTRIAL MUSEUM
Cusworth Hall, Doncaster.
Tel.: Doncaster (0302) 61842.
Mon.–Fri. 9–5; other times by appointment.

SHEFFIELD: CITY LIBRARIES
Central Library, Surrey Street, Sheffield,
S1 1XZ. Tel.: Sheffield (0742) 78771/7,
Ext. 36.
Mon.–Sat. 9–5.30. Advance notice advisable
for Sat. visits.

SHEFFIELD: UNIVERSITY LIBRARY
Western Bank, Sheffield, S10 2TN.
Tel.: Sheffield (0742) 78555.
Term: Mon.–Fri. 9–9.30, Sat. 9–1;
Vacation: Mon.–Fri. 9–5 (Easter
vacation 6); Sat. 9–12.30.

Staffordshire

STAFFORDSHIRE RECORD OFFICE
(in association with the William Salt
Library, Stafford, and the Lichfield Joint
Record Office).
Eastgate Street, Stafford.
Tel.: Stafford (0785) 3121, Ext. 156.
Mon.–Fri. 9–1, 2–5. On Sat. MSS. may be
seen at The William Salt Library by prior
arrangement.

BURTON UPON TRENT: PUBLIC LIBRARY
Union Street, Burton upon Trent, Staffs.
Tel.: Burton (0283) 3042.
Mon., Tues., Thurs. 9.30–6; Wed. 9.30–1;
Fri. 9.30–7; Sat. 9.30–5.

KEELE UNIVERSITY LIBRARY
Keele, Staffs, ST5 5BG.
Tel.: Keele Park (0782 71) 371.
Mon.–Fri. 9.30–5; Sat. 9.30–12.

LICHFIELD: JOINT RECORD OFFICE
Bird Street, Lichfield, Staffs, WS13 6PN.
Tel.: Lichfield (0543 2) 2177.
Mon.–Fri. 10–1.30, 2.30–5.15.

LICHFIELD DIOCESAN REGISTRY: *see*
LICHFIELD JOINT RECORD OFFICE

STAFFORD: WILLIAM SALT LIBRARY
19 Eastgate Street, Stafford. Tel.: Stafford
(0785) 52276.
Tues.–Sat. 10–12.45, 1.45–5. On Mondays
MSS. may be seen at the Staffordshire
Record Office by prior arrangement.

Suffolk

BURY ST. EDMUNDS AND WEST SUFFOLK
RECORD OFFICE
8 Angel Hill, Bury St. Edmunds, Suffolk.
Tel.: Bury St. Edmunds (0284) 2375,
Ext. 50.
Mon.–Fri. 9–1, 2–5; Mon. 7–9; Sat. 9–12 by
appointment. 24 hours' notice of a visit is
advisable.

IPSWICH AND EAST SUFFOLK RECORD
OFFICE
County Hall, Ipswich, IP4 2JS.
Tel.: Ipswich (0473) 55801.
Mon.–Fri. 9.15–5.30.

Surrey

SURREY RECORD OFFICE
County Hall, Kingston upon Thames.
Tel.: 01-546 1050, Ext. 158.
Mon.–Fri. 9–5; Sat. 9–12 by appointment
only.

GUILDFORD: MUSEUM AND MUNIMENT ROOM
Castle Arch, Guildford.
Tel.: Guildford (0483) 66551.
Mon.–Fri. 9–5; Sat. (usually) 9–4; preferably
by appointment. Closed for an hour at
midday.

CROYDON PUBLIC LIBRARY: *see* LONDON

KEW: ROYAL BOTANIC GARDENS: *see*
LONDON

KINGSTON UPON THAMES CORPORATION
MUNIMENT ROOM: *see* LONDON

NATIONAL ARMY MUSEUM: *see* LONDON

Sussex

EAST SUSSEX RECORD OFFICE
Pelham House, Lewes.
Tel.: Lewes (0791 6) 5400.
Mon.–Fri. 9–5.

WEST SUSSEX RECORD OFFICE
West Street, Chichester.
Tel.: Chichester (0243) 85100.
Mon.–Fri. 9.15–12.30, 1.30–5.

CHICHESTER CORPORATION
Greyfriars, Chichester.
Tel.: Chichester (0243) 4255.

HASTINGS: PUBLIC MUSEUM
John's Place, Cambridge Road, Hastings.
Tel.: Hastings (0424) 1952.
Mon.–Fri. 10–1, 2–5.

HOVE: CENTRAL LIBRARY
Church Road, Hove, BN3 2DJ.
Tel.: Brighton (0273) 70472–3.
Mon.–Fri. 10–6.30; Sat. 9.30–5.

LEWES: SUSSEX ARCHAEOLOGICAL SOCIETY
Barbican House, Lewes.
Tel.: Lewes (0791 6) 4379.
Mon.–Fri. 10–5, Sat. by arrangement.

WORTHING: PUBLIC LIBRARY
Chapel Road, Worthing. Tel.: Worthing
(0903) 39189.
Mon., Tues., Thurs., Fri. 10–7; Wed., Sat.
9.30–5.

Tyne and Wear

NEWCASTLE UPON TYNE: CITY ARCHIVES
OFFICE
7 Saville Place, Newcastle upon Tyne,
NE1 8DQ. Tel.: Newcastle upon Tyne
(0632) 21916.
Mon.–Fri. 9–5.30; Sat. and evenings by
arrangement.

NEWCASTLE UPON TYNE: CITY LIBRARIES
Central Library, P.O. Box 1MC, Newcastle
upon Tyne, NE99 1MC. Tel.: Newcastle
upon Tyne (0632) 610691.
Mon.–Fri. 9–9; Sat. 9–5.

NEWCASTLE UPON TYNE UNIVERSITY
LIBRARY
Queen Victoria Road, Newcastle upon Tyne,
NE1 7RU. Tel.: Newcastle upon Tyne
(0632) 28511, Ext. 2161.
Mon.–Fri. 9–9; Sat. 9–4.30. Long Vacation:
July, Aug., Sept., Mon.–Fri. 9–5; Sat. 9–1.

NORTHUMBERLAND RECORD OFFICE
Melton Park, North Gosforth, Newcastle
upon Tyne, NE3 5QX. Tel.: Wideopen
(0894 26) 2680.
Mon. 9–5.30; Tues.–Fri. 9–5; (open 9–9 last
Mon. of each month).

Warwickshire

WARWICKSHIRE COUNTY RECORD OFFICE
Shire Hall, Warwick.
Tel.: Warwick (0926) 43431.
Mon.–Fri. 9–1, 2–5.30; Sat. 9–12.30.
Records belonging to the Corporation of
Warwick can be seen at the County Record
Office by arrangement.

BIRMINGHAM: CITY LIBRARY
Reference Library, Ratcliff Place,
Birmingham, B1 2AR. Tel.: 021-643 2948,
Ext. 17.
Mon.–Fri. 9–9; Sat. 9–5.

BIRMINGHAM: UNIVERSITY LIBRARY
The Main Library, P.O. Box 363, The
University, Edgbaston, Birmingham,
B15 2TT. Tel.: 021-472 1301, Ext. 171.
Mon.–Fri. 9–10 (MSS. reading room open
9–8.45); Sat. 9–12.30 (during term);
Mon.–Fri. 9–5; Sat. 9–12.30 (during
vacation). Closed all Saturdays during
August.

COVENTRY: CITY RECORD OFFICE
9 Hay Lane, Coventry, CV1 5RF.
Tel.: Coventry (0203) 25555, Ext. 2767.
Mon.–Fri. 8.45–4.45.

LEAMINGTON SPA: PUBLIC LIBRARY
Leamington Spa.
Tel.: Leamington Spa (0926) 25873.
Mon., Tues., Thurs., Fri. 10–8; Wed., Sat.
10–5.30.

Westmorland

See CUMBERLAND, WESTMORLAND, AND
CARLISLE RECORD OFFICE (*Cumbria*)

West Yorkshire

DEWSBURY: PUBLIC LIBRARY
Central Library, Wellington Road,
Dewsbury. Tel.: Dewsbury (0924 2) 5151,
Ext. 218/9.
Mon.–Fri. 9–7; Sat. 9–5.

HALIFAX: CENTRAL PUBLIC LIBRARY
Belle Vue, Halifax, Yorks. Tel.: Halifax
(0422) 65105.
Mon., Tues., Thurs., Fri. 10–1, 2–5.30, Wed.
and Sat. 10–1. Documents requested in
advance may be consulted in the Reference
Library, Mon., Tues., Thurs., Fri. 5.30–8,
Sat. 1–5.

HUDDERSFIELD: PUBLIC LIBRARY
Central Library, Princess Alexandra Walk,
Huddersfield, HD2 2SU. Tel.: Huddersfield
(0484) 21356.
Mon.–Fri. 9–8.30; Sat. 9–5.

LEEDS: PUBLIC LIBRARIES
Sheepscar Branch Library, Chapeltown
Road, Leeds, LS7 3AP. Tel.:
Leeds (0532) 628339.
Mon.–Fri. 9–12.30, 2–5.30 (till 8.30 by
arrangement); Sat. 9–12.30.

LEEDS: BROTHERTON LIBRARY
University of Leeds, Leeds, LS2 9JT.
Tel.: Leeds (0532) 31751.
Mon.–Fri. 9–9 (July–September 9–5);
restricted service till 10 p.m. during term,
Sat. 9–1.

LEEDS: YORKSHIRE ARCHAEOLOGICAL
SOCIETY
Claremont, Clarendon Road, Leeds,
LS2 9NZ. Tel.: Leeds (0532) 27910.
Mon. (unless open the previous Sat.), Thurs.,
Fri., 9.30–5; Tues., Wed. 2–8.30. First and
third Sat. in each month 9.30–5, and *closed*
on following Mon. Closed all August.

WEST RIDING REGISTRY OF DEEDS
County Hall, Wakefield.
Tel.: Wakefield (0924) 73231–1.

Wiltshire

WILTSHIRE RECORD OFFICE
County Hall, Trowbridge.
Tel.: Trowbridge (0221 4) 3641.
Mon. 8.50–12.30, 1.30–5.50; Tues.–Fri.
8.50–12.30, 1.30–5.20.

SALISBURY: DIOCESAN RECORD OFFICE
The Wren Hall, 56c The Close, Salisbury.
Tel.: Salisbury (0722) 22519.
Mon.–Fri. 10.30–12.30, 1.30–4.

SALISBURY: MUNIMENT ROOM
The Council House, Bourne Hill, Salisbury.
An archivist from the Wiltshire Record
Office is in attendance on 2nd and 4th
Friday of each month, and records are
available at other times by arrangement at
the Diocesan Record Office.

Worcestershire

WORCESTERSHIRE RECORD OFFICE
Shirehall, Worcester, *and* St. Helen's, Fish
Street, Worcester. (Letters to Shirehall).

Tel.: Worcester (0905) 23400.
Mon.–Fri. 9–12.30, 2–4.45.

DUDLEY: PUBLIC LIBRARIES
St. James's Road, Dudley.
Tel.: Dudley (0384) 56321–5.
Mon.–Fri. 9–7; Sat. 9–5.
The Director of Libraries also acts as
Archivist to Dudley Corporation.

KIDDERMINSTER: PUBLIC LIBRARY
Market Street, Kidderminster.
Tel.: Kidderminster (0562) 62832.
Mon.–Fri. 9.30–7, Sat. 9.30–5.

REDDITCH: PUBLIC LIBRARY
Church Road, Redditch.
Tel.: Redditch (0739 2) 4252.
Mon., Tues., Thurs., Fri. 10–7; Wed. 10–1;
Sat. 10–5.30.

WARLEY: PUBLIC LIBRARIES
Central Library, High Street, Smethwick,
Warley. Tel.: Smethwick (021-558) 0497,
3919.
Mon., Tues., Wed., Fri. 9–7; Thurs. 9–1;
Sat. 9–5.

WALES

Clwyd

FLINTSHIRE RECORD OFFICE
The Old Rectory, Hawarden, Deeside,
CH5 3NR. Tel.: Hawarden (0244 53) 2364.
Mon.–Fri. 9–12.30, 1.60–5.30.

RHYL: PUBLIC LIBRARY
Wellington Road, Rhyl. Tel.: Rhyl (0745)
3814.
Mon.–Sat. 10–7 (Thurs., Sat. to 5).

Dyfed

NATIONAL LIBRARY OF WALES
Aberystwyth. Tel.: Aberystwyth (0970)
3816–7.
Mon.–Fri. 9.30–6; Sat. 9–5.

PEMBROKESHIRE RECORD OFFICE
The Castle, Haverfordwest.
Tel.: Haverfordwest (0437) 3707.
Mon.–Fri. 9.15–5.15 (5.45 Mon.).

CARMARTHENSHIRE RECORD OFFICE
County Hall, Carmarthen.
Tel.: Carmarthen (0267) 6641.
Mon.–Fri. 9–5.

Gwent

MONMOUTHSHIRE COUNTY RECORD OFFICE
County Hall, Newport, Mon., NPT 5XJ.
Tel.: Newport (0633) 64431.
Mon.–Fri. 10–1, 2–5.
(Serves Monmouthshire County Council and
Newport County Borough Council.)

Gwynedd

ANGLESEY COUNTY RECORDS OFFICE
Shire Hall, Llangefni.
Tel.: Llangefni (1048 81) 3262, Ext. 12.
Mon.–Fri. 9–5.

BANGOR: UNIVERSITY COLLEGE OF NORTH
WALES
Department of Manuscripts, The Library,
University College of North Wales, Bangor.
Tel.: Bangor (0248) 2501, Ext. 316.
Term: Mon.–Fri. 9–5 (Thurs. to 9), Sat.
9–12.30; vacation: Mon.–Fri. 9.30–5, Sat.
9–12. Closed for a week at Christmas and
Easter.

CAERNARVONSHIRE RECORD OFFICE
County Offices, Caernarvon.
Tel.: Caernarvon (0286) 2341.
Mon.–Fri. 9–5.

MERIONETH COUNTY RECORD OFFICE
County Offices, Lombard Street. Dolgellau.
Tel.: Dolgellau (0341 4) 341.
Mon., Tues., 9–1, 2–5.30; Wed.–Fri. 9–1,
2–5.15.

South Glamorgan

GLAMORGAN COUNTY RECORD OFFICE
County Hall, Cathays Park, Cardiff,
CF1 3NE. Tel.: Cardiff (0222) 28033,
Ext. 282.
Mon.–Fri. 9–5.

CARDIFF: CENTRAL LIBRARY
The Hayes, Cardiff, CF1 2QU.
Tel.: Cardiff (0222) 22116.
Research Department (MSS. and local
records) open Mon., Tues., Thurs., Fri.,
9.30–6; Wed. 9.30–1;, Sat. 9.30–5.30.
Except Sat. MSS. can be seen by special
arrangement up to 8 p.m. July–Oct. and
9 p.m. Nov.–June.

CARDIFF: NATIONAL MUSEUM OF WALES,
WELSH FOLK MUSEUM
St. Fagan's Castle, Cardiff, CF5 6XB.
Tel.: Cardiff (0222) 561357.
Archivist: Delwyn Tibbott, M.A.
Mon.–Fri. 9–1, 1.40–5. Closed extra day at
Easter, Spring Bank Holiday, Christmas.
Prior notice of a visit should be given.

SWANSEA: THE LIBRARY, UNIVERSITY
COLLEGE OF SWANSEA
Singleton Park, Swansea, SA2 8PP.
Tel.: Swansea (0792) 25678, Ext. 664.
Librarian: F. J. W. Harding, M.A., B.Litt.,
F.S.A.
Mon.–Sat. 9–5 (term), 9–12 (vacation).

SCOTLAND

Dumfries & Galloway

DUMFRIES: BURGH RECORDS
Municipal Chambers, Buccleuch Street,
Dumfries. Tel.: Dumfries (0387) 3166 (Town
Clerk), and Dumfries (0387) 3374 (Curator).
Mon.–Fri. 9–5; Sat. by prior arrangement.

DUMFRIES: EWART PUBLIC LIBRARY
Catherine Street, Dumfries.
Tel.: Dumfries (0387) 3820.
Mon., Wed., Fri. 9–8; Thurs., Sat. 9–5.

Fife

ST. ANDREWS: UNIVERSITY LIBRARY
The University, St. Andrews, Fife.
Tel.: St. Andrews 933.
Mon.–Fri. 9–10, Sat. 9–12.15 (term);
Mon.–Fri. 10–4 (vacation).

ST. ANDREWS: UNIVERSITY MUNIMENTS
North Street, St. Andrews.
Tues. and Thurs. 2–5; other times by
appointment.

Grampian

ABERDEEN: CHARTER ROOM OF THE
CORPORATION
Torn House, Aberdeen, AB9 1AQ.
Tel.: Aberdeen (0224) 23456.
Mon.–Fri. 9–12.45, 2–5.30.

ABERDEEN: UNIVERSITY LIBRARY
Manuscripts and Archives Section,
University Library, King's College,
Aberdeen, AB9 2UB.
Tel.: Aberdeen (0224) 40241.
Mon.–Fri. 9.15–4.30.

Lothian

EDINBURGH: CITY ARCHIVES
City Chambers, Edinburgh, EH1 1PL.
Tel.: 031-225 2424.
Mon.–Fri. 9–5.

EDINBURGH: SCOTTISH NATIONAL
MONUMENTS RECORD
Royal Commission on the Ancient and
Historical Monuments of Scotland, 52–54
Melville Street, Edinburgh, EH3 7HF.
Tel.: 031–225 5994/5.
Mon.–Fri. 9.30–5.
(Plans, drawings and photographs of ancient
monuments and historic buildings in
Scotland, comprehensive library of Scottish
architectural history.)

EDINBURGH: UNIVERSITY LIBRARY
Department of Manuscripts, George Square,
Edinburgh, EH8 9LJ. Tel.: 031-667 0011,
Ext. 6636.
Mon.–Fri. 9–5; Sat. 9–12.30.

NATIONAL LIBRARY OF SCOTLAND
George IV Bridge, Edinburgh, EH1 1EW.
Tel.: 031-225 4104.
Mon.–Fri. 9.30–8.30; Sat. 9.30–1. Closed on
Christmas Day, New Year's Day and the day
following, and Good Friday.

SCOTTISH RECORD OFFICE
P.O. Box 36, H.M. General Register House,
Edinburgh, EH1 3YY. Tel.: 031-556 6585.
(Annexe) West Register House, Edinburgh,
EH1 3YT. Tel.: 031-226 5101.
Mon.–Fri. 9–4.45 (Historical and Legal
Search Rooms, H.M. General Register
House; West Register House Search Room
and Museum); Sat. 9–12.30 (Historical
Search Room only).

Strathclyde

GLASGOW: CITY ARCHIVES OFFICE
P.O. Box 27, City Chambers, Glasgow, C.1.
(Callers use 249 George Street).
Tel.: 041-221 9600, Ext. 2021.
Mon.–Fri. 9–5.

GLASGOW: ANDERSONIAN LIBRARY,
UNIVERSITY OF STRATHCLYDE
Richmond Street, Glasgow, C.1.
Tel.: 041-552 4400.
Mon.–Fri. 9.30–5, Sat. 9.30–12. MSS.
requested before 4.30 may be consulted until
9 on Mon.–Fri. during term.

GLASGOW: MITCHELL LIBRARY
North Street, Glasgow, C.3.
Tel.: 041-248 7121.
Mon.–Sat. 9.30–9; Sun.
(October–March) 2–8.

GLASGOW: UNIVERSITY ARCHIVES
The University, Glasgow W.2.
Tel.: 041-339 8855, Ext. 543.

GLASGOW: UNIVERSITY LIBRARY
The University, Glasgow, W.2.
Tel.: 041-334 2122.
Mon.–Fri. 9–9.30, Sat. 9.30–12.30 (term);
Mon.–Fri. 9–5, Sat. 9–12.30 (vacation).

Tayside

PERTH: ART GALLERY AND MUSEUM
George Street, Perth.
Tel.: Perth (0738) 24241.
Mon.–Sat. 11–5; Sun. 2–4.

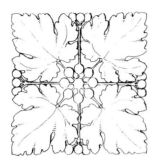

Inventory of Woodcarving in the United Kingdom

THE following abstracts represent only a small selection of entries from a much larger work currently in preparation. Due to the fact that research is continuing, no entries appear for Scotland, the Isle of Man or Ireland, but 27 counties are nevertheless represented. There is no suggestion that the county inventories which appear in this abstract are complete in themselves. They appear at this time for the benefit and the interest of readers who wish to see representative examples of carving pending the future publication of the complete Inventory.

Compilation of such an Inventory is a task of some magnitude. Information for the basis of entries is drawn from many sources, supplemented by the voluntary efforts of people who are willing to report the sites and the nature of carvings to the compiler. It is hoped that the number of reporters will increase as a result of publication of this abstract.

That the need for such an Inventory exists is self-evident, for many notable and even less notable examples of the architectural heritage of the United Kingdom have already vanished in the last few decades, a high percentage without benefit of detailed documentation.

Reports will, therefore, be welcomed by the compiler, Frederick Oughton FRSA, c/o Stobart and Son Ltd, 67/73 Worship Street, London EC2A 2EL.

In this abstract from the Inventory the following counties are represented: Bedfordshire, Buckinghamshire, Cambridgeshire, Cornwall, Cumbria, Devon, Dorset, Essex, Gloucestershire, Gwent, Herefordshire, Humberside, Kent, Lancashire, Leicestershire, Lincolnshire, Norfolk, Nottinghamshire, Oxfordshire, Shropshire, Somerset, Staffordshire, Suffolk, Sussex, Wiltshire, Worcestershire, Yorkshire.

ABBESS RODING, ESSEX

Medieval church with screen said to be finest in country in small church. Deep band of elaborate tracery carved in closing years of 15th century fills one-third of opening below low pitched arches. Panels have tracery at both ends and rich ornamentation along rail. Canopy of 18th century pulpit is richly carved.

ABERGAVENNY, GWENT

Church. Probably the earliest English carving extant, situated in south choir aisle, depicting the knight, Sir George Cantelupe (d. 1273).

ADDLETHORPE, LINCOLNSHIRE

15th century marshland church. Partly restored roof. Nine carved long-skirted figures. South aisle has carved floral bosses and human figures. Oak benches have carved armrests and poppyheads, one showing two birds in a tree, preening their feathers, also a little man in a treetop. In the nave are eleven poppyheads.

ALDHAM, ESSEX

Church, Anglo-Saxon with carved timber porch, 14th century.

ALGAKIRK, LINCOLNSHIRE

Restored medieval church with 13th century tower. Carved oak furnishings.

ALLINGTON, LINCOLNSHIRE

Holy Trinity church with 12th century arcade. Carved Jacobean pulpit.

ALPHAMSTONE, ESSEX

Church, 12th century. 17th century font cover, Communion table, and two chests.

ALTARNUM, CORNWALL

Church. Bench end, medieval, showing musician playing the vielle, an early form of violin. Others in same series show piper, two sword dancers and a jester.

ANCASTER, LINCOLNSHIRE

Church, 14th century with 15th century spires. In restored nave roof are eight wooden figures with shields and musical instruments.

APPLEBY, LINCOLNSHIRE

Church, partly rebuilt in last century. Crowning nave is modern roof with fourteen angels carved on hammerbeams. On pedestal pulpit are carved coats of arms and fifteen sacred scenes, believed to be 16th century Flemish. Chancel has finely carved altar-rail.

ARDLEIGH, ESSEX

Church, medieval with 15th century tower. Sixteenth century door with traceried heads, rich in character. Screen has grotesque heads and dragons with tracery at base.

ASHBY-CUM-FENBY, LINCOLNSHIRE

13th century church has a medieval oak screen.

ASHEN, ESSEX

Norman church. 18th century carved chair. Curious panel dated 1620 says it has been a marrying stool and 'so it shall be still'.

ASHDON, ESSEX

Guildhall, now cottages, built 1500. Overhanging storey ornamental brackets. Church 14th century with chancel roof set up at time of Agincourt, including beam with pierced ornament and other carved ornamentation. Also moulded roof beam, 15th century chest and Jacobean altar-rails.

ATHELINGTON, SUFFOLK

Church contains heads carved in the Elizabethan style with helmets and ruffs.

AVELEY, ESSEX

Church has Norman nave and 13th century tower. Screen is 16th century and has five openings with traceried heads on each side of the entrance to the chancel. Pulpit is 1621, six-sided with richly-carved sounding board. Lectern carved in ancient oak from Winchester. Elaborate chair is dated 1620, crowned with Dacre crest, a local family.

BAG ENDERBY, LINCOLNSHIRE

Church is 15th century and contains fragments of oak screen of same period.

BALDERTON, NOTTINGHAMSHIRE

Church contains some accomplished carvings of rabbits.

BARKESTONE, LEICESTERSHIRE

Church in which are desk and finely carved stall ends, incorporating lions and, in niches, representations of St James of Copostela and St John the Baptist. They are attributed to Bromflet, probably incorrectly.

BARLING, ESSEX

Church with medieval tower. Jacobean pulpit with great carved sounding-board.

BARMING, KENT

In church are some fine stall carvings believed to be of Flemish origin, representing St Michael and the Dragon, Lion of St Mark, Harrowing of Hell and Samson and the Lion.

BARNSTON, ESSEX

Church has Norman nave, rebuilt 13th century. 17th century oak chest and 15th century carved communion table.

BAUMBER, LINCOLNSHIRE

Georgian church with Anglo-Saxon origins. Screen of painted wood with coat-of-arms and decoration over three arches.

BECKINGHAM, LINCOLNSHIRE

Church has 15th century tower. Tall traceried screen is modern, also richly carved reredos depicting the Crucifixion.

BELCHAMP WALTER, ESSEX

Clark's Farm has 15th century Tudor fireplace and carved bargeboards.

BELCHAMP ST PAUL, ESSEX

Fifteenth century church with ten chancel stalls with tip-up seats carved in 15th/16th century. Poppyheads with foliage, a king and a monk holding a book. Jacobean altar table.

BELTON, LINCOLNSHIRE

Belton Park, ancestral seat of Lord Brownlow. Designed by Wren, completed 1689. Some carvings attributed to Grinling Gibbons adorn the cedar-lined private chapel. Jacobean pulpit with carved back and high canopy.

BERECHURCH, ESSEX

Church renovated 15th century. Tudor door with linenfold and traceried panels by Tudor craftsman. Hammerbeam roof in Audley Chapel with carved heads and flowers.

BEVERLEY ST MARY'S, HUMBERSIDE

One of the great repositories of misericords, including the following examples: two griffins

and two rabbits; a wodehouse, or wildman, of the woods between two lions and two wyverns below, all symbolic of evil, though the lion also symbolises good; a rare example of half-eights, being a medieval design device; milkmaid milking cow (early 16th century)—one of 68 in series; jester playing the then popular game of grimacing, also three other misericords featuring jesters; an ape misusing a dog as a set of bagpipes; Reynard the fox being nursed by a friendly ape—other versions of this can be seen at Bristol, Fairford and Padstow.

BIRDBROOK, ESSEX

15th century houses with overhanging storeys, resting on curved brackets. The church is 13th century with a 15th century choir. Graceful 18th century altar-rails.

BISHOP'S HULL, SOMERSET

In the parish church there is a 16th century bench end, probably the work of Simon Werman. The subject is an interpretation of the Resurrection. In the same carving is the Pious Pelican feeding her chicks. The pelican was the symbol of redemption.

BLACK NOTLEY, ESSEX

Norman church with oak-framed sedilia (a seat for the priest). Stanton's, a farm, is 600 years old and notable for its woodwork of the 14th century, including moulded capitals.

BOCKING, ESSEX

Woolpack Inn, Tudor, has beams richly carved with grotesques and foliage. At Wentworth House there is a carved 17th century canopy.

BOSTON, LINCOLNSHIRE

15th century church with lantern tower. Roof bosses installed in the Thirties but coloured in the medieval style. 18th century wooden vault with original wooden bosses, painted red and green. Chancel has medieval stalls and an outstanding reredos across east wall, 32 feet high, done in oak and with golden canopies

with coloured figures, including the Disciples and 38 small saints. 64 stalls dated 1390 with original hinged seats and misericords, including an armoured knight on horseback picking up a horseshoe; two sailors in a boat listening to a siren or mermaid; wolf in clerical garb preaching to geese. Jacobean pulpit.

BRADENSTOKE PRIORY, WILTSHIRE

14th century roof, formerly above the refectory and the priory, now in church. Highly decorative and richly carved with ball-flower ornamentation.

BRADFORD ABBAS, DORSET

In parish church are some finely carved bench ends, featuring a pig, owl and monkey. They probably formed part of the choir stalls in an earlier period.

BRADWELL, ESSEX

Church 12th century with 14th century porch. Fine timberwork and 14 traceried openings. The medieval screen has lost some of its tracery but retained the panelling behind its vanished rood loft. Traceried panels from another screen, also some good modern woodwork, including priest's desk with carved hares. Jacobean font cover.

BRANSTON, LINCOLNSHIRE

Carving in parish church by rector, Rev. Atwill Curtois, and daughters. The Curtois family held the living here from 1680 to 1891. Chancel screen by Rev. Curtois, with arches and tracery. One of his daughters carved panels with shamrock, roses, snowdrops and thistles, also a frieze of saints to represent the history of Christianity. Screen and other woodwork destroyed in 1962 fire, but a few bench ends remain.

BRANT BROUGHTON, LINCOLNSHIRE

14th century church. Modern oak stalls and font cover, which has door within which are carved and coloured figures of St Agnes, St Michael with Dragon, and St Nicholas with three children in a tub.

BRAUNTON, DEVON

Parish church contains 46 bench ends in chestnut, carved with the initials of patrons who commissioned them. Eight have inverted letters to denote the humility of the donors. But it is possible that the illiterate carver read and copied them upside down.

BRIGHTLINGSEA, ESSEX.

Jacobes Hall is one of the oldest timbered buildings in the United Kingdom. 13th century addition of ceiling with carved oak beams.

BROCKLESBY, LINCOLNSHIRE

Church contains a fine chair with carved fan-shaped back. Organ is dated 1773 with floral festoons and carved musical instruments as decoration.

BROUGHTON, LINCOLNSHIRE

Church has chest with linenfold panels, and a cupboard with three carved panels taken from an Elizabethan pulpit.

BROXTED, ESSEX

Church is 13th century. 17th century processional cross with flowered ends and raised bosses. The pulpit was carved in the 17th century.

BUCKNALL, LINCOLNSHIRE

Church is partly 13th century and contains a carved pulpit, also a Jacobean chest with a band of carving. There are modern oak carvings of St George standing over the Dragon, given by two friends of Langton Benson-Brown, killed in action in France, 1916.

BULPHAN, ESSEX

Church has 16th century timber porch with elaborately carved bargeboards. 15th century screen with two bays on either side of entrance, their heads containing bold tracery.

BURGH, LINCOLNSHIRE

In the parish church are floral roof bosses. The screens of the tower and chancel embody much of the 500-year old woodwork from the former chancel and aisle screen. There is also a carved and canopied Jacobean font cover. A gilded dove holds in its beak an inkform for entering baptisms and a sandsifter for drying ink. The lectern features an eagle with half-closed wings, carved in the last century by Jabez Good, a local man, and given in memory of Wm. George Tozer, vicar from 1858-63.

CANEWDON, ESSEX

Norman church, rebuilt 14th century. Pulpit brought from City of London after Great Fire of 1666. Carved cherubs, foliage and fruits on panels. Dubious attribution to Grinling Gibbons' workshops.

CANON PYON, HEREFORDSHIRE

Parish church contains grotesque carving of a bishop sitting on a monkey, which holds a book, probably the Bible.

CARLISLE, CUMBRIA

In cathedral a misericord showing man attacked by his wife, who is swinging a washing beetle, also 15th century example showing hyena devouring a corpse, based on a bestiary illustration.

CARTMEL, CUMBRIA

In priory the stalls are early 17th century while the misericords date from the 14th century, one of which features a finely carved peacock as a symbol of immortality. Another depicts the Pious Pelican feeding her young by giving them blood from a self-inflicted breast wound, symbolic of the Redemption. Another shows an ape doctor holding a bottle urinal. In the Middle Ages great importance was attached to the analysis of urine.

CASTLE HEDINGHAM, ESSEX

Norman church with 15th century screen with six bays of fine oak tracery, richly carved arches, moulded cornice adorned with bosses. The 15th century stalls, numbering five in all, are carved with shields, heads of wolves and leopards, a wolf carrying what appears to be a monk on a stick thrown over his shoulder, a fox with a distaff in his mouth. Also 18th century cupboard with carved panelling showing Daniel in the Lion's den and Jonah beneath the gourd. Panelled chest with three locks. Jacobean altar table.

CHARLTON MACKRELL, SOMERSET

In parish church a medieval bench end showing Tutivillus, the demon charged with the recording of the sins of the word, especially those mumbled or dropped during the recitation of the divine office. Carving depicts him with a scroll and a sack in which sins are stored. Also included are bell, book and candle.

CHELMSFORD, ESSEX

Guy Harling's, the house of the provost, has Tudor panelling and carved heads which look down on the hall. Tudor period.

CHESTERSON, CAMBRIDGESHIRE

Parish church has a series of finely carved upright figures in place of the more usual poppyheads. They have been compared in quality to similar figures in Jesus College, Cambridge.

CHIGNAL ST JAMES, ESSEX

Church dates from 11th century. Oak arch cover roodstairs which now lead to pulpit. Carved with the emblems of St James, a cockle shell and a fisherman's creel.

CHISHALL, ESSEX

In 15th century church are 16th century carved pews and fine carvings of kneeling women.

COATES-BY-STOW, LINCOLNSHIRE

In 15th century church a fine carved oak screen of the same period, much restored.

COGGESHALL, ESSEX

An area rich in carved beams. Paycocke's House is Tudor and displays carved ornamentation with timbers overhanging road. Upper storey has frieze of running foliage, small heads, a shield with a merchant's mark of an ermine tail, also the initials of Thomas Paycocke, d. 1580. Both storeys are divided by buttresses into five bays. On sideposts of an arch are moulded pedestals. Under canopies are two figures of a man with a shield and another with a load on his shoulder. The interior contains elaborately carved ceilings, original doorways, linenfold panelling and fireplaces carved with grotesque beasts.

COLCHESTER, ESSEX

Mill at Bourne Pond built as fishing lodge. Two gabled ends shaped in four stages, each stage adorned with pinnacles. St Peter's church is 14th century with a carved 18th century pulpit. 17th century oak memorial to Richard Sayer, who died in America in 1670 and his son who died at Colchester. St Martin's church is mainly 14th and 15th century. Midway in chancel is rare and fine timber arch dating back to 14th century. Screen is 15th century. Jacobean chests, poor box and pulpit are all carved. St Leonard's church is 14th century with 16th century hammerbeam roof, richly moulded. Marquis of Granby inn has 16th century beams with three odd figures clad in costumes of the period.

COMBEINTEIGNHEAD, DEVON

In parish church there is a carving of a fox taking a goose and being chased by a hound, also some fine niche carvings of saints.

CROFT, LINCOLNSHIRE

Parish church of All Saints is 14th century with 15th century chancel screen and modern cornice. Benches have simple tracery and doors,

211

but no poppyheads. South door is panelled with 'God Save the Queen' in carved raised letters. Carved and canopied pulpit was given in 1615 by the vicar, Dr Worship, in memory of his wife, Agnes.

CROWBOROUGH, SUSSEX

In parish church reredos is the work of women who attended carving classes given by female relative of Baden-Powell, founder of Scout Movement. It occupied three years and includes symbols of the Four Apostles and figures of Meditation and Adoration. Panels were executed by professional carver, identity unknown.

CROWCOMBE, SOMERSET

In parish church a medieval bench end depicting the Green Man, a popular subject on West Country bench ends. In this example mermen are emerging from his ears. For explanation and speculation connected with Green Man legend see *The Green Man* by Kathleen Barford (Brewer), 1978.

CROWLAND, LINCOLNSHIRE

In 15th century church is a 15th century oak chancel screen, enriched with tracery and still retaining some of the original colour. It once enclosed the lady chapel. In spandrels of the lower panels are leaves and flowers, a man in a boat, a bat-like grotesque, a dragon and a man's head

DANBURY, ESSEX

Church was renovated but founded in the 14th century. Three knights of St Clere sculpted in oak. Each has legs crossed and feet resting on a lion, face partly enclosed with chain mail. Each wears a tabard with its folds realistically carved. One has a drawn sword, the second vigorously thrusts his sword in a backward sweep, the third has hands folded in prayer. In the 18th century one of the coffins of the knights was discovered and opened. It contained the body of a man, perfectly preserved, wearing a linen shirt with lace crudely sewn around the neck. The coffin

was resealed and buried. There are 15th century carved benches with moulded rails and three poppyheads with beasts. Modern carvers have continued the patterns and all the pews are ornamented with lions and dragons. The 15th century gallery has Elizabethan balusters.

DENNINGTON, SUFFOLK

Church is medieval. A fine carving of the Pious Pelican on a finial, depicting the bird with chicks in a boat, or nest. Bench end shows a Sciapod, a human being with a huge foot which he used as a parasol while sleeping in the sun. In this example the carver made an error and endowed the Sciapod with two feet.

DENTON, LINCOLNSHIRE

15th century church has been largely rebuilt, including the screen. Other carving is modern, and there are six angels with outspread wings looking down from the roof.

DODDINGTON, LINCOLNSHIRE

Church was rebuilt in 1771 by Lord Delaval. The carving is by Col. Payne Jarvis, who served in the Peninsular War and is buried here. One shows Peter and John at the Gate Beautiful with life-like figures of the cripple on the floor with St Peter holding his hand, women passing by with baskets on their heads, and a small boy with two birds. The other depicts St Paul preaching.

EAST BUDLEIGH, CORNWALL

In parish church the arms of Sir Walter Raleigh, also carving of shears, which were the badge of the mercer.

ENVILLE, STAFFORDSHIRE

In parish church a 15th century misericord which illustrates a scene from the Romance of Sir Ywain. It shows the knight trapped by a portcullis as he chases another knight into the castle. There is a third figure, apparently a guard.

EPWORTH, LINCOLNSHIRE

The church is 14th and 15th century and has strong associations with the Wesley family. It contains a finely carved Elizabethan chair.

EXETER, DEVON

Exeter museum contains part of a medieval misericord showing a woman examining her daughter's head for nits. The museum houses the Harry Hems collection of medieval woodwork.

EYNESBURY, CAMBRIDGESHIRE

In parish church some interesting representations of cumbersome beasts, such as the hippopotamus with sawlike horns. Elsewhere in the church are other idiosyncratic carvings, derived probably from bestiaries.

FAIRFORD, GLOUCESTERSHIRE

In church a medieval misericord showing Reynard the fox. Other misericords show two wyverns with interlaced tails. In bestiaries wyverns have two legs rather than four, as here.

FISHTOFT, LINCOLNSHIRE

Church is Norman with later alterations. Modern oak roof with golden bosses adorned with carved angels and faces. Two fine 15th century oak screens, one from original chancel screen, the other, in the tower arch, is from the neighbouring church at Freiston.

FLEET, LINCOLNSHIRE

Church is said to have been built by monks from Castle Acre. Neat, modern hammerbeam roof rests on old corbels carved with gallery of medieval figures. Altar rail is Jacobean.

FOLKINGHAM, LINCOLNSHIRE

Church is 15th century and contains a dark oak screen with tracery, roses and vine leaves. About 500 years old, and probably one of the finest screens in Britain.

FORNHAM ST MARTIN, SUFFOLK

In the church a 15th century misericord showing the martyrdom of St Thomas á Becket in act of saying mass. It now forms part of the lectern.

FRAMPTON, LINCOLNSHIRE

Church is medieval, restored 1891. Modern oak roof, but barrel roof of nave still has old tie-beams. 15th century oak screen has been restored. There is also an ironbound chest of the period. The Jacobean pulpit was bought from Bourne church in 1891 for £3 3s. 0d.

FRECKENHAM, SUFFOLK

In medieval church is bench end showing a devil pushing one of the damned into the jaws of Hell.

FRESSINGHAM, SUFFOLK

In church are medieval bench ends carved with emblems of the Passion of Christ, including the seamless robe and the dice used by the Roman soldiers, the hammer and nails and ladder, the spear used by the soldiers to pierce Christ's side, the vinegar-soaked sponge and the symbols of Pilate's hand washing.

GAINSBOROUGH, LINCOLNSHIRE

All Saints church is restored but originally medieval. The lectern is a carved oak eagle. In the vestry is a carving of Leonardo's 'Last Supper' by a local craftsman.

GOSBERTON, LINCOLNSHIRE

Church is 15th century, restored 50 years ago. Ancient oak screen has modern cornice and over it a fine roof-loft with figures carved by Belgian refugees of World War I. The original rood stairway is still in situ. Pulpit with figures of St Peter and St Paul and two bishops is modern, also reredos.

GRIMSBY, LINCOLNSHIRE

Church of St James was founded 1110. Contains two Jacobean chairs with carved backs. There is also a curious old seat adorned with flowers and scrolls. Panelled chest with

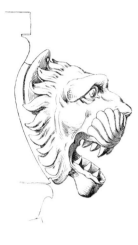

carved ornamental banding. The low chancel screen with panels of delicate pierced carving is modern.

HADLEIGH, SUFFOLK

In church is a medieval bench end depicting the legend of the finding of the head of St Edmund in the jaws of a wolf. The hidden meaning is a lampoon of the 14th century. The beast is wearing a robe and neck collar, similar to those worn by the monks of the period.

HALIFAX, YORKSHIRE

In church of St John are nine stalls with misericords in three groups of three, including one notable carving of a mermaid holding a mirror and comb.

HALSALL, LANCASHIRE

In church of St Cuthbert a carving of a lion on a bench composed in the Lancastrian manner, sleek and comfortable, although it has been likened to the East Anglian carving style, as a result of which it looks more like a lamb than a lion. There is also a unique misericord showing a wrestling match.

HALTON HOLGATE, LINCOLNSHIRE

Church is 15th century. Numerous bench ends of original period, but others are work of local carpenter and copies of those in Winthorpe church. Profusion of old and new poppyheads with a great variety of decoration, including angels, owls, double heads, a man with a pitcher, foxes chasing geese, and around base of one poppyhead are six monkeys and the crouching figure of a man held by his hair.

HONINGTON, SUFFOLK

In medieval church a carving of a piper atop a bench end, wearing a kilt.

IVINGHOE, BUCKINGHAMSHIRE

In parish church some naive carvings of poppyheads and unfinished human heads, also unfinished human figure.

IXWORTH, SUFFOLK

In 15th century church a carved figure on a bench end representing a thatcher with rake and knife, showing interesting costume detail, also female figure, probably by same carver, walking a dog on a lead. Church has thatched roof.

KETTLETHORPE, LINCOLNSHIRE

Church is 15th century, rebuilt 1896. The black oak pulpit was carved by a 17th century Brittany craftsman.

KIRKBY-LA-THORPE, LINCOLNSHIRE
(known in 13th century as Kirkebi et Leitorp)

Local cottage has two small oak panels on which are carved the Creed and the Commandments. They were located originally in the now vanished chapel-of-ease. The church of St. Denis is brother to the church of Asgarby, nearby, and is 14th century. Three bays of 15th century chancel screen are now in the tower arch, also medieval lectern.

LAKENHEATH, SUFFOLK

In church are carved finials with figures on elbow rests and carved backs, typical of East Anglian style. There is also an arm-rest showing a beaver biting off its testicles, said to possess medicinal properties for which the animal was hunted. The beaver castrated itself in order to gain peace from its pursuers.

LANGTON-BY-HORNCASTLE, LINCOLNSHIRE

The red-tiled church was restored in 1890. Flat oak cover of font was carved with odd-looking cherubs and a dove by the rector, J. Conway Walter, in 1891 and the golden dove was added later. Pulpit, reading desk and lectern were also carved by Walter as memorials to his father, Edward Walter, minister here for nearly 50 years from 1828.

LUDLOW, SHROPSHIRE

In parish church is 15th century misericord showing fireside scene with woman sitting on three-legged chair, warming her hands and feet before a fire. Also shown are two sides of bacon on hooks and a pot on a separate fire. Carving of St John the Baptist cradling a lamb in his arms. Also carving of a cardinal and a bishop.

MALVERN, WORCESTERSHIRE

In medieval priory a series of misericords symbolising the months of the year. January is represented by a man holding two goblets, toasting the new year with one and using the other to bid farewell to the old year.

MERTON, OXFORDSHIRE

In parish church there are several unique poppyheads with carved praying angels and eagles in a back-to-back design.

MILVERTON, CORNWALL

The parish church contains the carved arms of Henry VIII.

MILVERTON, SOMERSET

In church a bench end shows Joshua and Caleb, the two spies, returning from the Promised Land, carrying a large bunch of grapes. It was probably copied from the *Biblia Pauperum*, printed in the Netherlands and widely circulated early in the 16th century.

MONK'S RISBOROUGH, BUCKINGHAMSHIRE

In parish church a most unusual carving of upright figures on a base composed of human heads.

NORTON DISNEY, LINCOLNSHIRE

The church is 15th century and earlier. It formerly belonged to Sempringham Priory, which had 13 religious houses throughout England. In chancel are wooden stalls with carved foliage and curious little men and angels back to back on the poppyheads. They have grave and gay medieval faces. The traceried screen is Elizabethan and the large pulpit is Jacobean. Roof of aisle has carved bosses incorporating foliage with a man's face and a lion with protruding tongue.

PEWSEY, WILTSHIRE

In church of St John the Baptist the Communion rail was carved by Canon Bouverie, using timber taken from the *San Joseph* which surrendered to Nelson. He also carved the altar, organ screen and font cover.

RIPPLE, WORCESTERSHIRE

In medieval church a carving of Lammas (Loaf Mass) at the manorial bakery. Disputes over the weight and quality of the loaves necessitated the presence of armed guards. This misericord is the only known representation of the event.

SKIRBECK, LINCOLNSHIRE

The church is Norman with 13th century nave arcades. Pulpit is richly carved Jacobean with desk supported by six grotesque birds. The font cover is tower-shaped with carved figures of St Mary with lilies and St Nicholas with bags of gold at his feet.

SPALDING, LINCOLNSHIRE

Church of St Mary and St Nicholas has hammerbeam roof adorned with 28 carved angels. In south chapel the oak benches are traceried, also carved rails and screen. The oak altar is graced by angels. Oak reredos has triptych with figures of St Hugh, St Mary, Our Lord, St Nicholas and a bishop.

STANTON FITZWARREN, WILTSHIRE

In church the carver of reredos, sanctuary screen, wall panels, font panels and cover was Canon Masters, rector 1885-1919. The altar and the Pelican lectern were carved by Owen Thomas, a friend of Canon Masters.

STANTON ST JOHN, OXFORDSHIRE

In parish church there is an outstanding selection of poppyheads, many in back to back designs and much good carving showing human beings and horses. Also some effective primitive faces which glare and threaten.

STOVINGTON, BEDFORDSHIRE

In the parish church a carving showing two elderly men crawling up the bench-end to put their lips to a bowl containing, perhaps, the local ale. There is also a naive carving of a man seated at a desk, reading.

STOWLANGTOFT, SUFFOLK

In the medieval church a bench-end shows a pig playing a harp. There are other representations of animal musicians.

THURGARTON, NORFOLK

In parish church a carving of an elephant on a finial with a castle on its back. The castle is an exaggeration of the howdah and the carver probably relied on traveller's tales and woodcuts of the period.

TRULL, SOMERSET

In medieval church some early 16th century bench-ends. Five of them in nave depict a religious procession, including a crucifer leading the throng which includes an acolyte with candle, a singing chorister, a deacon carrying a casket and a priest.

UFFORD, SUFFOLK

The parish church contains an exceptionally fine 15th century carving of a kneeling woman wearing a striking butterfly headdress. Elsewhere in the church is a wealth of fantastic carving of unreal birds and beasts.

WEST HALTON, SOUTH HUMBERSIDE

St Etheldreda's church contains carved ends of choirstalls, done in 1874 by the self-taught wife of the Rev. James Murray.

Note: References in square brackets denote page numbers

AN EXPLANATION OF THE DECORATIONS

Note: References in square brackets denote page number.

[v] Supporter in demi-human form with animal hoof. Originally a heraldic term for ornamental accessories but introduced in furniture carving in the France of Louis XVI, it appeared in Egyptian forms in 19th century English furniture carving, particularly in the design of fireplaces.

[vii] Side elevation of [v] showing how the wing and calf of leg provided support.

[9] The akroter and antefix were used originally to provide an ornamental flourish to a gable apex. The roots are in the architecture of the Acropolis, and the Parthenon, but it was adopted by English carvers in the Middle Ages and Renaissance. It can also be seen in a variety of forms in the poppyheads of bench-ends.

[11] Carved horses appear in the design repertoire at an early date, most notably following the inclusion of the White Horse of Hanover in the Queen's Beasts. This design is a double-Pegasus, culled from Greek mythology.

[14/15] Vine leaves and grapes were carved as a rule on 18th century screenwork in churches. The design has a long lineage, from China, where it developed eventually into a scroll; to Egypt, where it was combined with ivy, lotus and papyrus in the carving of stone capitals; also Graeco-Roman, Byzantine, Gothic and Renaissance. After falling from use, it was revived in the 18th and 19th centuries.

Carvers frequently combined vines with wheat ears to symbolise the Eucharist. This drawing represents the 'English' vine most favoured by 18th century carvers.

[19] Acorn quatrefoil design used in repetition, or as roof bosses, by carvers from the 14th to the 18th centuries, also as ornamental terminals on furniture. Oak leaves have featured in antiquity and were associated with Jupiter, signifying valour.

[22/23] Oak leaves and acorns were favoured by carvers charged with the embellishment of columns, entablatures and cornices, copied from the stone mason in the decoration of classical and Gothic architecture.

[26/27] Repetitious use of the akroter and antefix (see 9), providing scope for fluting and other detailed carving. It appeared in profusion in the Regency period, when it was gilded or polychromed.

[28/29] Design decoration for pilaster or wall-pier, exemplified in Renaissance carving, and drawn directly from organic forms. In extravagant distortion it was brought to richness by the Gibbons' school.

[46] The rosette was a formalised rose and previously a sun symbol in religious decoration in India, Assyria and Persia, later passing into Greek and Roman use, when it featured in

panelled coffered ceilings. English carvers used the device on parish chests and furniture, either singly or in series. When carved in overlapping series they are known as 'strung coin' or 'money moulding.'

[51] Lion-head ornamentation best exemplified in carved English furniture of about 1810. The lion motif was common in ancient Egypt, it appeared in Persian architecture, and in Ceylon. English carvers drew it from the Royal Arms of England, often featuring the head and body in grotesque poses. The Lion is one of the Queen's Beasts.

[52/53] Decoration schemes in two variations for a carved frieze embodying classical motifs, and drawing, however vaguely, on ancient Greek forms.

[56/57] Moulding variations adapted from the chevron, which originated in Paleolithic and Neolithic line patterns, and is thought to symbolise the serpent, lightning or water. It appeared in Romanesque and Norman stone carving, and was adapted by English wood carvers.

[60/61] An elaborate scheme for the carved altar rail of a church, employing the acanthus (see 18). Such carving was done in deep relief, based on a curvilinear motif with a C-scroll of Graeco-Roman origin. In some early versions Christian symbols are evident.

[64/65] Free ornamentation drawn from organic forms, serving to enrich mouldings on furniture and architectural features, such as door-cases. Although the foliation appears naturalistic, it is freely adapted. The carved English versions of the 16th and 17th centuries are relatively inelegant in comparison to those created in the Italian Renaissance.

[83] Design for a carved heraldic Tudor rose, being the combined red and white roses of Lancaster and York. It appears in profusion in English carving, often as roof bosses. In medieval times it was the symbol of Paradise and the Virgin Mary, later becoming the Royal Badge of England.

[86/87] Fanciful floriation design was common in the carved decoration of cottage, or country, furniture (see p. 32). In this example the leaf-edges have been rounded off in the Roman style.

[90/91] Crudely designed frieze employing mock-natural forms in which the leaves have been contorted to fit into available space. It fell to Gibbons to free such design from its limitations and bring to it a new richness.

[92/93] The traditional enrichment of mouldings has many forms, including the Greek egg-and-tongue (p. 92) and its elaboration (p. 93). Taken from the Greek ovolo in architecture, it was widely applied by carvers in the Georgian period. Like other ornamentation, egg-and-tongue suffered many corruptions and innovations in which carved motifs were applied to the egg surfaces.

[98/99] A further graceful variation of the akroter and antefix (see 9) in which there is an attempt to provide a virtually independent series of motifs.

[100] Carvers of the Middle Ages drew their patterns from stone masons. When naturalistic foliated friezes were required they took as models the leaf carving which the mason used to connect items of stonework. Known as link borders, they appeared in architectural cresting and cornices, also in the fringes of the textiles of the period.

[106/107] The artificial leaf was widely used in the decoration of private houses and public buildings in Georgian times. This is the type of working drawing which served as a basis of elaboration, the leaves being carved flat and later given detail. The Continental influence was apparent when the design was spaced out (p. 107), evolving into scrollwork, when it was exploited by the plasterwork artist.

[111] In the evolution of the acanthus there were occasional attempts at a new enrichment, as in the carving of Jonathan Mayn and Edward Pearce, until the basic shape of the plant became obscured.

[114/115] Cross-fertilisation of design was common after Gibbons' death. The combination of the neo-Greek scroll and tulip-like shapes (p. 114) made an unhappy marriage, as did the unnatural acorns (p. 115).

[120] 19th century ornate decoration created from segments grew out of the previous century's application of classical forms. In both these examples the roots were in a conventional floral motif, the athemion, based on the honeysuckle or Egyptian lotus, and typified by the flowers joined by an enclosing scroll or compartments.

[124/125] Certain carvers specialised during the Georgian period in the representation of man in relation to special gifts and attributes, intermingling the human form with vices and virtues against symbolic backgrounds in the Classical style. Many mix together the tender and the slightly horrific (p. 124), while others portray the purely heroic (p. 125).

[128/129] Further examples of Greek egg-and-tongue moulding, the carving of which occupied the labours of apprentice and master-carver alike (see 92/93).

[132/133] Designs for furniture supports, the surrounds of fireplaces and pedestals which featured in carvers' design books in the second quarter of the 18th century, executed as a rule in pine painted to imitate mahogany. The design incorporates not only Greek features in portraiture but also egg-and-tongue moulding (see 92/93 and 128/129).

[136/137] The carver of Georgian times was unable to escape the temptation to add often incongruous touches, such as the unidentifiable vertical flowers between the otherwise strictly classical segments (p. 36). The embellishments occasionally got out of hand to such an extent that it was impossible to identify the source (p. 137).

[140] A conventional representation of The Good Shepherd favoured by 18th and 19th century carvers and church restorers. The element of ecclesiastical statuary remained in the classical mould until well into the 20th century.

[141] Carved decoration of the Cross, a symbol of antiquity with possible origins in the swastika, was uncommon in medieval England but came to fruition in the Victorian period, when carvers surrounded the shape with vine leaves and wheat sheaves.

[143] Design for a carved wreath, a device from the past when the wreath was regarded as a victory emblem. Robert Adam's designs of about 1765 occasionally used it as an embellishment of such items of furniture as pier tables, and the device remained in use until at least 1780.

[144] The multiple-figure carving containing several classical figures in a series of poses. Many carving shops specialised in these items in the 17th and 18th centuries, selling them to architectural carvers who used them for the finishing of beam-ends and the crowning of internal porches and overmantels.

[166/167] The Greek pillar was utilised by William Kent (1684-1748) to act as a carrier, or medium, for fine and detailed carving for the decoration of furniture based on classical architecture.

[171] Design for a door of the Adam period (1728-92) in which many classical elements, including Egyptian and Greek, were harmoniously blended.

[175] A further variation of the acorn quatrefoil design (see 19) in which the oak leaves are relegated to a minor role.

[178/179] Designs for drops and their realisation reached a zenith in the age of Gibbons. Innumerable designs abounded in 18th century France, many of them representing ingenious combinations of symbols to suggest the arts, trades and agriculture. Holding the various elements together is the carved ribbon, known in an early form in 5th to 7th century Celtic design but given greater elaboration in the mid-18th century, especially in Thomas Chippendale's designs.

[180] The carved pedestal of the 18th century embodied many firmly-based classical elements. In this design the support is given by the swan, which was sacred to Apollo and Venus. In France the black swan was the device of Josephine Bonaparte, and imported into Britain by furniture carvers.

[186] A non-natural rosette created by the juxtaposition of disparate leaves and petals. Early carvers in the medieval period tended to invent foliation to fit awkwardly-sized friezes, hence this design.

[186/187] Bead, otherwise known as astragal, half-round mouldings, carved as part of egg-and-tongue moulding or alone, particularly in the Middle Ages. From a simple line of disks (p. 186) it was possible to progress to the complication of depicting them as seen from a side-view (p. 187), alternating with elongated versions of the bead.

[188] A cross between the rosette and a formal geometric design, most apparent in the decoration of Tudor and Elizabethan furniture.

[192/193] Design of carved panels demanded compression of detail while still suggesting a balanced design. The late Georgian carvers excelled in adapting Italian and French characteristics (p. 192), while an earlier generation relied largely on the manipulation of the acanthus (p. 193). See 18.

[196/197] Panel carving in the 14th century (p. 196) was relatively simple and uncomplicated, but in less than a century the carver was beginning to lose natural forms and convert them into geometric figures (p. 197).

[200/201] A few years after the death of Queen Anne furniture became baroque, design being influenced by French and Italian styles. The arbiter of taste was William Kent (1684-1748), who introduced such architectural elements as columns, architraves and entablatures with heavily scrolled supports bringing into play such items as flowers, fabulous beasts, sea shells and scrolls.

[204/205] Medieval stonework provided a wealth of inspiration for the carver, who displayed ingenuity in fitting natural forms into restricted spaces.

[206] A 15th century design obtained by placing four leaves within the area of a square. With the addition of formalised fruits and spines, the natural forms merge to create a complicated pattern.

[207] The refined rosette was finally brought to a delicate representation in the 19th century, and carved as a rule in mahogany.

[208/209] Medieval carvers frequently adapted their designs in such a way as to suggest the influence of the guilloche, a continuous pattern of interlaced bands (p. 208). Other designs of the same period brought into conjunction the Graeco-Roman scroll combined with leaf forms.

[210/211] Designs for friezes developed early in the 18th century for the Gothic revival, which sprang from the founding in 1707 of the Society of Antiquaries of London, to make a study of medieval ruins, the elements of which were to appear in furniture and architecture.

[212] The Green Man, a medieval folk figure, had tendrils emerging from the mouth to form a frame of foliation. There are parallels elsewhere in the world, including China and the Semitic civilisations. The tree is said to represent life while the face suggests the guardian.

[213] The sweeping scroll has here totally discarded its pagan origin and grown into a lyrical composition for furniture decoration of the late Gothic revival.

[214/215] The English lion taken from the Royal Arms of England, made a flamboyant appearance as decoration of mahogany furniture in the William Kent period (see p. 200/ 201).

[216] The stele, or Greek tombstone, decorated with deeply carved scrolls and the features of a deity, resting on the egg-and-dart moulding.

To John Rost Sculpture

For a white and veined marble Chimney Peice with Slips and
slab of the same, with Coverings and Hearth pace in the ⎫ 20 : 00 : 00
Communication Gallery att _____ ⎬
                                       ⎭
                    20 : 00 : 00

To Grimling Gibbons Carver

In the Communication Gallery

For 2 members enricht in the Cornish in the Communication ⎫ 21 : 13 : 06
Gallery Cont: 172 foot 5in ~~inches~~ att 1s. 7d ⅌ ft ————⎬
~~Ditto~~ 74 ft 3inches att 9d ⅌ ft ——————————— 03 : 14 : 03

                    Chapell
            In the Kings Closett
For 59 ft 10 inches in the Coved Cornish 2 members enricht ⎫ 17 : 19 : 00
att 7d ⅌ ft ————————————————————⎬
                    43 : 06 : 09 ½

To Charles Haughton For his attendance & pains in ⎫ 01 : 10 : 00
setting downe ye Rates, Casting ym up, & Ingrossing ye Acct ⎬
                    01 : 10 : 00